DATE DUE

DEMCO 38-296

Volume 22

Advances in
Librarianship

Volume 22

Advances in
Librarianship

Edited by

Frederick C. Lynden

Rockefeller Library
Brown University
Providence, Rhode Island

Elizabeth A. Chapman

Taylor Institution
University of Oxford
St. Giles, Oxford, United Kingdom

Academic Press

San Diego   London   Boston   New York   Sydney   Tokyo   Toronto

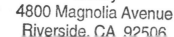

This book is printed on acid-free paper. ∞

Academic Press
a division of Harcourt Brace & Company
525 B Street, Suite 1900, San Diego, California 92101-4495, USA
http://www.apnet.com

Academic Press Limited
24-28 Oval Road, London NW1 7DX, UK
http://www.hbuk.co.uk/ap/

International Standard Book Number: 0-12-024622-8

PRINTED IN THE UNITED STATES OF AMERICA
98 99 00 01 02 03 QW 9 8 7 6 5 4 3 2 1

Contents

Guidelines for Evaluating E-Journal Providers with Applications to JSTOR and Project Muse
Mary Jean Pavelsek

Data Preparation for Electronic Publications
Norman Desmarais

Metropolitan Area Networks and the Future of Networking in the United Kingdom
D. G. Law

The Quest for Access to Images: History and Development
Christine L. Sundt

Here Today, Gone Tomorrow: What Can Be Done to Assure Permanent Public Access to Electronic Government Information?

Daniel P. O'Mahony

Past, Present, and Future of Library Development (Fund-Raising)

Joan M. Hood

Cooperation in the Field of Distance Education in Library and Information Science in Estonia

Sirje Virkus

Historiography and the Land-Grant University Library
Douglas J. Ernest

Contributors

Numbers in parentheses indicate the pages on which the authors' contributions begin.

Norman Desmarais (59), Phillips Memorial Library, Providence College, Providence, Rhode Island 02918; normd@seqent1.providence.edu

Douglas J. Ernest (155), Morgan Library, Colorado State University, Fort Collins, Colorado 80523; dernest@manta.library.colostate.edu

Rick B. Forsman (1), Denison Memorial Library, University of Colorado Health Sciences Center, Denver, Colorado 80262; rick.forsman@uchsc.edu

Joan M. Hood (123), University Library, University of Illinois at Urbana–Champaign, Urbana, Illinois 61801; j-hood1@ux1.cso.uiuc.edu

D. G. Law (77), King's College London, London, WC2R 2LS, United Kingdom; derek.law@kcl.ac.uk

Daniel P. O'Mahony (107), Brown University Library, Providence, Rhode Island 02912; daniel_o'mahony@brown.edu

Mary Jean Pavelsek (39), Bobst Library, New York University, New York, New York 10012; pavelskm@elmer4.bobst.nyu.edu

Christine L. Sundt (87), Visual Resources Collection, Architecture & Allied Arts Library, University of Oregon, Eugene, Oregon 97403; csundt@oregon.uoregon.edu

James L. Terry (21), Bobst Library, New York University, New York, New York 10012; terryj@elmer4.bobst.nyu.edu

Sirje Virkus (141), Department of Information Studies, Tallinn University of Educational Sciences, EE0001 Tallinn, Estonia; sirvir@tpu.ee

Preface

This volume marks the end of an editing era. We pay tribute to the editorship of Irene Godden, who took a dwindling series in 1991 and brought it back to the vitality envisaged by the founding editor, Melvin Voigt. We hope that a new joint transatlantic editorship, backed by a vigorous editorial board, will build on existing strengths and bring a wider perspective to future volumes. We will look back on developments and look forward to trends—and we will not be alone in doing this as the millennium draws to a close. We will seek experts in the field to cover all areas of librarianship and intend to publish comprehensive and scholarly articles that will report on advances and serve as a benchmark for the future.

This volume paints a picture of the way librarianship is advancing, moving through broad technical advances to specific applications of technology, and then examines three more focused issues: fund-raising, distance education, and library history.

Rick Forsman provides a useful introduction to the other papers on technology in the university library by giving an overview of research on the evolving roles of the information professional and the library, the issues of licensing and fiscal management, and the future adaptation of librarians as they work with electronic resources. He urges librarians to shape this new environment rather than react to it.

James Terry takes us on a fascinating tour of the development of automated systems for libraries. He charts the move from homemade systems in university computing services to the current concentration in the hands of a few large corporations. It is instructive to revisit the early dreams of fully integrated systems and compare these dreams with the commercial imperatives of today's developments on the Web.

Mary Jean Pavelsek considers one particular service on the Web, the provision of electronic journals, or e-journals. We are faced with a multiplicity of such services in today's libraries, and Pavelsek provides us with guidelines to evaluate these services and put them in an arena where they can be compared. These guidelines are used to look at two particular projects, JSTOR and Project Muse.

Norman Desmarais takes us further into the realm of electronic publishing with one librarian's experience of authoring electronic publications. This author worked on a project to produce a CD-ROM on the American Revolution. Here we see the librarian as a producer, moving one step further from the librarian as a consumer. Once again, commercial pressure provided a series of opportunities and constraints.

Derek Law examines electronic cooperation between libraries in the context of Metropolitan Area Networks in the United Kingdom. He considers networking for libraries in the UK to be at a crossroads where disparate initiatives could coalesce via Metropolitan Area Networks. The capacity for sharing resources between libraries and the organizations to which they belong can spread to cognate institutions such as local councils, schools, hospitals, museums, and art galleries.

Art, and the true images in art galleries, is central to the paper by Christine Sundt, which looks at the history of access to images to support study on a global basis. She examines the recent use of electronic access via the Web with a particular focus on the Image Directory. We have moved a long way from the days when a painter had to be employed to depict the items in a collection, but we must still take care that our current digital access to images is available to all who need it.

Accessibility is the theme of Daniel O'Mahony's paper on public access to electronic government information. The author is concerned about the fleeting nature of government information when presented in an electronic format. Paper formats have long seemed vulnerable, and in need of preservation, but on the whole they have survived. Digital information can disappear in a matter of months, either because the public files are no longer available or because the technology employed to access them has become obsolete. O'Mahony recommends a program to preserve electronic government information.

To preserve any of our resources in libraries, we need sufficient budgets, but because we seldom have this, many libraries are committed to development fund-raising. Joan Hood looks at the founding of some of the most famous U.S. library collections and considers the growth of "Friends of Libraries" to support continued development. She discusses the development of these groups and the publications that have supported their work. Hood also examines foundations that give grant aid to libraries, along with government agencies, as libraries reach out for new financial support. In addition, she covers how best to attract individual donors, the major source of donated funds.

Sirje Virkus takes us to Eastern Europe to consider cooperation in distance education for information professionals in Estonia. She covers the history of cooperation between Nordic (Finnish, Norwegian, and Swedish) librarians and Estonian librarians. After describing a pilot project for school librarians and the opportunities and threats to distance education in Estonia, Virkus reports that a major project supported by the Open Estonian Foundation, begun in 1996, will last until 2005 and improve information technology and distance education in Estonia.

The last article focuses on the histories of U.S. land-grant university libraries. (In the last century, the U.S. Federal Government granted each state land, the proceeds from the sale of which were to be used to establish colleges in agriculture and mechanic arts.) Douglas Ernest discusses the library historiographical thinking since World War II and examines how this thinking has been applied throughout the histories of land-grant institutional libraries. He stresses the importance of university library histories and expresses hope that better trained historians, who include the context of changes, will produce them.

Advances in Librarianship will continue to report and analyze significant trends in librarianship. Clearly, information technology will dominate in future papers, but major advances in library education, special collections, library histories, and library operations, among others, will also receive attention. It is also our intent to produce a millennium volume that will consider 20th-century advances and look forward to the 21st century.

Elizabeth A. Chapman

Frederick C. Lynden

Managing the Electronic Resources Transforming Research Libraries

Challenges in the Dynamic Digital Environment

Rick B. Forsman
Denison Memorial Library
University of Colorado Health Sciences Center
Denver, Colorado 80262

I. Introduction

Is this an era of exciting and unprecedented library opportunities, a crisis of professional self-determination, a time of unmatched mayhem and madness, or a bit of all three? This question and much of the turbulence experienced in today's libraries stem from the intertwined mix of threat and boon that results from the rapid proliferation of electronic information resources. The Internet and its applications have exploded into every library, changing user expectations, forcing librarians to rethink the services that they provide, and altering the very work we do. The incredible impact of the World Wide Web has been likened to the development of the printing press and movable type, the creation of the world's largest vanity press, and a basic platform for re-creating the process by which scholarly communication occurs. Whatever the complex nature of the Web and its effects, libraries sit directly in its juggernaut path.

The number of electronic journals has increased steadily throughout the 1990s, and this trend is widely predicted to continue. Khalil and Jayatilleke (1996) provide an overview of the factors that limit the usefulness of online journals at this early point in their development, describing The University Licensing Program (TULIP) Project, the *Online Journal of Current Clinical Trials*, and other examples of significant visibility and early innovation. Tenopir (1997) and other researchers note that variations in quality and accessibility make it unlikely that libraries can soon substitute electronic publications for print publications, but these limitations can be expected to change rapidly as the marketplace and its products mature. Shortcomings of the first online journals are being overcome by their successive iterations, with new features and sophistication enhancing retrieval and display options. Concurrent refinements in Web browser software allow electronic journals to create resources with new allure and convenience.

By their very nature electronic information resources are volatile, and they exist in a dynamic marketplace in which librarians are compelled to reassess assumptions and roles on a daily basis. The broad realm of information technology mutates at an incredible pace, with formats, programming languages, new companies, and new ideas emerging faster than standards can be shaped to control and normalize the structure, retrieval, or display of the content for today's products. From that perspective, this article represents a snapshot in time, a look at factors, predicaments, and opportunities confronting libraries at the time the manuscript was completed. It reviews selected trends in the impact of digital products, comments on the professional and managerial challenges they pose, and suggests likely conditions that will affect libraries in the future. As technology and the market continue to evolve, some of these issues will recede in importance while others grow more acute. Readers may find this article useful, however, in reviewing key trends and in being prepared for decisions we will face as conditions continue to change. The author has not attempted to provide a comprehensive bibliography, but has chosen representative reports and articles that highlight key issues or topics. Given the nature of the subject, it is not surprising that many references are to information located on World Wide Web sites, in papers, and in reports that will not be issued in print unless the reader sends them to a local printer.

II. Evolving Roles for the Information Professional

We begin by considering the impact of electronic information resources on the librarian's work. Soete (1997), a long-time consultant to the Association of Research Libraries (ARL), briefly describes a number of traditional library functions that undergo change as a result of electronic products, including collection development, acquisitions, cataloging, and user instruction. He notes that local, in-house acquisition decisions take on new complexity when libraries enter into collaborative licensing arrangements. Software can provide data on actual usage of electronic products, which may improve collection development decisions. Training becomes a critical factor in allowing staff and users to successfully interact with powerful and intricate software interfaces. The library must define what educational role it will claim compared to other units, such as academic computing or even the institution's central systems or telecommunications department.

The role of consultant and instructor is stressed by Haack (1997) as he argues for librarians to extend their traditional skills. Bibliographic instruction takes on a new importance and complexity as librarians attempt to impart competencies to users who must use continually changing electronic products. As new versions of each product appear, the entire Internet and its interface software also evolve. Students and faculty who learned to search a Web-based product last term may face a different interface when they next log on. Teaching and providing one-on-one assistance to users have become truly demanding and unending tasks. Lenzini (1996) elaborates on what happens in collection development as the complexity of database selection becomes a new responsibility. Decisions now require direct contact with indexing and abstracting services, other types of information aggregators, local system vendors who offer content created by third parties, publishers who are promoting new World Wide Web services, and even companies that are aiming products directly at the end user. Information gathering for selection decisions often requires multiple contacts with these different parties as new information and questions come to light.

Duranceau (1997) points out that electronic serials are more complex to purchase, more complex to provide access to, more complex to manage, and more complex to both order and renew. Her article notes that when the libraries at the Massachusetts Institute of Technology (MIT) ordered new serials in the first half of 1997, nearly 25% of the orders were for titles distributed in electronic format. Although MIT may be unusual in its rapid move toward acquisition of such a significant number of digital journals, other libraries should anticipate the same trend over time. Duranceau then provides a detailed comparison of workflow for print versus electronic serials, highlighting differences in tasks in a process that is no longer linear. For example, the acquisition of a digital journal often involves some type of online trial period, review and negotiation of a license, and possibly price negotiation, all extra steps that take considerable time and effort. She also describes the development of a new specialty position in a variety of academic libraries, with position titles ranging from "electronic access librarian" to "scholarly communications librarian."

Kara *et al.* (1995) further describe the opportunities for serials librarians to reshape their roles in the electronic environment. They highlight the change from simple purchase of a print product to negotiation of a series of complex factors, all of which affect the lasting value and the daily usability of electronic journals. Previously, serials librarians selected and managed the inventory. With digital tools, there is increased room for variation and, at times, more is at stake because of hidden costs such as training or potential restrictions lurking in the licensing agreement. Librarians engaged in selection and acquisition of these tools make more intricate decisions that also require continued vigilance and reconsideration as conditions change.

Hawkins (1997) offers an annotated listing of Web-based serials, which exemplify cataloging problems encountered by the National Serials Data Program at the Library of Congress. These problems include specifying the details about the file format of a given title (especially if this changes over time) and describing the intricacies of variant publisher practices in making available complete or partial back files of electronic issues. He remarks on the shift from organization by physical publication issue, with its standard numbering system assigned to a collection of tangible and often interrelated papers, to emphasis on the individual article that may appear to exist independently or in loose relation to the other digitized documents being released with it at a particular point in time. Hawkins stresses that the current multiplicity of file and image formats presents libraries with numerous user support problems, as do serials that are released with embedded audio or multimedia components that require special add-on software. Does one reflect these details of display requirements in a cataloging record if they may change periodically?

Sleeman (1996) describes electronic serials cataloging at the University of Virginia, where they are entering into the online public access catalog (OPAC) records from journals that are available only through the Web. Xu (1997) represents the truly updated cataloger, advocating the library's responsibility for creating repositories of metadata as an enrichment of the OPAC. Her paper examines the importance of metadata in global information retrieval and discusses its function within the framework of the Internet.

In addition to the impact of electronic resources on traditional collection development and technical services roles, one also finds that information professionals are beginning to approach electronic resources in other ways. For example, Bailey (1997) maintains an updated bibliography of scholarly electronic publishing. This Web site organizes a selected set of sources that assist in understanding what is happening in networked access to information. Machovec (1997a) has gone a step further in his Web overview of the electronic journal market, producing an online paper that synthesizes important trends as a tool to aid decision makers in wrestling with strategic investment choices within the Colorado Alliance of Research Libraries consortium.

York (1997) recounts the local development of an automated periodicals index tailored to the needs of students at East Carolina University. The index includes titles specific to North Carolina that were not previously indexed to the depth needed locally. He views this as an essential way to add value to library services. McCue (1994) repeats this theme, reminding librarians that we benefit both users and institutions by adding value, not simply by processing materials. The electronic dissemination of information affords opportunities for inserting value in ways unique to our profession, such as offering new services related to numeric, full-text, and bibliographic information.

Working in the digital era requires state-of-the-art competencies in using advanced information technologies. In academic institutions, this has resulted in changes in the levels of tension and cooperation and in roles for librarians and information professionals in other units. For example, in some institutions a librarian has become the official organizational Webmaster with responsibilities far broader than merely the library Web pages. Cunningham (1997) provides a practical guide for planning and developing a library Web site, including discussion of programming and technical skills needed by the would-be Webmaster. By extension, this expertise allows the librarian to develop and manage any Web site, and today's library school graduates find such work in many different organizational structures, both within and outside libraries.

Many of the same skills are covered by Saunders (1996), one of numerous authors who comments on the blurring of lines between librarians and computer professionals, despite their different academic preparation and credentials. Some of the best discussion about the relatedness of these two professions is found in Woodsworth (1997) and Woodsworth et al. (1992) who argue that job content is often similar and that librarians deserve salary equity and greater recognition for their valuable knowledge and skills. Our traditional professional humility serves us poorly when computer or telecommunications experts boldly press for high salaries despite having little customer service experience and poor responsiveness. Foote (1997) documents the median starting salary of a systems librarian as $32,000 per year, truly a bargain compared to the compensation commanded by other information technology professionals.

Some authors stress the vital communication role that librarians must embrace. Rapple et al. (1997) observe librarians reaching out to form new partnerships within and outside their institutions, taking on participation and leadership in campus planning and governance, and enlarging their roles in a networked environment. Similar ideas come from Rice-Lively and Racine (1997), who see technology requiring technical, cognitive, and behavioral changes. They believe librarians must be capable of multitasking, be more self-directed, engage in critical evaluation of information rather than simply passing unfiltered information to the user, and undertake continual innovation in library services.

Tennant (1995) opines that the knowledge and skills required in the virtual library have only recently become a part of the library school curriculum and may still be lacking in some programs. He outlines what he believes to be essential expertise as an outcome of the learning process. The New

York State Department of Education (1997) has taken the same approach at its Web site. It recommends that organizations that provide funding and training for librarians produce programs that impart critical technological knowledge and skills. The advent of new information technology and the emergence of products aimed at end users have produced changes in the definition of the essential educational base both at the entry level and for the duration of a career. New librarians receive a different education than earlier generations, while the existing population of practitioners must pursue updated knowledge at an ever faster rate. Library schools often have not been responsive to the continuing education needs of the profession, but this market has tremendous opportunities for growth as a revenue stream for programs that have concentrated on graduating master's degree candidates. Practitioners have passed the point of being able to pursue an entire career based solely on their initial library degree. The technological imperative calls for periodic reinvestment in current knowledge and skills. The Medical Library Association (MLA) (1991) is one example of a professional organization that addresses personal and institutional responsibilities for lifelong professional development in its educational policy statement, *Platform for Change.* Both practitioners and their employers must heed the call for acquisition of new knowledge and skills across their careers.

III. Evolving Roles for the Library

While technology has clearly altered the ways in which library staff work, the impact at the broader organizational level has been equally evident as we continue in the migration from print to electronic dissemination of information. Klemperer and Chapman (1997) provide a broad review of issues related to digital libraries and services. This review covers retrospective conversion, preservation, and archiving dilemmas; project management; imaging technology and quality problems; standards; and late-breaking news sources. Not surprisingly, the full text of the review is also available on a Web site because so many librarians are disseminating new information through the Web. Most libraries are also compelled to develop Web sites as communication vehicles that can reach users with new information and in different ways. The libraries at the University of Texas at Austin seek to educate users by including an overview of publishing statistics at their Web site (http://www.lib.utexas.edu/cird/publishing.html) to show the annual growth in both print and digital publications. The number of electronic journals grew 150% from 1995 to 1996, and it seems reasonable to expect an even steeper growth rate for the remainder of the 1990s as publishers retool the more than 165,000 existing print serials for digital distribution. As this large-scale conversion gains momentum, the library as a whole will experience further changes.

Soete (1997) reports on 14 significant information projects that typify new directions, from envisioning the development of the California Digital Library to the Online Computer Library Center's (OCLC's) growing array of electronic journals available through the FirstSearch Electronic Collections Online service, from partnering with commercial publishers to mounting local online products that compete with publishers. He concludes these vignettes by commenting on eight trends: the amount of electronic content will continue to mushroom, especially in the science, technical, and medical fields; consortia will offer attractive leveraged buying opportunities; new acquisitions options will emerge; the Web will dominate access and delivery; publishers will adjust their business to this format; specialized intermediaries, such as licensing experts, will be required; archiving issues will be solved through cooperative ventures; and technical advances will continue.

In many areas consortia are experiencing renewed energy and stronger ties through the cooperative licensing of electronic products. In the West, for example, the Colorado Alliance of Research Libraries has assisted its members in purchasing integrated library systems, mounted shared Silver Platter and Ovid Technologies products for subsets of its member institutions, and joined with other libraries in the state to obtain lower priced access to OCLC's FirstSearch. The Alliance libraries must also confront technical complications resulting from the Web becoming the newly dominant delivery mechanism. For instance, Alliance technical staff have been hired to augment the systems experts located in member institutions. The Alliance staff help libraries deal with the technological intricacies of supporting users of Web-based tools and telecommunications protocols. They troubleshoot connectivity problems, tweak interface software, and expedite Internet linkages in a more responsive manner than is generally the case for campus systems staff who see the library as only one of many customers needing service.

The eight trends described by Soete (1997) are complemented by Marcum's (1997) framing of four broad questions facing libraries: Should libraries concentrate on adding digital resources or put some effort into actually digitizing print documents? How do we shift our focus and budgets from local holdings to electronic access? How do we factor in our new reliance on network infrastructures for such access and delivery? What should we now count; that is, what measures give us useful management information? This last question is echoed by Jenkins' (1997) analysis of and speculations on usage statistics for electronic journals compared to their print predecessors. Do we know what data should be captured and tracked, and is it possible to obtain from today's digital products the data that depict significant measures of value?

Most libraries have lost the battle of keeping their serial budget even with annual publisher price increases. Individually and collectively, libraries have gradually cut subscriptions year after year, in part because they have a difficult time demonstrating the impact of or value derived from investing in a library. In recent years libraries have sometimes found that administrators, legislators, or other budget decisions makers are more willing to fund technology projects. This allure may not continue, however, as libraries keep coming back for dollars. Forward-thinking managers must begin to build their case for ongoing infusions of technology funds. We must show concretely how online databases and full-text resources enhance learning and scholarship, how the availability of access to the record of scientific data can improve peoples' daily work or civic participation. One boon of electronic journals is the promise of strong management data that shows usage details, how well searches were structured, and what resources were used to support actual learning experiences or interpersonal communication.

Many issues concerning electronic resources are currently being tackled through revitalized consortium arrangements. Geffner (in press), Lynden (1996), and Davis (1996) describe the Committee on Interinstitutional Cooperation (CIC) consortial endeavor to provide seamless electronic resource access to titles in the humanities. Lynden also mentions similar efforts by the Chesapeake Information and Research Library Alliance, TexShare, VIVA (Virginia), GALILEO (Georgia), and OhioLINK, all of which seek to offer broad benefits by cooperatively providing many users with access to electronic resources. Lynden further suggests that retrospective conversion of journals into digital full text may be a productive resource-sharing project for consortia.

Neff (1997) provides a detailed account of the digital delivery of chemistry information in Ohio that results in shared savings for the participants. In this project Case Western Reserve University and its partners scan chemical journal pages into an automated system that includes rights management software for tracking royalties due to copyright owners. Participants monitor and report on their access of the scanned pages, which can be less costly than purchasing the printed journals. Neff points out the importance of adopting clear technical standards for such a system to operate effectively.

Librarians have preceded some technology users in their recognition and adoption of standards at an early stage in automation, such as development and adherence to the MARC record formats. As online catalogs became the norm, OPAC features became more similar in some respects, and the Z39.50 standard grew as a mechanism to expedite multi-OPAC searching. In the commercial marketplace, libraries face true challenges as disparate vendors create electronic products with unique search interfaces, none of which seem to be quite as intuitive as developers claim or users prefer. Library efforts to augment access to electronic products will be enhanced as vendor products in turn make increased use of standards, but are currently hampered by the paucity of industrywide conventions. For instance, as more and more electronic books are released, it will be important to have their contents organized, searchable, and able to be manipulated in similar ways. Users and library staff alike are frustrated when having to use multiple, dissimilar tools.

As long as libraries struggle with serial price inflation, cost remains a critical issue in all phases of their operations. Varian (1997) analyzes electronic journals from an economic perspective, while also noting that archiving costs must be considered as a major expense factor for traditional shelving or in any alternative. If shelf space is saved by digitizing print materials, whomever stores the data on a Web server incurs new costs that can be substantial and that will be ongoing as technological advances require periodic reformatting due to evolving hardware and software. A number of libraries have undertaken digitization projects, and almost all academic libraries are mounting Web servers. Have these libraries considered the multiyear costs and commitments of such decisions? Have they planned in advance for personnel time and staff development costs for creating a Web presence? Have they budgeted for hardware and software depreciation? Have they compared internal costs with the costs of contracting out for the same end result?

Soete (1997) and Guthrie and Lougee (1997) report on the Journal STORage (JSTOR) Project, which, following initial funding from the Mellon Foundation, must devise an economically viable model for the continuing digitization and storage of print journals. By sharing the costs across a subscriber base, JSTOR developers hope to arrive at reasonable costs for libraries, another example of cooperative buying. Related to the JSTOR Project is the ambitious agenda of the HighWire Press, which operates under the aegis of the Stanford University Libraries. McGee (1997) gives a thumbnail description of this electronic publishing enterprise. One of the early products of HighWire Press is *JBC Online*, the electronic version of the *Journal of Biological Chemistry*. Institutional pricing for *JBC Online* went from $200 in 1996 to $1100 in 1997, a price jump and level of unpredictability that greatly complicate planning and budgeting. Although HighWire Press was originated by a library, institutional access and pricing have not been easy for readers to understand. Indeed, access to this title is sufficiently complex that a "frequently asked questions" page and explanation of pricing were created on the main Web page for the journal (http://www.jbc.org/). Can we hope that electronic journals as a whole will simplify our decisions and tasks at some future date, or will they remain complex and difficult to manage? As is true for all innovations, the competition of the marketplace will rapidly refine the digital resources now being offered. Pricing options and schedules will become more normalized, predictable, and understandable or buyers will cease to subscribe. Commercial and library publishers will learn how to generate the revenue they need and satisfy customers or products will disappear.

Libraries are moving into the publishing realm in other ways as well. The Colorado Alliance of Research Libraries (Cochenour and Jurries, 1996) has acted as an aggregator, bringing together at one Web site a large list of electronic journals with online links for accessing each title. More and more libraries are entering the world of publishing by expanding their Web sites with an array of digitized information never before available to users in such a convenient fashion. Sittig (1996) reports that technology also has an impact on the national libraries, causing them to offer new forms of access and even altering the content of what they choose to collect. No library can remain unchanged as the digital era unfolds.

IV. The Licensing Quagmire

One particular impetus for collective activity has been especially noteworthy as libraries adjust to the burgeoning production of electronic resources: Libraries have moved out of the era of one-time purchasing of print materials and into the annual leasing of digital information. Legal considerations have come to the forefront as librarians begin to understand the ramifications of licensing agreements offered to them by vendors and producers. The advent of licensing as a library concern can be seen in *Library Literature*, where the index subheading "licensing agreements" was added in 1994 and has included a growing number of citations each year thereafter. The Yale University Library, the Commission on Preservation & Access, and the Council on Library Resources (with the latter two organizations now merged to form the Council on Library and Information Resources) collaborated to create LIBLICENSE-L, a moderated Internet discussion list devoted to discussion of licensing issues for academic and research libraries. Instructions for subscribing to this listserv may be found at http://enssibhp.enssib.fr/miroir/liblic/mailing-list.shtml. The list will continue to reflect the latest dialogue on licensing issues and legal considerations as the marketplace adopts new practices.

Cramer (1994) offers suggestions for decisions related to licensing agreements, and Warro (1994) adds to these suggestions by offering a model rider that was developed at Loyola University as a way of deleting unacceptable terms and inserting important rights for the licensee. This rider serves as a useful mechanism that a number of libraries have employed to counter one-sided licenses offered by vendors. Most librarians have come to realize they are not well served by simply signing an agreement as originally written by the vendor. After all, the vendor's lawyers have slanted original agreements in the best interest of their client. Warro's article further argues the need for joint action by libraries and library organizations to influence the development of fairer contracts with electronic resource producers. Crews (1995) summarizes copyright law and implications evident at that date. Davis (1997) mentions some of the same points, but goes on to describe how contract law often supersedes standard library policy based on copyright law. Davis offers a useful comparison of rights guaranteed by copyright and rights assigned to a licensee via a written agreement. Librarians cannot afford to be ignorant of the legal issues.

As this article goes to press, the U.S. Congress is considering a variety of bills dealing with changes to copyright and intellectual property legislation. It is impossible to predict what will emerge as law or how readily all parties will be reconciled to one view. Information producers want to maximize the economic controls they believe are merited by ownership, while libraries cannot permit the abandonment of the principle of fair use. Due to the huge financial ramifications of this legislation, however, it seems safe to predict that a stable outcome is unlikely for some time. If nothing else, producers and consumers of electronic information products will gain more experience and insights after new legislation is passed. Presumably, both will alter their opinions and legal stance as well as attempt to influence interpretations in the courts.

The ARL rose to the ownership and fair use challenge by producing its *Licensing Electronic Resources* booklet (Brennan *et al.*, 1997). More important, ARL coordinated the development of a set of *Principles for Licensing Electronic Resources* in 1997, which was ratified by ARL and the American Association of Law Libraries, the American Library Association, the Association of Academic Health Sciences Libraries, the MLA, and the Special Libraries Association. The National Humanities Alliance (1997) offers principles for managing intellectual property that reflect discussion by participants from 15 professional associations related to learning and libraries. Many of these principles argue for application and interpretation of copyright law to avoid restricting the availability of information. ARL (1996) also maintains a directory of online serials at its Web site and sponsors a listserv (arl-ejournal@arl.org) that fosters discussion of all aspects of electronic journals.

V. Fiscal Management Implications

Duranceau (1997) discusses licensing in the context of the serial acquisition process and describes a database developed by the libraries at MIT for recording key data about a title and for tracking digital journal renewals. Chen (1986) calls to our attention the fact that information technology in general requires a new approach to budgeting because most libraries lack an adequate capital budget to cover depreciating hardware and software. Although it has been easy for many libraries to repurpose print subscription dollars for the annual licensing of electronic journals, does this simple substitution assist libraries in the long run? If a library administrator is asked how much is being spent to support electronic information services, only a fuzzy answer is available if personnel costs are buried in the overall human resources line, special supplies are not tracked, or licensing costs are not kept in some discrete fashion. Digital resources and the many costs required to support them will become larger components of every library's budget. Good management will necessitate tracking these expenditures and using the data for strategic decision making and budget justification.

Getz has authored numerous articles on the economics of libraries. Getz's 1997 paper on the ARL Web site focuses on electronic publishing. Using the example that the *Encyclopedia Britannica* costs less to produce in electronic format, Getz predicts a dramatic increase in the quantity of electronic information that libraries can expect. He provides a detailed economic discussion of electronic information as marketed through three typical arrangements: site license for access within the institution, personal subscription, and pay-per-view of individual articles. After commenting on the various role choices available to publishers, libraries, and agents, Getz concludes that American higher education is driven by competition and the ultimate incorporation of electronic resources into learning will be determined by which products and options optimize the institution's cost effectiveness as a learning organization. This conclusion underlines the necessity for libraries to concentrate on creating solid cost–benefit data.

Consonant with Getz's example, Fisher (1997) compares the cost of producing the *Chicago Journal of Theoretical Computer Science* in print and electronic formats, determining that the latter was easier, cheaper, and less of a financial risk. Libraries should anticipate that more and more publishers will see the proverbial "handwriting on the wall" and move away from print. Printed words that lasted for centuries will be more likely to appear tomorrow as temporary pixels on a screen. Hobohm (1997) describes the migration of the *International Journal of Special Libraries*, a publication of the International Federation of Library Associations, to online form. He worries that electronic products disenfranchise the "information poor" and suggests that uneven distribution of telecommunications systems and computer access will seriously impede the complete disappearance of print versions. Like Fisher (1997), Getz (1997), and Varian (1997), Hobohm states that production of an online journal is less costly than print format, but loss of revenues from subscriptions and advertising make the transition a risky business move in his analysis.

Meanwhile, other forces are promoting the rapid emergence of online journals. The Internet Free Press (http://www.free-press.com/), with the support of the MCB University Press Ltd., wants to assist electronic publishers in introducing new digital titles. Countering this one finds libraries joining together to oppose publisher efforts to broaden monopolies or otherwise extend their pricing control. Enserink (1997) reports that Dutch and other European libraries are uniting to act against the merger of publishers Reed Elsevier and Wolters Kluwer. This blocking effort may be brought to the Association of European Research Libraries for endorsement in 1998 and could encourage further international action to thwart publisher maneuvers that may adversely affect libraries. Other authors (e.g., Kiernan, 1997) document the ambivalence of libraries toward publishers and their products. In reference to online products from Academic Press and Elsevier Science, Kiernan remarks that some libraries are quite satisfied with pricing and value for the dollar, while some see publishers focused on a perpetual search for greater, even excessive, profit margins.

VI. Looking Ahead

Riggs (1997) reminds us that historically higher education and its academic libraries have been rather slow in changing the ways in which they conduct their business. But we can no longer afford our past practices of cautious consideration and lengthy debate prior to reaching a decision or implementing a change. The tools of our trade are mutating daily, resulting in new and sometimes startling user expectations. Riggs points out that librarians must come to terms with a less secure environment, a time of much greater ambiguity, and the imperative to engage in calculated risk taking and creative endeavors. We must embrace what is good about the move toward greater digital distribution of information and take an active part in resolving what remains problematic about electronic resources.

Not only will we experience the continued development of new electronic products as publishers reformat from what has been released to date in print, but growth in the sheer volume of scientific information will not abate. Getz (1997) reminds us that the quantity of new information continues to double in an increasingly shorter time span. Because the majority of this new information is processed in some digital form on its way to being shared, we can anticipate that an increasing amount may never appear in print as publishers and vendors become more skillful at shaping marketable products.

Pullinger (1997) remarks that the success of journals was not determined by their availability in print, but rather by their timely delivery through surface mail. The authoring and distribution of an entire book were slow. The value of the journal to the scientific community was due to the shortening of the time lag from the point of discovery to awareness by other colleagues.

If this observation is accurate, it seems inevitable that the electronic journal will win the hearts and dollars of users who depend on timely information delivery.

Pullinger (1997) predicts that the journal of the future will include specialized information content, an editorial policy on what is accepted and what criteria are used to screen contributions, a means to access the information, some citation conventions for referring to items, and a long-term archive. These elements could also describe the traditional print publications we already know, underlining that the enduring qualities we value in journals will not change. Today's digital products are perhaps weakest in means of access and lack of standardization. As publishers become more sophisticated in organizing the content of products and allowing users to easily retrieve relevant data, current problems with finding and displaying content will gradually recede. As producers redress the shortcomings of electronic tools, the advantages of faster distribution will quickly drive more users toward a preference for the digital format. This change will be complicated and held back, however, until the user is not frustrated by requirements for multiple pieces of add-on software. Web-based electronic products incorporate more multimedia that necessitate the user's loading supplemental software on his or her computer. At some point, these plug-ins and proprietary programs will need to become standard components of all basic system configurations to foster user acceptance and satisfaction.

Neff (1997) believes that greater standardization will emerge as existing technologies mature, thus adding impetus to the adoption of electronic resources as a preferred medium. If nothing else, the marketplace provides countless examples of the forces that impel the adoption of standards. Videotape and CD-ROM formatting standards arose in large part from the struggle for market share, but served ultimately to foster the convenience of both producers and users as one dominant version emerged. Microsoft and Netscape are battling for domination of the Internet, and this conflict will eventually benefit everyone through the abandonment of numerous alternative ways to code and retrieve information. Conventions for these codes and search engines will usher in an era in which digital information tools are more predictable and more easily understood. At the same time, new technologies will continue to arise, causing difficulties due to their own lack of initial standards.

For librarians, this means an abiding emphasis on our roles as organizers and instructors. Users and administrators want to believe in a vision of perfected interfaces that allow any user to rapidly and effortlessly home in on the right information required by a problem at hand. This is unrealistic in light of perpetual changes to hardware and software, the inevitability of newly emerging technologies with far from perfect interfaces, and the unrelenting growth of the information base. No interface is likely to remain static for long. Developers are compelled by competition to embark on development of a new, improved version as soon as they have released the latest software, such as we see with word processing or spreadsheet programs. The introduction of gopher technology was almost a flash in time given how quickly the World Wide Web eclipsed this simpler Internet approach. The Web serves as a wonderful case study in itself, a unique environment that expands, twists, and turns in ever-changing directions on a daily basis. How can standards be imposed, and how can interfaces become stable in such a frenzy of growth and change?

Meadows *et al.* (1997) stress the considerable difficulties that users face in navigating through electronic journals and in using the varying capabilities of different titles. An exciting aspect of the mutability of Web-based resources is the creativity that can be injected into developing products and the generation of revolutionary features and conveniences. Yet this same dynamism baffles and even angers infrequent users who cannot keep up with, let alone master, the evolving digital products. Training and user assistance, long a forte of librarians, will endure as vital enablers for the user populations we serve. Schools at all levels are beginning to understand the importance of information retrieval and handling competencies as foundations for the successful exploitation of electronic resources in lifelong learning. It is not sufficient for users to learn how to use specific tools. Instead, they must learn a conceptual framework that allows them to define an information problem, devise iterative strategies for retrieving relevant information from the huge and growing knowledge base, evaluate the amount and appropriateness of the information they found, and then apply it to the original problem. Librarians have traditionally taught or at least touched on many of these skills, although often by way of demonstrating particular tools. As a profession, however, we hold critical expertise in the organization of information, structures such as sophisticated controlled vocabularies, and rules for assessing relevance. On our own or in collaboration with others, we have the ability to teach on a more generalized level that stresses the learning of competencies for interaction with advanced technologies that continue to change.

Saunders (1996) advocates such teaching and outreach to our users while also observing that librarians have knowledge and skills that enable them to be active partners with other information technologists. Access to electronic content serves users only to the extent that they can successfully interact with the tools and that the network infrastructure also supports rapid and convenient connection. There is a three-fold interdependence of skills, information content, and infrastructure, with librarians able to assist users in all three aspects. With the swift advent of the Web, libraries and larger institutions face a new demand for security and restriction of access to valid user populations through some authentication process. This has large importance for complying with licensing agreements. Machovec (1997b) analyzes current problems and alternative solutions for handling authentication in a library context, but parent institutions need strategies for controlling access to other technological resources as well. Librarians have an opportunity to devise pilot projects or to participate in solving an important problem for the larger organization, a chance to demonstrate the value and scope of our expertise and abilities.

Delving into such systems issues can also take other directions. Rorvig and Wilcox (1997) describe the use of visual access tools to give users a new perspective on the relationship among items retrieved in a Web environment. By displaying a chart that depicts the content overlap of the Web search results, the visual access tool shows an easily understood summary of the relatedness of all items in the set. This may provide a useful overview that complements or surpasses the value of a ranked or weighted list of items, especially for a large set where a list would extend over numerous screen displays. The authors predict widespread commercial incorporation of these tools into products within 5 years. This will create another specific need for user education and an opportunity for librarians to begin adding the same visual tools into the Web pages and products we develop. Other applicable tools and programs are certain to come forth. Librarians will need to search for them and fold them into continual innovation in our electronic products and services.

Tennant (1997) has undertaken a new monthly *Library Journal* column on digital libraries, another indication of the rising prominence of this topic within the profession. In his introductory column he asserts that digital resources and collections enhance rather than replace traditional libraries, and he encourages librarians to leave their past comfort levels and experiment with the riskier electronic world. We must not only learn to function in this environment, but also help to shape it. We know that users struggle on a daily basis with imperfect interface software, and we know that software developers often lack insight into user behavior or cognitive models. We can become involved first hand in helping to improve interface design. Eliasen *et al.* (1997) report, for example, on work done by the University of Washington Libraries to study the effect of terminology and screen display on database selection. They show that use of expansive terminology and grouping of databases by type result in significantly better success in selecting the databases with greatest relevance to a given information problem. The authors conclude by recommending further active research, especially in Web design. This recommendation has been taken to an even broader plateau in *Using Scientific Evidence to Improve Information Practice: The Research Policy Statement of the Medical Library Association* (MLA, 1995). MLA advocates the prevalent conduct

Automated Library Systems
A History of Constraints and Opportunities

James L. Terry
Bobst Library
New York University
New York, New York 10012

I. Introduction

For nearly a quarter of a century, we have been told by social theorists, journalists, self-proclaimed prophets and futurists, and yes, even by librarians, that we have entered the postindustrial age. Driven by technological advances (especially in the computer and telecommunications fields), the service sector of the economy has come to predominate over manufacturing, white-collar brain work has come to replace blue-collar muscle work, and knowledge rather than capital is the new basis of power. The effect on libraries is reflected in the shift from collection building to information access, from libraries as places to the virtual library, and from traditional concepts of librarians to new concepts of librarians as information professionals. It is commonly assumed that technology has dramatically increased the range of opportunities and choices available.

It is certainly unarguable that, when we consider the developments in computer technology, telecommunications, and the accessibility of electronic information, a world of possibilities exists that was hardly imaginable prior to the 1970s. Yet, technology itself cannot explain these developments but must be examined as an element in social processes embedded in history. A rather well-known nineteenth-century social theorist framed the nature of sociohistorical processes quite simply, yet elegantly:

> [People] make their own history, but they do not make it just as they please; they do not make it under circumstances chosen by themselves, but under circumstances directly found, given and transmitted from the past. (Marx, 1963, p. 15)

This premise expresses the dual nature of social life. People's actions are bound at any historical moment by the parameters of a given political economic order, that is, a structure of relationships inherited from the past.

Within this structural framework, people make their own history; they are not passive agents totally determined by the imperatives of a given order. While action is shaped by structure, structure is transformed by action in the course of historical process.

Technology, rather than existing as an autonomous force in history, advances in response to conscious decisions made by those who control its development as well as by consumers of technology. But neither is technology neutral (Balabanian, 1993). As historian Noble (1977) reminds us,

> technology is always . . . more than information, logic, things. It is people themselves, undertaking their various activities in particular social and historical contexts, with particular interests and aims. (p. xxii)

Moreover, once implemented, technologies become embedded within the social structural arrangements, thus shaping the parameters of constraints and opportunities. As Winner (1977) observes, technology "enters into and becomes part of the fabric of human life and activity" (p. 320).

Rochell (1993), Dean of Libraries at New York University, succinctly frames the types of questions libraries, as consumers of technology, face today:

> The emergence of today's information technology has created new sets of options, responsibilities, and opportunities for America's libraries. What it most offers are choices. To be understood, these choices must be considered in an economic, political, and even philosophical context, for the decisions American librarians are making now involve far more than the technological options available to them. They relate in a powerful way to the historic goals and role of librarians and libraries. (p. 436)

If library decision makers are going to make intelligent choices related to library automation, they must be aware of the historical development of the structures of constraints and opportunities. In recent years a body of literature has developed that contextualizes the development of information technologies.[1] In this article, the author intends to provide a modest addition to that literature by examining the development of automated library systems in that context.

II. Early Development: From the University to the Marketplace

When we think of automated library systems today, we likely think of the names of a relatively small number of commercial vendors who dominate the market (e.g., Geac, DRA, Innovative Interfaces, Dynix). Commercial vendors, however, were not always predominant. In fact, in the early days of library

---

[1] See, for example, Mosco and Wasko (1988), Buschman (1993), Harris and Hannah (1993), and Crawford and Gorman (1995).

automation—the 1960s and early 1970s—major research libraries in cooperation with their university computer centers worked to develop and implement
in-house library computer systems.

The early automation efforts were a response to the dramatic expansion
of higher education in those decades and were facilitated by increased federal
funding and foundation support. As part of the "Great Society" initiatives,
the Johnson administration pushed for legislation and programs to support
education, including libraries (Henry, 1971). For example, the Library Systems and Construction Act and the Higher Education Act of 1965 made
millions of dollars available to support library expansion and research projects
in universities and libraries (Veaner, 1974). College and university enroll-
ments increased dramatically. Universities expanded and modernized their
physical facilities. They established computer centers to support both administrative functions and scholarly research. Many universities also expanded
their graduate studies programs and established new disciplinary and interdis-
ciplinary programs, ranging from women's studies to computer sciences. The
growth in higher education stimulated a growth in scholarly research and
publication. Academic libraries were faced with increasing public service
demands from both students and faculty, and demands to acquire and process
an increasing number of monographs and serials. Working with manual
systems, academic librarians were inundated with increased workloads in
circulation, acquisitions, and technical processing.

It was within this context that automation projects were undertaken
at Florida Atlantic, the Massachusetts Institute of Technology (MIT), the
University of Chicago, Stanford University, University of Minnesota, University of Oregon, University of California at Berkeley, University of British
Columbia, Northwestern University, Ohio State University, Washington
State University, University of Toronto, Harvard University, Yale University,
and the New York Public Library (De Gennaro, 1976; 1983). Largely supported by government and foundation grants, the purpose of these projects,
according to De Gennaro, was to create totally integrated in-house systems
that use a single bibliographic database to support multiple library functions
(i.e., online public catalog, circulation, acquisitions, serials control, catalog).

Several early developers of automation systems intended to sell or transfer
the systems to other libraries at cost. Under the terms of the Council on
Library Resources grant to the University of Chicago in 1966, the comprehensive system was to have been made available to other libraries as a stand-
alone system or a central system for a regional network (De Gennaro, 1976).
A similar grant to Stanford University in 1967 was to have allowed the system
to support a large-scale network in California. The University of Minnesota
Bio-Medical Library, thanks to a grant from the National Library of Medicine
in 1972, developed an integrated online system that was suitable for other

libraries of comparable size (200,000 volumes) and could be linked with regional networks and databases.

Although these early noncommercial efforts were promising, few of the experiments survived the 1970s. According to De Gennaro (1983), the level of technology at the time, its prohibitive costs, and the difficulty of sharing systems doomed these ambitious automation projects. Veaner (1974), in an extensive study of these early developments in library automation, also discovered major institutional, political, and fiscal factors that inhibited the success of these efforts. Libraries competed with other university constituents (e.g., students, faculty, and various administrative units) for scarce computer time. The computer centers did not assign high priority to library system development work.

According to Veaner, the university computer centers, in their early stages of development, were semi-autonomous entities operated by "technicians" who lacked managerial skills. Veaner describes computer facility staff, at the time, as elitist, protective of their autonomy, and threatened by potential loss of control over the direction of library system development and operations to librarians. At the same time, the expert programmers, according to Veaner (1974), "resisted participation in establishment of a production environment [for the library], with its concomitant requirement of 'dull' maintenance support work" (p. 8) Librarians, in turn, had difficulty working with the computer facilities. Unfamiliar with computer technology, they were unable to clearly write system specifications or to view automation as a developmental process rather than a purchased product, and generally had difficulty communicating with computer experts.

Whether these factors doomed the development of in-house library systems is arguable. Veaner (1974) observes that the trend toward professional management in computer centers was improving their operations and creating a service-oriented environment. In addition, librarians were becoming more knowledgeable about computers. Large academic libraries were hiring full-time technicians and professional system development managers to oversee automation development. The prospects for joint computer facility and library cooperation, however, were severely curtailed in the early 1970s, with a sudden economic downturn that affected higher education. With a depressed economy and increasing inflation, federal, state, and local government cut their financial support of education and libraries (Henry, 1971). Endowment and gift monies also declined. By the 1970s, income could not keep pace with the costs of higher education. Cheit (1971) observed the following:

> After a decade of building, expanding, and undertaking new responsibilities, the trend on campus today is in the other direction. The talk, the planning, and the decisions now center on reallocating, on adding only by substitution, on cutting, trimming, even struggling to hang on. (p. 3)

The funds that had fueled the library automation projects of the 1960s were no longer available. On university campuses, computer facilities and libraries both suffered cutbacks, and each competed for their share of a decreasing pool of resources (Veaner, 1974).

Meanwhile, other developments in the 1970s shaped a new course for library automation. In the late 1960s, the Library of Congress developed the MARC format and, in 1969, introduced a magnetic tape database that allowed for standardized online cataloging. In 1971, the Online Computer Library Center (OCLC) shared cataloging system came online, soon followed by a host of regional computer networks, initiating a new era of library networking. Faced with declining library budgets and inflationary prices, libraries turned in droves to the rapidly developing cooperative networks for shared computer systems, shared cataloging, and shared resources by way of interlibrary loan (Avram, 1978) The 1970s became, in De Gennaro's (1983) words, "the golden age of library cooperation and cooperative networks" (p. 632).

Equally significant technological developments resulted in the availability of minicomputers, affordable to most large and medium-size libraries, rapid access storage devices that allowed for online record transactions in real time, and machine-readable bar code technology. According to Barrentine and Kontoff (1990),

> Certainly, it was the capability to record circulation transactions automatically in real time on cost-effective mini-computers that allowed commercial organizations to develop products to automate circulation control, one of the most labor-intensive operations of a library—effectively and economically. (p. 476)

Thus, while libraries were devoting their attention to cooperative networking efforts, commercial vendors applied the newly developed technologies to create marketable automation products. It is understandable that the first commercial products targeted the labor-intensive circulation functions. Throughout the 1970s, for commercial vendors, automated library systems really meant automated circulation systems. Vendors typically marketed "turnkey systems," packages that included hardware, software, installation, training, and maintenance service.

CLSI installed its first turnkey circulation system in 1973. By 1983, more than a dozen other companies had entered the market, but CLSI continued to dominate with 180 of the 365 total systems installed (Mathews, 1983). Librarians will likely recognize some familiar names among these early competitors (e.g., DRA, Geac, SIRSI, Gaylord). Most competitors (e.g., Cincinnati Electronics, Easy Data Systems, M/A-COM Sigma Data, Computer Translations) are remembered only by the most erstwhile historian of library automation.

As noted earlier, the technology for integrated library systems was developed during the late 1960s and 1970s, largely in academic libraries. NOTIS (Northwestern University), VTLS (Virginia Polytechnic and State University), and multiLIS (Université de Quebec à Montréal) were each developed during this period. Commercial vendors did not began marketing online catalogs and other functional applications until the early 1980s, about the same time that NOTIS and VTLS were being made available to other libraries. By the mid-1980s, most turnkey vendors were offering integrated systems, although with varying configurations and functionalities (Genaway, 1984).

Although it appeared that more choices were being made available to libraries seeking to automate, the typical pattern of library automation severely narrowed the range of options available. Rather than purchasing a complete integrated system, many libraries, for budgetary reasons, would begin with the installation of a circulation system and then gradually add additional system components, such as an online catalog or an acquisitions module. As late as 1985, for example, only about one third of CLSI's customers had purchased its online catalog (Saffady, 1994a). The initial selection of a circulation system, however, would "preselect" the future adoption of an online catalog or acquisitions or serials module. Because vendors were offering proprietary systems, hardware and software could not be interchanged among different vendors' systems. Of course a library could change vendors, but for many libraries the cost was too high.

III. Market Segmentation and Globalization

The automated library systems market in the 1980s was characterized by two trends: market segmentation and globalization. A segmented market developed with vendors focusing on a particular market niche based on type of library (academic, public, special, school) and size (large, medium, small). Some vendors, such as Dynix, CLSI, and Geac, maintained significant market shares in both academic and public libraries of varying sizes. NOTIS specialized exclusively in systems for large academic libraries. Gaylord marketed almost entirely to small public libraries, and multiLIS to public libraries of varying sizes. SIRSI was especially strong in marketing to special libraries.

A lower-end market also developed based on sales of microcomputer software. Even though clients for these products could be found among each type of library, because of the relative inexpensiveness of these systems, school libraries tended to be the major customers. By 1994, 70% of all sales of microcomputer-based library systems software were to school libraries (Barry et al., 1995). Although some vendors of minicomputer-based systems also sold microcomputer software (e.g., IME, VTLS), the major competitors specialized solely in minicomputer-based systems (e.g., Follett, Winebego, CASPR, Brodart, Data Trek).

As Table I illustrates, competition in the minicomputer market increased as new vendors entered the marketplace. As competition intensified in the U.S. market, the major vendors increasingly marketed their systems in other countries. In 1986, Geac and CLSI dominated the international market, with foreign systems installations largely in Canada and Europe (Walton, 1987). In 1985, CLSI was purchased by TBG, Inc., a multinational conglomerate based in Monaco (Mathews, 1986). In 1986, CLSI signed an agreement to automate the National Library of China in Beijing. In addition to Geac and CLSI, DRA, Dynix, NOTIS, OCLC, and VTLS also had a small number of foreign installations.

As the 1980s progressed, vendors increasingly focused on the global market. According to Walton and Bridge (1988), in 1987 the foreign market was growing faster than the domestic market. Most of the top vendors had opened sales offices in other countries or had contracted with foreign brokers for distribution of their products. Most of the sales were in Europe, Canada, Australia, and New Zealand, with a small number in Asia and South and Central America. By 1989, Dynix, Inlex, CLSI, VTLS, and other companies increasingly pushed the sales of automated systems overseas (Walton and Bridge, 1990). Walton and Bridge (1990) observe that "the tremendous growth of the overseas marketplace tends to skew the view of what is happen-

Table I Market Shares of All Systems Installed at End of 1983 and 1987

1983			1987		
Company	Rank	installations (%)	Company	Rank	installations (%)
CLSI	1	44	CLSI	1	22
Geac	2	14	Geac	2	11
Data Phase	3	14	OCLC[a]	3	10
DRA	4	5	Dynix	4	9
Others		17	NOTIS	5	7
			Innovative	6	6
			DRA	7	5.5
			Universal	8	2
			Sobeco	9	1.6
			ALI	10	1
			Utlas	11	1
			Others		12

[a] OCLC acquired the Data Phase library systems in 1986.

Sources: Compiled from data presented in Mathews (1984, p. 855), Walton (1987, p. 41), and Walton and Bridge (1988, p. 34).

ing here at home" (p. 57). In other words, vendors were relying increasingly on foreign sales, reflecting yet another segmentation of the overall market. Table II presents both worldwide and U.S. market shares of the major integrated library systems vendors at the end of 1990.

By the 1990s, technological developments in computing and telecommunications were significantly changing the potential accessibility of information in various formats from various information suppliers. Open systems (usually UNIX based), as opposed to proprietary system platforms, and client/server architectures (which require open systems) provided standardized computer connectivity across vendors' products and allowed transparent access to data across systems (Boss, 1994). One client/server application, the *scholar workstation* would allow users to have seamless access to remote databases and multimedia materials. The Internet expanded rapidly and held the promise of accessibility to large amounts of information (Hart *et al.*, 1992). Increasingly, information of various types and formats was being produced and disseminated in electronic form. The development of the virtual library appeared to be coming closer to realization.

The library and university communities, without much dissent, welcomed these developments. At a series of workshops of 60 university provosts and library directors of major research institutions organized by the Research Libraries Group in 1991, the participants reflected on their "preferred futures for libraries." Although they disagreed on strategies, according to the Executive Summary report of the workshops,

Table II Market Shares, Total Installed Systems by 1991

Company	Worldwide			United States only		
	Rank	No.	Systems (%)	Rank	No.	Systems (%)
Dynix	1	478	18	2	248	13
CLSI	2	335	12	1	267	14
Geac	3	222	8	10	93	5
Innovative	4	196	7	3	184	10
Info Dimensions	5	190	7	7	122	6.5
VTLS	6	187	8	5	145	8
DRA	7	174	6	4	156	8
DOBIS	8	167	6	13	21	1
NOTIS	9	145	5	6	133	7
Ameritech	10	116	4	9	111	6
Sobeco	11	105	4	13	12	0.6
Inlex	12	86	3	11	76	4
SIRSI	13	81	3	10	79	4

Source: Adapted from data presented in Bridge (1991, p. 51).

Provosts and librarians share an image of the future of information resources on their campuses. They all strongly prefer a future in which there is universal access by faculty and students to multiple information sources in all possible media via a single multifunctional workstation. (Dougherty and Hughes, 1991, p. 3)

In the early 1990s, vendors, who were accustomed to the stable climate of marketing turnkey automated library systems based on proprietary computer platforms, responded to the changing electronic information environment and expressed library preferences. Some companies (e.g., Innovative Interfaces, MARCorp, SIRSI) had developed new UNIX-based systems (Saffady, 1994a). Other companies (e.g., NOTIS, VTLS) developed UNIX applications for systems previously developed as proprietary. Still other companies chose to acquire the open systems technology through the acquisition of other companies. Geac, for example, purchased Advance Libraries and Information, Inc., in 1989, thus acquiring what would become their major product, the Advance library system (Saffady, 1994b). DRA, another major vendor whose systems were proprietary, purchased Sobeco's UNIX-based multiLIS system in 1994 (*Library Systems Newsletter*, 1994c).

Geac and DRA's acquisitions were part of a general trend toward increased consolidation, or concentration of ownership, within the automated library systems market. Although mergers and acquisitions have occurred throughout the history of the market, the scale of consolidation and concentration within the market in the 1990s is unprecedented. Table III presents some of the major acquisitions in the 1990s.

IV. The 1990s: The Ameritech Story

The entrance of Ameritech, the multinational telecommunications giant, into the library systems marketplace has had a profound effect on competition within the market. The Ameritech story is not only one of acquisitions but also of the death and birth of library systems. The story actually begins in the late 1970s, long before the deregulation of telephony in the United States and the incorporation of Ameritech.

In 1977, the Lister Hill Center for Biomedical Communications of the National Library of Medicine (NLM) developed the Integrated Library System (ILS), a fully integrated minicomputer-based system (Geneway, 1984). Following testing at the Army Library in the Pentagon, the system was made available for release in the public domain through the National Technical Information Service (NTIS) in 1980. Enhanced versions of the ILS system were jointly developed by two private companies: Avatar Systems and Online Computer Systems (OCS). In 1983, OCLC purchased Avatar and entered a joint agreement with OCS to market the ILS, which OCLC named LS/2000,

Table III   Recent Acquisitions in the Library Systems Market

Year	Acquisition
1989	Geac acquired Advanced Libraries and Information, Inc.
1990	Ameritech acquired OCLC Local Systems Division.
1991	Ameritech acquired ALICE-B software from Tacoma Public Library.
1991	Ameritech acquired NOTIS.
1991	CARL Systems acquired Utlas T/Series 50 System.
1991	Inlex acquired The Assistant software.
1991	Sobeco (multiLIS system) merged with Ernst & Young, an actuarial and management consulting firm.
1992	Ameritech acquired Dynix.
1992	Geac acquired CLSI.
1993	Dynix acquired PALS system from Unisys.
1993	Data Trek acquired The Assistant software from Inlex.
1993	Gateway acquired Library Management System from National Computer Systems.
1994	Data Trek acquired OASIS from Dawson Holdings, a multinational textile company based in England.
1994	DRA acquired multiLIS from Sobeco/Ernst & Young.
1995	Endeavor Information Systems, an employee-owned company of former NOTIS employees formed in 1994, acquired the MARCorp automation systems (Voyager).
1996	Data Trek acquired IME to form Electronic Online Systems International (EOSi).
1997	Innovative Interfaces acquired SLS Information Systems (Great Britain).

Sources: Compiled from various issues of *Library Systems Newsletter* and *Advance Technology Libraries.*

and to provide enhancements and support to clients. In 1984, the NLM discontinued further development of the ILS system, leaving the market for the product to OCLC. The market for the LS/2000 quickly became quite lucrative. In 1987, OCLC's revenues were more than $10 million. By the end of the year, OCLC ranked third in total system installations, behind only CLSI and Geac (Walton and Bridge, 1988).

Ameritech, the Midwestern telecommunications giant, was incorporated in 1983 following the divestiture of AT&T. Following a 13-year U.S. Department of Justice antitrust suit against AT&T, in 1982, a court-ordered consent decree divested the corporation of its 22 local telephone operating companies (Cole, 1991). The local companies were divided into seven regional holding companies, including Ameritech, which was comprised of the local telephone companies in five Midwestern states. Among the provisions in his "Modification of Final Judgment" opinion, presiding Judge Harold Greene allowed the holding companies to seek permission to enter nonregulated competitive businesses. Ameritech soon diversified its operations into various unregulated businesses allowed by the court.

In 1990, Ameritech entered the library marketplace with the purchase of OCLC's Local Systems Division (which included the LS/2000 and LS/2 systems) and the Tacoma Public Library's Alice-B system (Bridge, 1991). It became apparent that Ameritech was not fully committed to maintaining the OCLC systems. Initially, Ameritech reported that it would continue future releases of LS/2000 and LS/2 (Bridge, 1992). Then, the company announced that it was discontinuing both systems. Finally, in 1992, the company decided to discontinue the LS/2 that year and not support the LS/2000 after July 1995. At the time of its purchase of OCLC's automated library systems in 1990, Ameritech was responsible for supporting more than 100 LS/2000 installations. Without vendor support of the systems, Ameritech's clients' only option was to migrate to a new system (Saffady, 1994a).

By the time Ameritech had made its announcement to discontinue the OCLC systems, it had already been casting for bigger fish in the library systems waters. In 1991, Ameritech acquired NOTIS, the leading vendor of integrated library systems for IBM mainframe computers and for major research libraries (Saffady, 1994a). By the end of 1993, 40% of ARL libraries were operating NOTIS systems (Saffady, 1994a). As discussed in Section II, the NOTIS-integrated library system was developed in the late 1960s at Northwestern University. When NOTIS began sales of its software to other libraries in 1981, it quickly became the preferred system for libraries with access to IBM mainframes.

In 1992, Ameritech acquired Dynix, the leading company in minicomputer-based integrated systems (*Library Systems Newsletter*, 1992). Since 1987, Dynix had installed far more of these systems than any other vendor. In 1994, Dynix clearly dominated the market, controlling more than 40% of the total minicomputer system sales (Barry *et al.*, 1995).

When Ameritech purchased the two major vendors, they were complementary in terms of market niches. Dynix's minicomputer-based systems were popular among small and medium-size libraries; NOTIS dominated the large academic library market of IBM mainframe-based systems. With the declining market for IBM mainframe systems, however, in 1993, NOTIS began development of a new product, Horizon, a Unix-based client/server system (*Library Systems Newsletter*, 1993). Carnegie Mellon University (CMU) became the alpha test site. CMU and NOTIS additionally signed a technology transfer agreement that allowed NOTIS to take advantage of technology developed at CMU's Mercury Electronic Library Project, a research program in existence since 1989. NOTIS's Horizon system, however, appeared to place NOTIS in direct competition with Dynix's Marquis system, a similar client/server system that had been successfully marketed since 1989. Within a year, Ameritech rethought not only the development of NOTIS Horizon but also the structure of its library division.

On the eve of the American Library Association (ALA) annual meeting in June 1994, Ameritech announced the consolidation of Dynix and NOTIS into a single entity, the Ameritech Library Services Division (ALS), with Dynix President, Paul Sybrowsky, as the new ALS president (*Library Systems Newsletter*, 1994a). NOTIS President, Jane Burke, left the company.[2] Ameritech also announced that it was discontinuing the NOTIS Horizon system. Keith Wilson, Executive Vice President at ALS, later explained that Horizon development was woefully behind schedule and was "struggling" at eight test sites in early 1994 (Rogers, 1995).

Confident that the Horizon system would soon be ready for the market, NOTIS sales staff had successfully arranged contracts with 27 additional sites for the installation of a system that no longer existed. According to Wilson, these libraries had "purchased a vision" (Rogers, 1995, p. 25). ALS decided to substitute its Dynix Marquis system, which Wilson claimed "adheres to [the same] vision" (Rogers, 1995, p. 25). The vision did not, however, include equivalent acquisitions or serial control modules, a reserve module, or Z39.50 standards, which were included in Horizon (Rogers, 1995; *Library Systems Newsletter*, 1994b). Ameritech assured its prospective clients that these features were targeted for early upgrades of the Marquis system. Although ALS claimed that 25 of the original 27 contracted sites were proceeding with the installation of Marquis, most of the eight test sites, including CMU, were looking for new vendors. To add an interesting twist to this tale, Ameritech has renamed the Marquis system Horizon.

Today, Ameritech dominates the minicomputer/server-based systems market as no company has since CLSI first introduced its automated circulation system in the early 1970s. Table IV presents market shares of server-based library systems for 1996. Ameritech had 30.6% of all system sales for that year. What is equally significant is Ameritech's strong showing in each type of library.

Ameritech's capital and technical resources give it a clear competitive advantage in the automated library systems market for several reasons. First, in contrast to most of its competitors, it has sufficient wealth to fund extensive research and development activities. As Griffiths and Kertis (1994) observe, "major investments in R&D are not feasible for vendors whose sole market is libraries, a relatively small area compared to other automated system markets" (p. 54).

A second, and related, competitive advantage relates to the type of R&D projects. Typically, library systems vendors devote most of their efforts to developmental enhancements of existing systems rather than engaging in

---

[2] Backed by $450 million in venture capital, several other former NOTIS employees formed a new employee-owned company, Endeavor Information Systems, to market automated library systems (*Advanced Technology Libraries*, 1995a).

Table IV Market Shares of Server-Based Systems, 1996

Company	Total (%)	Academic (%)	Public (%)	School (%)	Special (%)
Ameritech	30.6	20.8	57	7	27
DRA	25.2	5.4	7	75	1
EOSi	7.5	19	1	—	14
Geac	5.3	5.4	12	—	6
SIRSI	5	8	3	4	8
Innovative	4.6	14	2	1	4
COMPanion	3.3	—	—	11	1
Sanderson	2.7	2	2	1	—
Gaylord	2.5	2	7	1	—
Ex Libris	2.4	6.9	1	—	3
VTLS	2.3	4.5	1	—	6
Best-Seller	1.4	1	3	—	3
Endeavor	1.3	4.2	—	—	2
Fretwell–Downing	1.3	2	1	—	4
Info Dimensions	1.3	—	—	—	9
Others			Less than 1%		
TOTAL SALES	**2006**[a]	**480**	**525**	**578**	**301**

[a] Total sales include 122 systems sold to consortia or other clients.
Source: Compiled from data from Pepin *et al.* (1997).

research related to new technologies (Griffiths and Kertis, 1994). In Griffiths and Kertis's (1994) words, "vendors tend to pace themselves with computer industry developments, adopting them as they are mainstreamed" (p. 54). Ameritech, however, with its technical resource base, is well positioned to apply its expertise in broadband, fiber-optic networks to the new generation of automated library systems.[3]

Lacking Ameritech's resources for R&D, some competitors are allying with university research centers to pursue technological development. SIRSI, as NOTIS had previously, has signed a technology transfer agreement with CMU (*Advanced Technology Libraries*, 1994). Similarly, Geac established an alliance with MIT in 1995 (*Advanced Technology Libraries*, 1995a).

A final competitive advantage for Ameritech results from its resources for advertising and marketing. Of course, most vendors advertise in the major library journals and may even distribute promotional canvas book bags at library conventions. Attendees at the 1995 annual conference of the ALA, however, could not avoid recognizing the major sponsorship by Ameritech. The opening general session, in fact, was named the "Ameritech Opening

---

[3] On the importance of telecommunications technology for the development of new library systems, see McKibirige (1991).

General Session." The ALA is careful to note that this sponsorship does not imply an ALA endorsement for Ameritech's products. Yet, the identification of Ameritech with the ALA has an impact far beyond mere advertising. Ameritech acquires legitimacy as a company committed to libraries and, through name identification, receives the implicit endorsement of the library community represented by the ALA.

Despite these competitive advantages, Ameritech's continuing dominance of the library systems market is far from assured. In 1996, the company realigned its ALS operations for a second time, consolidating its units, laying off 15% of its employees, and appointing its fourth new president in 3 years (*Library Systems Newsletter*, 1996). This appearance of instability, and the company's appointment of top-level managers who have had no library automation experience, may affect the choices of current or prospective customers.

V. Freedom to Choose

With the emergence of a new generation of automated library systems, many libraries are faced with migrating from an obsolete system to a new system, developed by either their previous vendor or another vendor. In 1994 alone, vendors reported migrating 151 clients to new systems (Barry *et al.*, 1995). The required investment in new systems comes at a time when libraries of all types are faced with increasingly scarce resources. The final section of this article discusses some of the constraints on choice related to migration and vendor selection. Geac provides an interesting case in point. When the company began marketing its new integrated online system, Advance, its clients who had come to know and love the older Geac GLIS system were faced with a rather narrow range of choices. They could either migrate to the new Advance system, which required a sizeable capital outlay, or they could shop for a new vendor and be faced with a likely higher capital expense.[4] Since Geac could not indefinitely support the outmoded GLIS system, staying with GLIS for any extended period of time was not an option. As an open system, Advance allowed greater interconnectivity and the promise of seamless access to remote databases, including the Internet. From the client's standpoint, however, the options for what system to select and when were limited.

Whether the Geac client chose to migrate to Advance or another vendor, the opportunities or range of choices the library can make to implement a system that meets that institution's needs are constrained in particular ways. Vendors generally sell a package system, certain features of which may or may

[4] Boss (1994) estimates that client/server systems, the latest technology in library automation, cost from 30% to 50% more than "hierarchical" systems, which have been the standard technology.

not be modifiable. Where modifications, or enhancements, are technically possible, they may not be financially possible for the library. Enhancements made for a particular library can be quite expensive. In addition, vendors will develop major enhancements that become part of the package system only if they are profitable. The formation of users groups, comprised of libraries that share the same vendor, systematized the enhancement process for major vendors. Users of a particular system will cooperatively specify which enhancements are most important to the group as a whole. The vendor will then, if technologically feasible, develop those enhancements for which there is the greatest demand. The users group thus performs marketing research work for the vendor, allowing the vendor to tailor its product to meet the greatest demand. Vendors discourage requests by particular libraries for more unique enhancements through the high prices they charge for such development work.

Libraries, assuming that they have the financial resources, have always been free to choose automated library systems from a range of commercial vendors. It is not a simple matter, however, to evaluate the strengths and weaknesses of the various technological systems. Neither is it easy to evaluate the stability, commitment, and future prospects of the companies themselves. Standard tools for company evaluation, in any industry, are financial statements from annual reports, company SEC filings such as the 10-K report, and investments surveys such as those done by Value Line or Standard & Poors. This information, however, exists only for publicly traded companies, and most library automation companies are privately held. As of April 1998, only Ameritech, Geac, and DRA were publicly traded. Since Geac and Ameritech are really conglomerates with multiple divisions, financial statistics for their library automation segments are not provided. In effect, financial statements for library automation companies are not a useful tool for evaluating these companies. News reports and industry surveys have regularly appeared in *Library Journal, Library Systems Newsletter, Library Technology Report,* and *Advanced Technology Libraries,* but the reports rely on information voluntarily supplied by the companies.

If the availability of company information is problematic, it is not a simple matter to compare library automation systems in terms of functionality. *Library Technology Reports* periodically analyzes and compares the functionality of competing vendors' systems. However, because of industry volatility and changes in technology, the *Reports* cannot be the sole source for evaluation. The information becomes quickly outdated. Typically, the Request for Proposal (RFP) procurement process is used for vendor comparisons. A library will send outlines of their system needs to several vendors. Vendors will respond with detailed written proposals, including estimated costs, of how their system can meet the library's needs. But detailed RFP's and time spent on system demonstrations are costly to both the vendor and the library. According to Barry *et al.* (1995), "The increased vendor costs end up in the cost of the systems. In many instances, the cost of procurement exceeds the cost of the system" (p. 48).

In summary, libraries are now free to choose among various providers of automated library systems. However, the concentration of ownership within the industry, the competitive advantage of large conglomerate corporations, the uncertainties of corporate commitment, the problematic nature of system and company evaluation and comparison, and the process of technological development itself, together structure a system of constraints and opportunities that concentrates the control and direction of technological development among a small group of large corporations. Although CMU and MIT have engaged in joint technology development projects with commercial vendors, most libraries have limited leverage in directing the course of system development.

VI. Conclusion

The author framed this brief history of automated library systems in terms of structures of constraints and opportunities. One opportunity forgone was the potential for the development of library systems outside the commercial sector. Although the constraints ultimately proved too formidable to overcome, given different historical circumstances, an alternative history of cooperative development among universities and libraries, comparable to the "golden age of networking" in the 1970s, can be imagined. Once commercialization occurred, however, the structure of constraints and opportunities became embedded in the marketplace with the profit motive as the ultimate arbiter for affecting the range of choices for both vendors and clients.

What about technology? Developments in telecommunications and computer technologies have clearly led to changes in library automation. Rather than working on the cutting edge of technological development, library systems companies have implemented new technologies as they have become marketable, profitable, and safe. Once implemented, however, the new technologies make the old obsolete. The death of the typewriter provides a simple but useful analogy. For some people it may still be an appropriate technology, but typewriters, as well as their maintenance and support services, have virtually disappeared from the marketplace.

Increasingly, people are questioning the postindustrial love affair with technology, from neo-Luddites such as Sale (1995), to technophiles with second thoughts such as Stoll (1995), to library leaders such as Crawford and Gorman (1995). Each is asking the question: What is appropriate technology?

For librarians, this question must be framed within the larger context of questions, such as what is the mission of the library, and what is the role of the librarian? These questions are especially important today as we observe the increasing commercialization of the Internet. As librarians collectively address these questions, it is wise to keep in mind that, despite structural constraints on opportunities and choices, people make their own history. If they cannot do so just as they choose, the challenge exists to make creative choices that preserve the values that we share.

References

Advanced Technology Libraries. (1994). **23**(12), 4.

Advanced Technology Libraries. (1995a). **24**(1), 1, 10.

Advanced Technology Libraries. (1995b). **24**(5), 1, 10–11.

Avram, H. D. (1978). Toward a nationwide library network. *Journal of Library Automation* **11**, 285–298.

Balabanian, N. (1993). The neutrality of technology: A critique of assumptions. In *Critical Approaches to Information Technology in Librarianship: Foundations and Applications* (J. Buschman, ed.), pp. 15–40. Greenwood, Westport, CT.

Barrentine, J., and Kontoff, T. (1990). Library automation software. *Library Technology Reports* **26**, 475–483.

Barry, J., Griffiths, J.-M., and Lundeen, G. (1995). Automated system marketplace 1995: The changing face of automation. *Library Journal* **120**(6), 44–54.

Boss, R. W. (1994). Client/server technology for libraries with a survey of current vendor offerings. *Library Technology Reports* **30**, 681–744.

Bridge, F. R. (1991). Automated system marketplace 1991: Redefining system frontiers. *Library Journal* **116**(6), 50–62.

Bridge, F. R. (1992). Automated system marketplace 1992: Redefining the market itself. *Library Journal* **117**(6), 58–72.

Buschman, J. (Ed.). (1993). *Critical Approaches to Information Technology in Librarianship: Foundations and Applications.* Greenwood, Westport, CT.

Cheit, E. F. (1971). *The New Depression in Higher Education.* McGraw-Hill, New York.

Cole, B. G. (Ed.). (1991). *After the Breakup: Assessing the New Post-AT&T Divestiture Era.* Columbia University, New York.

Crawford, W., and Gorman, M. (1995). *Future Libraries: Dreams, Madness, and Reality.* American Library Association, Chicago.

De Gennaro, R. (1976). Library automation: Changing patterns and new directions. *Library Journal* **101**(1), 175–183.

De Gennaro, R. (1983). Library automation and networking: Perspectives on three decades. *Library Journal* **108**(7), 629–635.

Dougherty, R. M., and Hughes, C. (1991). *Preferred Futures for Libraries: A Survey of Six Workshops with University Provosts and Directors.* Research Libraries Group, Mountain View, CA.

Genaway, D. C. (1984). *Integrated Online Library Systems: Principles, Planning and Implementation.* Knowledge Industry Publications, White Plains, NY.

Griffiths, J.-M., and Kertis, K. (1994). Automated system marketplace 1994. *Library Journal* **119**(6), 50–59.

Harris, M. A., and Hannah, S. A. (1993). *Into the Future: The Foundations of Library and Information Services in the Post-Industrial Era.* Ablex, Norwood, NJ.

Hart, J. A., Reed, R. R., and Bar, F. (1992). The building of the Internet: Implications for the future of broadband networks. *Telecommunications Policy* **16**, 666–689.

Henry, D. D. (1971). *Challenges Past, Challenges Present: An Analysis of American Higher Education Since 1930*. Jossey-Bass, San Francisco.

Library Systems Newsletter. (1992). **12**(2), 9–10.

Library Systems Newsletter. (1993). **13**(8), 62–63.

Library Systems Newsletter. (1994a). **14**(7), 49–51.

Library Systems Newsletter. (1994b). **14**(8), 61–62.

Library Systems Newsletter. (1994c). **14**(11), 83.

Library Systems Newsletter. (1996). **16**(9), 69–70.

Marx, K. (1963). *The Eighteenth Brumaire of Louis Bonoparte* [originally published in 1869]. International Publishers, New York.

Mathews, J. R. (1983). The automated library system marketplace, 1982: Change and more change. *Library Journal* **108**(5), 547–553.

Mathews, J. R. (1984).

Mathews, J. R. (1986). Growth and consolidation: The 1985 automated library system marketplace. *Library Journal* **111**(6), 25–37.

McKibirige, H. (1991). Information communication highways in the 1990s: An analysis of their potential impact on library automation. *Information Technology and Libraries* **10**, 172–184.

Mosco, V., and Wasko, J. (1988). *The Political Economy of Information.* University of Wisconsin, Madison.

Noble, D. (1977). *America by Design: Science, Technology, and the Rise of Corporate Capitalism.* Knopf, New York.

Pepin, T., Barry, J., and Penniman, W. D. (1997). Automated system marketplace, The competative edge: Expanded access drives vendors. *Library Journal* **122**(6), 47–56.

Rochell, C. C. (1993). The library and new technologies: Bringing students and scholars on-line. In *Research Libraries—Yesterday, Today, and Tomorrow* (W. J. Welsh, ed.), pp. 436–450. Greenwood, Westport, CT.

Rogers, M. (1995). Ameritech looks to move beyond the Horizon. *Library Journal* **120**(1), 25.

Saffady, W. (1994a). Integrated library systems for minicomputers and mainframes: A vendor study, part I. *Library Technology Reports* **30**(1), 5–150.

Saffady, W. (1994b). Integrated library systems for minicomputers and mainframes: A vendor study, part II. *Library Technology Reports* **30**(2), 157–323.

Sale, K. (1995). *Rebels Against the Future: The Luddites and Their War on the Industrial Revolution, Lessons for the Computer Age.* Addison-Wesley, Reading, MA.

Stoll, C. (1995). *Silicon Snake Oil: Second Thoughts on the Information Highway.* Doubleday, New York.

Veaner, A. B. (1974). Institutional, political and fiscal factors in the development of library automation, 1967–71. *Journal of Library Automation* **7**, 5–26.

Walton, R. A. (1987). The 1986 automated system marketplace: New perspectives, new vistas. *Library Journal* **112**(6), 36–43.

Walton, R. A., and Bridge, F. R. (1988). Automated system marketplace 1987: Maturity and competition. *Library Journal* **113**(6), 33–44.

Walton, R. A., and Bridge, F. R. (1990). Automated system marketplace 1990: Focusing on software sales and joint ventures. *Library Journal* **115**(6), 55–66.

Winner, L. (1977). *Autonomous Technology: Technics-Out-of-Control as a Theme in Political Thought.* MIT, Cambridge, MA.

Guidelines for Evaluating E-Journal Providers with Applications to JSTOR and Project Muse

Mary Jean Pavelsek
Bobst Library
New York University
New York, New York 10012

I. Introduction

As technology advances, libraries are presented each day with new and innovative ways to access, archive, and search for information. This huge increase in technology creates both opportunities and confusion. For some time, the Internet has been a vehicle for specialized and experimental publications, but now commercial publishers, university presses, and others are using World Wide Web technology to bring their journals to the global community. Barnes (1997) states that

> The impetus of this giant leap is undoubtedly the emergence of the Web and reduction in entry costs and the complexity it is providing to the information provider. This, in turn, is providing the essential standardization and critical mass of electronic journals that the library is looking for to finally start the migration from paper. (p. 407)

The term *e-journal provider* as used here is not meant to describe individual journal offerings but, instead, ventures ranging from commercial publishers offering their own journals to services acting as distributors of e-journals from multiple publishers. Products such as these are proliferating, and it is becoming increasingly difficult not only to keep abreast of them but also to evaluate them. Just a few examples of initiatives providing the journals of single publishers include Academic Press IDEAL, Blackwell Science, and Project Muse; products providing journals from a variety of publishers include OCLC Electronic Collections Online, Information Access Company, JSTOR, and Dialog@Carl.[1] E-journal providers are using similar World Wide

---

[1] For an overview of current e-journal providers see Machovec (1997). For discussion and profiles of producers and distributors of electronic databases, see Tenopir and Barry (1997).

39

Web technologies to provide full-text journals, but important differences still remain in many areas.

Much has been written on the technologies and issues surrounding e-publications, but little practical advice on how to evaluate e-journal providers and services to decide which are right for which situations. This article has a two-fold purpose: first, to provide a general checklist that can be applied to any e-journal provider to give a clearer picture of the product and its features, and second, to use these guidelines to examine and become familiar with two very different but excellent providers. These providers are JSTOR, an archiving service supplying only back files, and Project Muse, which provides only current journals. In the process, not only the products but also some of the concepts of e-publications in general are explored. Evaluating resources against prescribed guidelines results in more informed decisions. As Tenopir (1997) puts it,

> With print, there is little choice about format and payment. With electronic journals, there is a complex mix of options. Those who consider replacing or supplementing part of a print journal collection with electronic alternatives must examine what they get, where they get it from, and how they pay. (p. 37)

There are many excellent resources currently available, but only through careful scrutiny can decisions be reached determining what features of each are most useful, not only to the electronic community as a whole, but also to individual libraries and institutions with specific needs and user populations.

II. Evolving Roles

Librarians have traditionally been the selectors for print materials and, more recently, have developed criteria used in the selection of electronic resources. Until just a short time ago, only a handful of scholarly journals were available in electronic format, and so the criteria developed have been used predominantly in the selection of single electronic journal titles or to decide whether to catalog or point to a resource available on the Web. The electronic landscape has changed again and has brought with it this explosion of e-journal providers. We must now not only have guidelines to select individual electronic titles, but we also need new guidelines by which to evaluate these providers of veritable digital libraries. To be sure, the value of individual titles offered by these providers must certainly be determined, but criteria are also needed by which to evaluate the e-journal providers as a whole. Issues range from new pricing strategies to wide variations in copyright and distribution restrictions. E-publications offer solutions to some of the more pressing problems facing libraries and are changing the world of scholarly publishing as we know it. This is not to say that they are complete solutions; far from it. There are still issues to be dealt with, and ultimately each library will have to decide what path to take depending on the research needs of its users and other factors, such as the budgetary constraints of the institution.

III. Guidelines for Evaluation of E-Journal Providers

This is intended to be a general set of guidelines. Many of these issues and others have been discussed throughout the literature from various viewpoints. Machovec (1997) provides an overview of common issues facing e-journal publishers, while Jones (1996) identifies which should be considered by libraries making the transition to e-journals. It should be noted that not every checklist point may be appropriate for every product, and certain products and situations may require specialized criteria that may not be included here. Indeed, some products offer specialized features and services that must be evaluated on their own merits. In addition, each library has individualized needs and requirements, and these must be considered when evaluating the suitability of providers. For instance, archival implications would be of no import to libraries that desire access to current publications only. In general however, this list provides the major points that a library should examine prior to subscribing to any e-journal service.

1. *Economics.* Does the library stand to save money? Even if the library must spend more money, will it be money well spent in the sense that remote and electronic access are value-added services and important to the user?[2] In this time of serials budget cutbacks, can the library justify purchasing the same journals in more than one format?

2. *Ease of Use/User Flexibility.* Are search utilities good? Is printing or downloading problematic? Are there hypertext links to related material? Can documents be downloaded and used in word processing programs?

3. *Archival Implications.* Have assurances been made by the provider to maintain an archive? If electronic back files remain available, are they in a form appropriate for an archive? That is, are they close enough to the print version—still considered the copy of record—to be acceptable for archives? Are the documents bitmapped images complete with photographs and graphical material, or are they HTML format? *Bitmapped images* are high-quality digital images

[2] For a discussion of the importance of print collections and future implications for digital libraries, see Crawford (1998).

created by individually scanning pages. *HTML* (hypertext markup language) *format* transfers only textual data, not images, and does not deliver an exact image of the printed page (Hahn, 1996). For many libraries, only electronic replicas of the print will be deemed adequate for archival purposes. Will the majority of users accept electronic archives, or will the library need to retain paper copies?

4. *Future Accessibility.* Many libraries subscribe to both print and electronic versions for fear that electronic versions may be canceled or may cease, leaving gaps in their holdings. There are two aspects to consider. First, if the electronic subscription is canceled, will there be continued electronic access to the material subscribed to up until the point of cancellation, or will all electronic access be lost? With print subscriptions, this was never an issue; whatever is paid for until cancellation is *owned.* Libraries retain journals even after canceling subscriptions. To ensure future accessibility, will libraries be forced to locally archive the material? With the increase in the number of e-journals being published, libraries who must rely on what they have archived locally, assuming that they even have permission to archive the material in question, may have to consider offline storage options that present problems ranging from loading procedures to preservations issues (Neavill and Sheble', 1995). What provisions, if any, has the provider made to ensure future availability in the case of cancellation?

Second, how do the prospects look for the provider? Does it appear that it will continue into the future? E-journal providers may go out of business, leaving no archives, or may discontinue individual titles leaving subscribers with gaps or with no holdings at all (Neavill and Sheble', 1995). Even if electronic back files remain accessible, subsequent issues may only be available in print, disrupting the consistency of the libraries' holdings.

5. *Access.* Are passwords necessary, or is there domain access? If passwords are used, they must be assigned and kept track of by the institution, requiring manpower and paperwork, and they present headaches for users required to remember them. Domain access works by recognizing IP addresses, unique addresses assigned to each computer on the Internet, necessitating no manpower. Despite the advantages to domain access, it is not without problems. Students and faculty using private Internet accounts such as America Online will be denied access because they will be outside of the domain, and those residing outside the local calling area will be charged for long distance calls (Yott and Hoebeke, 1997), obliging institutions with large commuter populations to consider alternative approaches.

Is there a limit to the number of simultaneous users? Is the information mirrored anywhere to diminish slow response times brought on by heavy traffic on the Web?

Are individual URLs provided for each journal? Unique URLs for individual journal titles enable users to quickly gain access to the journals that they need without having to navigate through the database. Individual journal titles may be cataloged and included in either Web-based online public access catalogs (OPACs) or Web pages, with direct access to the journals and sometimes the search engine, or listed in the online OPAC with the URL provided for the patron's later use.

6. *Licensing, Copyright, and Distribution Restrictions.* The electronic age is seeing changes in intellectual property rights. The regulations that apply to print format or even first-generation ASCII text e-journals published by individuals or scholarly groups who normally waived copyright restrictions may not be the same for World Wide Web-based publications (Duranceau *et al.*, 1996). World Wide Web-based e-journal providers are now often university presses, commercial publishers, or distributors representing multiple publishers, who "cannot be expected to take the generally relaxed attitude toward copyright characteristic of first-generation publishers" (Duranceau *et al.*, 1996, p. 50).

Copyright, licensing, and distribution restrictions may vary among providers and, as Okerson (1997) has noted, many electronic publishers have now turned from copyright to licensing to establish the rights of the owners and users. Although processes such as scanning printed materials and creating bitmapped images or converting them to ASCII text is probably protected under the archival reproduction exemption of the Copyright Act of 1976, making such copies available to multiple terminals simultaneously is not likely to be allowed. Due to such changes, libraries and providers are entering into licensing agreements (Quandt, 1996).

Because licenses are becoming standard practice for providing access to and use of electronic information in library settings, we must pay attention to both the details and the cumulative effect of these agreements on users, institutions, and the process of scholarly communication. (Brennan *et al.*, 1997, p. 1)

On a practical level, it is important to review the rights and restrictions involved, to determine how practices such as interlibrary loan, making copies for class distribution, archiving, and accessing material on multiple terminals may be affected.

7. *Is the Provider a Single Publisher, or Does it Handle Publications of Multiple Publishers?* This is an important consideration, as it may

have direct implications on the *subject scope* of the product now and in the future. Providers who contract with multiple publishers have the flexibility to offer any journals that are in demand or will have the most users. However, if the provider is a single publisher, the scope of the resource will be limited to the publications of that publisher only. As Malinconico (1996) points out, a shortcoming of earlier providers was that they did not include "a critical mass of journals of interest to potential users" (p. 218); a problem easily remedied by involving multiple publishers.

8. *Is the Electronic Version as Comprehensive and Complete as the Print Counterpart? Are the Articles Refereed?* Currently, a relatively small percentage of scholarly journals is available electronically, and they may not be as complete as the printed versions, assuming that a printed counterpart even exists. In addition, it is sometimes the case that electronic versions are not subject to the same strenuous peer review that print publications must undergo.

9. *User Support.* Does the product provide good user support? Is there online help available? Are there e-mail lists for announcements and updates? Is there a listserv that subscribers can use to communicate with each other and the providers?

10. *Are Individual Titles Available?* With serials budgets as tight as they are, the ability to subscribe to single journals or selected journals is helpful. For institutions that cannot afford or justify subscribing to an entire database, decisions can be made to include only heavily used titles, or to tailormake their database to more closely fit the particular research needs of the institution, or a particular program, without subscribing to journals that will receive little use. This is especially useful for academic departments, special libraries, or smaller institutions. Past technologies such as CD-ROMs made it impractical or impossible to allow libraries to select individual titles. World Wide Web technology makes it possible for libraries to select only the journals they need and should demand that e-journal providers not require libraries to purchase "prepackaged" content bundles (Barnes, 1997).

11. *Upcoming Plans or Enhancements.* Electronic publishing is an evolving industry, and there is much room for improvement and change. What does the provider have planned for the future?

IV. JSTOR

JSTOR, a not-for-profit organization established in 1995, was provided with initial funding from the Mellon Foundation. It provides the full text of all the back issues of selected core academic journals in the areas of economics, political science, history, ecology, and population studies, with plans to add additional titles in mathematics, philosophy, sociology, and other fields (Garlock *et al.*, 1997). JSTOR's emphasis is on becoming a reliable and comprehensive archive. They do not publish current issues of journals but instead have worked out agreements with publishers and established a lag period ranging from 3 to 5 years. With each passing year, another year is added to the archive, ensuring continuous updating (JSTOR Phase 1 Pricing and Availability). Within 3 years, JSTOR will provide the complete runs of at least 100 academic journal titles in 10 to 15 fields.

Taking advantage of the latest imaging technologies, JSTOR uses high-resolution (600 dpi) bitmapped images to provide faithful reproductions of original journal articles, including tables, charts, photographs, and other graphic material. These bitmapped page images are linked to a separate text file allowing complete search and retrieval of journal material (JSTOR Background).

JSTOR hopes to demonstrate that by converting back issues of journals into digital formats, it is possible to save shelf space, decrease capital costs associated with the space, and improve access to the journals through better indexing and making them available electronically. In addition, the project could solve preservation problems, as journals in electronic format need not be bound, repaired, or replaced, thereby reducing not only the operating and capital costs incurred by the storage but also by the maintenance and preservation of print journal collections (JSTOR Mission and Goals). (Access: http://www.jstor.org)

A. Economics

JSTOR has digitized an enormous amount of material that might otherwise never have been available due to prohibitive costs or lack of interest by publishers. Due to this, and because JSTOR is a work in progress, the pricing structure is unique. There is a one-time database development fee that includes permanent access rights, and an additional annual access fee that will remain fixed for the first 3 years of participation. The initial development fees are substantial, ranging from $10,000 for the smallest institutions to $40,000 for the largest. Annual access fees range from $2000 to $5000, depending on institution size and class, and are incurred to help cover the costs of maintaining and updating the database. The rationale behind offering varying prices was to create pricing that would enable as many institutions as possible to participate, while distributing the huge costs of the effort in a fair way.

Although the $10,000 to $40,000 participation fees represent substantial amounts for most libraries, the sums seem small when measured against the amount of money libraries stand to save. Space and storage problems are very real issues faced by libraries today, and in the case of institutions with immediate and pressing storage problems, even the $40,000 paid by the largest institutions is minor compared to the costs of building or renting offsite storage. For libraries with incomplete or deteriorating back files, or that lack certain journals altogether, JSTOR presents the opportunity to get complete journal runs, in perfect condition, for a fraction of the cost of purchasing printed copies. In addition, the associated costs of building and maintaining library space, and for preservation and processing of these journals, would not be incurred. For institutions who already have substantial paper back files, having them electronically gives them the option of either moving them to offsite storage or, for the very brave, discarding them altogether (Bowen, 1995).

Some preliminary figures to calculate possible savings were given in a paper by Bowen (1995), President of the Mellon Foundation. Using the journal *Ecology* as an example, it was estimated that the costs involved in storing the entire 76-volume run of the journal would far exceed the capital charge for both the storage and acquisition of this journal in the JSTOR electronic archive. In addition, figures compiled at the University of Michigan and at five other college test sites show that, with JSTOR's electronic access, costs involving retrieving and reshelving paper copies will be substantially lower, especially for closed-stack libraries (Bowen, 1995).

JSTOR admits that these figures are preliminary but maintain that the economics are driven by scale effects, since tasks such as storage and retrieval now repeated at thousands of institutions need to be done only once, far more effectively, and at much lower cost. When both capital and operating costs are combined and expressed on a yearly basis, it is estimated that "the continuing costs of storing, retrieving, conserving, processing, and binding one journal, such as *Ecology*, in paper format are at least twice (and perhaps three times) greater than what they would be if the library contracted with JSTOR" (Bowen, 1995). Guthrie and Lougee (1997) state that

> The underlying proposition that JSTOR proposes to address is that selective retrospective conversion to digital formats is economically feasible . . . when the costs can be distributed among a large number of libraries. Furthermore, these costs will be justified by economies in the use of space, reduced library operating costs, and added convenience and value to users. (p. 43)

In addition, a separate report commissioned by the Research Libraries Group and the Commission on Preservation and Access (1996) contends that, although there is much more to be learned, digital archives such as JSTOR do appear to be cost effective.

A model put together at the Massachusetts Institute of Technology (MIT) shows that it is not economically feasible for any single institution to attempt to electronically archive its own holdings and, in fact, the vast majority of research libraries have decided against it. The rough cost of archiving and maintaining 100 journals during a 5-year period was estimated to be $500,000, or about $1,000 per title per year, which is significantly more than the cost to maintain the same number of print titles. These costs are based on the outlays needed for the purchase of fast servers, additional technically proficient manpower, and disk space (Duranceau *et al.*, 1996). Considering that these figures do not even reflect the costs of digitizing vast back files and that research libraries are giving up their depository roles for electronic formats, JSTOR represents an extraordinary value and an indispensable service.

On the down side, Yale University's associate librarian points out that with JSTOR libraries are actually purchasing the same material for the third time—print, microform, and electronic format—and that although the individual journal price is low, it is still difficult to finance the $40,000 start-up fee. She concedes that JSTOR may save on labor costs, but at the moment, "the university can't measure that in any way that passes for cash on the barrel head" (DeLoughry, 1996, p. A32). In fact, an important consideration is that money may only be saved if paper back files are actually discarded. If they are not, they must still be stored, and they will presumably be used, necessitating retrieval and reshelving, as well as binding and preserving. Unless the radical step of actually eliminating the paper back file altogether is taken, libraries are spending $10,000 to $40,000 for electronic access only. Presumably electronic access will be readily accepted in the future, but that time is not here yet. It may take time for some institutions to realize savings on their initial investment, but it does appear that they will save. The difficulty will be convincing administrators and users that this is money well spent and, in the long run, money saved.

B. Ease of Use/User Flexibility

The advanced imaging technology used by JSTOR makes it possible to replicate not only the text of the journal exactly as it appeared on its publication date, but also, perhaps more important, to replicate the nontext material such as tables, photographs, and drawings. This faithful replication, however, comes with a high price in terms of ease of use. In fact, if a document is predominantly character based (i.e., only text, including no graphical content), it is clearly preferable to offer text-based rather than image-based delivery. The image-based files in JSTOR are considerably larger than text files, making downloading and printing somewhat problematic. Hypertext links to page numbers corresponding to occurrences of search terms appear at the top of retrieved articles, allowing users to go directly to desired pages, but links to endnotes or illustrations are not available within JSTOR articles, which may be disappointing to those who have come to expect them when using World Wide Web technology. Last, these image-based files provide no flexibility for manipulation by the end user in terms of word processing abilities such as cutting and pasting.

Although the lack of more extensive hypertext links and the inability to perform editing tasks still remain, the printing problem has been somewhat resolved. Previously, articles from JSTOR could only be printed using a special helper application called JPRINT, which is supplied by JSTOR. JPRINT speeds up printing, aids higher quality printing, groups the individual page images so that articles can be printed in their entirety instead of just one page at a time, and allows users to select from a variety of resolutions, including an archival-quality, 600-dpi version (JSTOR Printing). Now, however, it is possible to use Adobe Acrobat to print articles in .pdf version, an option with which users may be familiar and, therefore, be more comfortable using. Those who want to print entire articles away from the library must install either application themselves or must be satisfied with printing one page at time. Instructions guide the user through the process of downloading JPRINT and configuring it to work with their Web browser, but the instructions are somewhat confusing, and thus some portion of the remote users may meet with frustration when attempting to download and configure. It should be noted that after successfully installing JPRINT, it worked quite well. Installing Adobe Acrobat was easier and, because many users may already have it, it may be the print option that is more often used.

Downloading also presents special problems for image-based materials. The process is difficult and is most useful to users on UNIX workstations or Linux PCs, for which JSTOR has not provided a print helper application. The articles must be downloaded in PostScript format and printed with corresponding PostScript software. The difficulties involved with downloading may lead most people to print the articles. Even if downloading is used, it is not be possible to edit or manipulate the articles, since they are images, not text. The ability to easily print and download is crucially important to most users; if they cannot print or download easily, they may be less likely to use JSTOR.

Although image-based files are not themselves directly searchable, JSTOR has linked them to a full-text ASCII file, which is easily searched by the full-text, or author, title or abstract fields. Searching may be done by specific journal or by all journals at once. The user may choose either a basic or advanced search mode, both of which support Boolean searching.

C. Archival Implications

By making high-resolution replications of back issues of core academic journals available electronically, JSTOR is ostensibly addressing many of the archiving problems faced by libraries today. The questions of space, preservation, and incomplete runs appear at first glance to be solved. JSTOR journals are not merely online *versions* of the print journals, they are exact reproductions of the originals, in pristine condition, that can never be lost, stolen, or taken off the shelves. The fact that they are exact replicas of the print counterparts is of utmost importance to many, especially if they are to be used as archival records. Electronic versions may lack advertising, letters to the editor, and more; thus, retaining them as archives would result in an incomplete historical record. Despite the fact that JSTOR journals are actual images of the print volumes, as librarians we are very aware of the need to supply information to users in a way that they find acceptable. In the future, space restrictions may make it absolutely necessary to move to electronic access, but the path there may not be easy. "[T]he initial hope that JSTOR would pay for itself by allowing libraries to move journals into cheaper warehouse space, is not yet considered feasible. Some suggest that libraries might be willing to get rid of journals if paper copies were still available from a library nearby, but most say faculty members will not tolerate such a change anytime soon"(DeLoughry, 1996, p. A32). Indeed, although many researchers will appreciate the ease of being able to access these materials electronically, the actual deed may be met with resistance by many, especially older faculty who are still distrustful of computers. This sentiment is succinctly summed up by Yale University's associate librarian: "If we took *Speculum*, or *The American Economic Review* and put it in off-site storage, we'd be killed. Prime journals are going to take up prime space, no matter what format you put them in" (DeLoughry, 1996, p. A32). In fact, an important consideration is that even now in a society in which World Wide Web access is commonplace, paper copies still remain essential. As far as discontinuing paper subscriptions, one e-journal provider puts it this way: "Don't cancel yet though—the edition of record is still the paper copy of these journals" (Project Muse Frequently Asked Questions). Who is to say that this will change any time soon?

D. Future Accessibility

Many libraries subscribe to both print and electronic formats, despite the added cost, for fear that if they decide to discontinue their subscriptions to the electronic format there would be a gap. With JSTOR, this may no longer be necessary. As North Carolina State's Director of Libraries puts it,

> Libraries can keep all the journal backfiles that they have paid for, unlike the common commercial practice of a database reverting to the vendor if a subscription is dropped. Also, participating publishers must agree to leave all their digitized backfiles in the JSTOR archive, even if they decide not to stay with the project. This arrangement finally gives libraries the assurance we need that the archive will be a permanent resource, and it allows

us to make management decisions about the long-term preservation and storage of print journals accordingly. (Davis, 1997, p. 145)

If JSTOR itself fails, subscribers will be supplied with either a complete CD-ROM set of the digitized journal images or an equivalent of JSTOR's choosing. Although granted $4 million to launch the project, JSTOR needs continued money to ensure its long-term viability. JSTOR hopes to become self-sustaining by having 750 participating libraries. The number of participants has grown quickly and, according to the JSTOR User Services Coordinator (K. Garlock, personal communication, November 1997), has now reached 240.

E. Access

JSTOR offers site licenses that allow unlimited simultaneous users. Passwords are not necessary because IP addresses are used to authorize access to the entire site. To stave off problems encountered by heavy Web traffic, JSTOR maintains its original database at the University of Michigan, as well as a mirror site at Princeton University. Unique URLs are provided for every journal title, allowing direct access to the needed journal and the search engine, as well as making it possible to include the URL in the OPAC record for the patron's convenience.

F. Licensing, Copyright, and Distribution Restrictions

Users may not download, copy, or store any JSTOR material except one stored electronic copy and one paper copy of any article, and users may not electronically distribute any JSTOR content. Downloading entire issues is prohibited. Libraries may use printed material only, not electronic for ILL purposes, and they must keep records of this use. This policy will remain in effect through 12/31/98, at which point the policy may be revised. Site licenses are used, allowing access to anyone, anywhere within the IP domain (JSTOR Library License Terms).

G. Is the Provider a Single Publisher, or Does it Handle Publications of Multiple Publishers?

JSTOR handles the works of multiple publishers, which will presumably have positive effects on the scope in the future, as they may contract with still other publishers to include any subject areas or titles for which there is demand. In fact, in a future, independent phase, JSTOR hopes to provide clusters of journal back files in specific subject areas.

H. Is the Electronic Version as Comprehensive and Complete as the Print Counterpart? Are the Articles Refereed?

The journals in JSTOR are as complete in every way as their print counterparts. The articles are replicated in their entirety, and all else that appeared in the original issues including advertisements is scanned and included. JSTOR includes only widely respected, core academic journals containing articles that undergo peer review.

I. User Support

Questions concerning any aspect of JSTOR may be directed to jstor-info@umich.edu or to a toll-free user services number for prompt and courteous help. Support resources including general information and archives of JSTOR announcements is available at http://www.jstor.org/support, and an e-mail group, jstor-contact@umich.edu, is used to send announcements and updates.

J. Individual Title Availability

At this point, individual titles are not available from JSTOR and participating institutions must subscribe to the entire archive. In a future, independent phase, JSTOR plans to provide clusters of journals devoted to specific subject areas, making it more practical for specialized libraries to take advantage of these electronic archives.

K. Upcoming Plans or Enhancements

JSTOR acknowledges the need for users to have access to both current and back issues, and the value in being able to search the entire run of a journal at once. To this end, they intend to work with publishers to establish linkages between JSTOR and the current electronic versions of the journals (Sully, 1997).

V. Project Muse

In one of the first ventures of its kind, the Johns Hopkins University Press and the Milton S. Eisenhower Library are working cooperatively on Project Muse, an initiative providing World Wide Web access to the full text of the Press's 40 scholarly journal publications in the social sciences, humanities, and mathematics, with plans to expand in the future. The project was supported through 1997 by grants from the National Endowment for the Humanities and the Mellon Foundation. Project Muse includes current issues only, which are made available before the print version. Although there is presently no substantial back file available, Project Muse is considering avenues to include more issues published prior to 1995 at some point in the future. (Access: http://muse.jhu.edu)

A. Economics

As Cochenour (1995) points out, university presses and university libraries have long been encouraged to work cooperatively to arrive at solutions to the problem of rising serials costs, and Project Muse is representative of just such a merger. Although the pricing structures of Project Muse are complex, they underlie the fact that one of the goals is to serve as a model for electronic publishing. As Lewis (1995) states, "The goal of our collaborative effort is to offer electronic journals and price them, at lower rates than their paper counterparts" (p. 176).

Subscription rates vary and range from $2500 annually for unlimited university use, with unlimited simultaneous users, to the $300 to $400 range for smaller school or public libraries, with a restricted number of users. The lower-priced plans allow up to 25 users at one building site, no ILL, and no accompanying print discounts. For high schools and special libraries for whom these restrictions have little bearing, these plans make it quite affordable to access Project Muse. Individual titles are 10% less than the print and, in the most expensive plan, if both the complete print and electronic versions are subscribed to, the cost for both is only 30% more than for just the print subscription alone. This pricing is arrived at by closely examining the costs associated with the print versus the electronic versions of the journals. Day (1995) states:

> They have carefully distinguished between those costs that are common to both print and electronic forms, those specific to the paper form and those specific to the electronic form. This is an essential step on the way to any well-thought out pricing scheme for a product being published in more than one form. (p. 54)

Despite these generous pricing structures, the economic reality for most academic institutions is that they will be spending more money, not less. To ensure future availability of these materials if they stopped subscribing to the electronic version, or if Project Muse itself were no longer available, libraries have two options: Either continue to subscribe to the print or create their own archives. As an MIT study shows, creating local archives is extremely expensive (Duranceau *et al.*, 1996) and much more costly and difficult than simply continuing to subscribe to the print. At this early date, many libraries would be reluctant to give up their paper subscriptions, so they will probably opt to subscribe to both the paper and electronic versions, thereby purchasing the same journal in two formats—a difficult position to argue for in a time of shrinking serials budgets. If the research requirements of a library are such that only current journals are needed, then Project Muse offers a true solution; the library only needs to subscribe to the electronic versions. Unfortunately, the research needs of most academic institutions require the assurance of reliable, uninterrupted journal coverage. It must be noted, however, that although libraries may be spending more money, they are getting an important value-added service; that is, remote access to full-text journals is a benefit much appreciated by most users and, many would agree, money well spent.

B. User Flexibility/Ease of Use

Project Muse uses a straightforward search utility called SWISH (Simple Web Indexing System for Humans), making Boolean searching possible on all 40+ journals simultaneously, or on individual journals or volumes. Extensive keyword indexing has been provided using Library of Congress subject headings, and searching can be done by full text, author, or title as well.

There are hypertext links in the endnotes, tables of contents, illustrations, and author bibliographies. Many of the illustrations are in color and can be enlarged from those appearing in the printed version, making screen viewing easier. The HTML format makes printing and downloading fast and simple. Although currently not available, the future may see access to audio and video files. The problem of pagination has been solved by the insertion of [End Page x] in the appropriate place (Wagner, 1997).

C. Archival Implications

The Johns Hopkins University Press acknowledges that creating a permanent archive is crucial, and they are committed to maintaining permanent electronic editions of their journals. As the current issues in the Project Muse database become older, they will be retained and will remain as fully accessible and searchable as the new issues. Project Muse is also seeking funding and electronic conversion options for back issues published before 1995, but the plans for such retrospective conversion remain tentative at this time. In addition, institutions with full subscriptions may archive journals electronically on a local domain Web server, on CD-ROM or on tape backup, but as discussed elsewhere in this article, archiving this amount of material represents a substantial amount of money and manpower.

The archival value of Project Muse documents can be viewed from two sides. It can be argued that any deviation from the original print version does not represent a true archive because the print version is regarded as the copy of record. Since the majority of the material in Project Muse is in HTML format, rather than exact bitmapped images of the journals, institutions saving these might be said to be archiving only reasonable facsimiles of the journals, which may not be historically valuable, since they are visually changed by the use of different typeface and graphic materials may have been altered from those appearing in the original print version. Currently, Project Muse does not include advertisements and classified ads but has plans to include them at some future point. Excluding advertising and classified ads poses problems not only for people needing access to them now, but also for those in the future studying advertising or popular culture. When portions of print publications are omitted or altered from the original, a part of history is lost, or at the least a somewhat different version is presented, and the results may not be suitable for archival purposes.

In contrast, some people may believe that Project Muse would represent a superior archive, since not only is all the intellectual content intact, but the graphics can be enhanced by the addition of color and the ability to enlarge them from the originals. The future may see audio and video in some of the journals, invaluable features that could never be made available in a paper archive.

D. Future Accessibility

Institutions who cancel their electronic subscriptions will have continued electronic access only to materials they have archived themselves. Institutions with full subscriptions may archive journals electronically on a local Web server, such as an organizational Website restricted by domain address, on CD-ROM, or tape backup. As with print subscriptions, the library owns everything they paid for until cancellation. There will not, however, be continued Web access to materials to which the library previously subscribed. Local archiving of large amounts of material is not economically viable in the majority of cases, making future availability an important consideration.

The future of Project Muse looks very promising. Johns Hopkins University Press is an established and respected publisher and is committed to electronic publishing. Electronic versions of individual journals cost 10% less than print, and deeply discounted electronic packages are offered to special libraries with no discounts available on the print, indications of their level of commitment to their future in electronic publishing.

E. Access

Project Muse is available without passwords within the domain name of the subscribing campus. The Basic Plan allows up to 25 users, IP addresses, or computers within a single building. The Campus Plan permits unlimited users, who can search anywhere provided they are using an account within the domain name. In case of power outages or Web traffic, there are two servers in Baltimore and plans for European and Australian mirrors. Unique URLs are provided for each journal title with the standard form http://muse.jhu.edu/journals/title_of_journal/, allowing the user direct access to the title if a link is provided from a Web-based OPAC or Web page, or if the user knows the URL or the standard form and the title.

F. Licensing, Copyright, and Distribution Restrictions

In the Full Campus Plan, there are no restrictions within the campus for noncommercial and educational and research purposes. Users may download, print, and archive articles on personal computers for their own use, and may send one copy via e-mail, print, or fax to another person at a different location for that person's private use. Libraries may print, download, and archive materials on CD-ROM or paper and place them on campus file servers, provided that access is restricted to the campus community. In the Basic Plan, access and distribution are permitted within the single building site only. ILL is permitted in the Full Campus Plan but prohibited in the Basic Plan. Neither plan permits dissemination of the digital content from Project Muse journals outside the contiguous campus, except as noted above.

G. Is the Provider a Single Publisher, or Does it Handle Publications of Multiple Publishers?

Although Project Muse represents a single publisher, the Johns Hopkins University Press works in conjunction with other respected societies and institutes and may continue to expand its holdings through such associations. Johns Hopkins University Press currently represents a broad subject scope and, if more publishers or university presses are contracted with, the range can continue to grow.

H. Is the Electronic Version as Complete as the Print Counterpart? Are the Articles Refereed?

The full text of each article in the Project Muse database is available in its entirety. Currently, Project Muse does not include advertisements or classified ads but plans to include them at some point in the future. Johns Hopkins University Press is an established, reputable publisher, and all articles are thoroughly peer reviewed.

I. Does the Product Supply Good User Support?

Project Muse provides an e-mail address to contact representatives with questions. In addition, there is a listserv for subscribers to communicate with each other and with the developers for discussion and questions about the project and related issues, as well as a separate mailing list for notification of new materials.

J. Individual or Selective Title Availability

Project Muse offers the option of selecting individual titles rather than sub-scribing to the entire database. This feature allows libraries with limited budgets to choose only heavily used titles for electronic format, while limiting less used titles to print only.

K. Upcoming Plans or Enhancements

While the emphasis of Project Muse is to provide current journals, it now includes back issues for four titles, and has tentative plans to continue to expand coverage of issues published prior to 1995. Although these plans remain preliminary, Project Muse is investigating funding and conversion options. At some future point, audio and video features will be incorporated into selected publications such as *Performing Arts Journal* and *Theatre Topics*. The inclusion of advertisements is also planned.

VI. Conclusion

Despite the huge advances in electronic publishing, it is still an industry in its infancy. Although it may be theoretically possible to have electronic access to anything imaginable, there will be obstacles encountered along the way. Electronic access appears to be the way of the future, and it is the privilege and responsibility of information professionals to develop criteria that can be used to evaluate electronic text providers to ensure that high-quality materials are made available in usable formats and with reasonable pricing and usage policies. Academic institutions must act as the testing grounds for these works in progress; without testing, there can be no advancement toward improved and economically viable solutions. It is also the responsibility of those with access to these services to determine whether these products are truly providing solutions to the problems they set out to tackle, through critically examining the issues to uncover problems or shortcomings with an eye toward finding solutions. By the same token, identification and acknowl-edgment of features or technologies that work will lead to further future improvements and enhancements.

The future looks bright for electronic publishing and particularly for projects such as JSTOR and Project Muse. It must be conceded, however, that as with all new ventures, until more time has passed, we simply cannot know the full implications academically or economically. Providing guidelines by which electronic journal providers can be evaluated, is a step toward this goal.

References

Barnes, J. H. (1997). One giant leap, one small step: Continuing the migration to electronic journals. *Library Trends* **45**, 404–415.

Bowen, A. (1995, September 18). *JSTOR and the Economics of Scholarly Communication.* Paper presented at the Council on Library Resources Conference, Washington, DC.

Brennan, P., Hersey, K., and Harper, G. (1997). *Licensing Electronic Resources: Strategic and Practical Considerations for Signing Electronic Delivery Agreements.* Association of Research Libraries, Washington, DC. (http://www.arl.org/scomm/licensing/licbooklet.html)

Cochenour, D. (1995). Project Muse: A partnership of interest. *Serials Review* **21**, 75–80.

Commission on Preservation and Access. (1996). *Preserving Digital Information: Report of the Task Force on Archiving of Digital Information.* Commission on Preservation and Access and the Research Libraries Group, Washington, DC.

Crawford, W. (1998). Paper presists: Why physical library collections still matter. *Online* **22**, 42–48. (http://www.onlineinc.com/onlinemag/JanOL98/crawford.html)

Davis, M. E. (1997). NC State happy with JSTOR backfiles. *College and Research Libraries News* **58**, 145.

Day, C. (1995). Pricing electronic products. In *Filling the Pipeline and Paying the Piper: Proceedings of the Fourth Symposium* (A. Okerson, ed.), pp. 51–56. Association of Research Libraries, Washington, DC.

DeLoughry, T. J. (1996). Journal articles dating back as far as a century are being put online. *Chronicle of Higher Education* **43**, A30, A32.

Duranceau, E., Lippert, M., Manoff, M., and Snowden, C. (1996). Electronic journals in the MIT Libraries: Report of the 1995 e-journal subgroup. *Serials Review* **22**, 47–61.

Garlock, K. L., Landis, W. E., and Piontek, S. (1997). Redefining access to scholarly journals: A progress report on JSTOR. *Serials Review* **23**, 1–8.

Guthrie, K. M., and Lougee, W. P. (1997). The JSTOR solution: Accessing and preserving the past. *Library Journal* **122**(2), 42–44.

Hahn, H. (1996). *The Internet Complete Reference* (2nd ed.). Osborne McGraw-Hill, Berkeley, CA.

Johns Hopkins University. *Project Muse.* http://muse.jhu.edu/muse.html

Jones, D. (1996). Electronic journals—Are we really ready for them? *Serials Review* **22**.

JSTOR. http://www.jstor.org

JSTOR Background. http://www.jstor.org/about/background.html

JSTOR Library License Terms. http://www.jstor.org/about/library.html

JSTOR Mission and Goals. http://www.jstor.org/about/mission.html

JSTOR Phase 1 Pricing and Availability. http://www/jstor.org/about/pricing.html

JSTOR Printing. http://www.jstor.org/about/printing.html

Lewis, S. (1995). From Earth to ether: One publisher's reincarnation. *Serials Librarian* **25**, 173–180.

Machovec, G. (1997). *Electronic Journal Market Overview–1997.* http://www.coalliance.org/reports/ejournal.htm

Malinconico, M. (1996). Electronic documents and research libraries. *IFLA Journal* **22**, 211–225.

Neavill, G. B., and Sheble', M. A. (1995). Archiving electronic journals. *Serials Review* **21**, 13–21.

Okerson, A. (1997). Copyright or contract? *Library Journal* **122**(14), 136–139.

Project Muse Frequently Asked Questions. http://128.220.50.88/proj—descrip/faq/

Quandt, R. E. (1996). Electronic publishing and virtual libraries: Issues and an agenda for the Andrew W. Mellon Foundation. *Serials Review* **22**, 9–24.

Sully, S. E. (1997). JSTOR: An IP practitioner's perspective. *D-Lib Magazine.* http://www.dlib.org/dlib/january97/01sully.html

Tenopir, C. (1997). The complexities of electronic journals. *Library Journal* **122**(2), 37–38.

Tenopir, C., and Barry, J. (1997). Database marketplace 1997: The data dealers. *Library Journal* **122**(9), 28–36.

Wagner, K. W. (1997). Review of Project Muse, Internet Reviews Section. *College and Research Libraries News* **58**(5), 348.

Yott, P., and Hoebeke, C. H. (1997). Improving valid access to site-licensed resources. *College and Research Libraries News* **58**(10), 698–700.

Data Preparation for Electronic Publications

Norman Desmarais
Phillips Memorial Library
Providence College
Providence, Rhode Island 02918

I. Introduction

Libraries have long been recognized as repositories of a wealth of information resources. As guardians of this material, much of it in the public domain, librarians can find themselves assuming some of the roles of electronic publishers (Stover, 1996). As funding becomes increasingly available to digitize library collections, many more libraries can be expected to embark on digital library projects, such as the Library of Congress's American Memory Project and similar projects undertaken by some of the United States' largest research libraries.

Not only may librarians be involved with converting their collections to digital format, they might also restructure and republish traditional library materials, combining them with original material to create entirely new publications. Many librarians are also the authors of original material and may find themselves wanting to shift from traditional print formats to electronic formats. Converting from analog to digital formats, however, involves many technical decisions and user issues that authors and developers must address if they want to produce a successful product. The nature of the original format or its intended use will initiate some of these decisions. Others will be conditioned by available funding, human resources, or technology.

This article examines some of the issues and decisions involved with the digitization of text, audio, and graphics for electronic publication (Adam, 1992; Anderson, 1990; Harrel, 1996; Holsinger, 1991; Maloney, 1992; Maughan, 1997). It attempts to cover most of the critical decisions and the trade-offs that a course of action will have on subsequent options. It draws on the author's experiences in creating two electronic publications: *The American Revolution*, a multimedia CD-ROM published by Research Publications in the *American Journey: History in Your Hands* series, and *Essential Documents of American History*, a text-only title published by EBSCO Electronic Publishing.

II. Converting Text

A. ASCII

Textual material accounts for the largest quantity of library material available; however, *full text* means different things to different people. For some people, it refers to the entire document being in ASCII (American Standard Code for Information Interchange) text. Others use the term to refer to a bitmapped image (see Section IV,A) of the original document, which some people now call *full image*. Still others refer to full text as anything with a substantial amount of textual information, minus charts, graphs, or photos.

ASCII documents contain all the words of the original but do not preserve the original page layout or any nontextual information such as graphics or illustrations. The ASCII character set is the lowest common denominator for text and is limited to 128 characters (256 characters in the extended set). Although it does not support diacritics, exponents, and many other types of characters, it does allow readers to search for any word or combination of words. However, ASCII documents require much less storage space than their image counterpart.

An ASCII document can be created by typing it as original, using virtually any word processor, or by scanning and converting it from a printed version or converting it from an already existing electronic version. Although typing is labor intensive, the advantage is that the typist can include formatting and structural information into the text during data entry. This can reduce the time necessary to prepare the text for the retrieval software.

1. Optical Character Recognition

The use of a scanner, computer, and OCR (Optical Character Recognition) software can convert printed or typed material into machine-readable form more quickly and at lower cost. However, some scanners and accompanying OCR software can read only a limited set of typefaces or must be "trained" by running samples through the scanner and calibrating its interpretation of the text. Specifications for many scanners indicate an accuracy rate of 99%. Although this seems acceptable, an average of one error for every two lines of text results, requiring considerable editing and proofreading. In addition, special symbols, such as diacritics or mathematical symbols can become garbled or lost. Complex formatting, such as tables or special fonts, can suffer a similar fate. High-quality printed material produces the best results.

OCR played an important role in the development of both *The American Revolution* and *Essential Documents of American History*. *The American Revolution* included approximately 300 primary source documents and material from a variety of sources that needed to be digitized and reworked. The scanning, conversion, and proofreading responsibilities fell on the principal author and editor. *Essential Documents of American History* included 1300 primary source documents in full text. The publisher was provided with more than one third of the documents in ASCII format, which were converted and proofread or obtained in electronic format from a variety of sources. The publisher undertook the conversion of the rest of the material, either through scanning or having it rekeyed in the Philippines. The authors were required to provide good photocopies, but sometimes the best photocopies available were of low quality, particularly those from microfilm.

2. Electronic Formats

The items were obtained in electronic format from a variety of sources, including Internet sites, and needed to be converted to a consistent format. HTML (HyperText Markup Language) codes needed to be stripped out, and tabs, indentations, and additional spacing needed to be eliminated. A series of macros dealt with the more common problems, but even so, proofreading became a gargantuan task.

Some of the texts, particularly those contained in *Essential Documents of American History*, included tables in the forms of rate charts and tariffs. The macros created havoc with these tables, making them illegible. Spaces that kept the data elements in the proper columns had to be replaced with tabs. Sometimes, the tables would not fit on a single screen with the most common 640 × 480 resolution, which was assumed to be the basic display for the installed equipment base of the readership.

Some of the texts, particularly those that were older, presented other problems such as the use of long *F*s and *S*s, which did not convert well and introduced errors that spell checkers did not identify. For example, "of" often converted to "oil." There were also the usual conversion problems. "Them" and "then" and "all" and "an" often became interchangeable. E and O, 1 (one) and l (ell), R and F, U and O, B and D, and M and N were often confused. In the early drafts of *The American Revolution*, the section on the Virginia Resolutions was changed to read the Virginia Revolutions; and the essay discussing the hardships endured during the winter at Valley Forge referred to "foraging for good" instead of "food." Mercy Otis Warren's play *The Adulateur* was constantly identified as *The Adulterer*, and repeated correction notices went unheeded (Desmarais, 1996).

In addition to problems with conversion, marks on the originals or foreign matter or scratches on the microfilm reader lens or on the photocopier glass introduced marks on the copies that, in turn, resulted in garbage characters in the converted file.

Futhermore, the editorial process sometimes introduced errors. Even though all text was run through a spell checker before submission, the copy editors of *The American Revolution* deleted sections that sometimes left incomplete sentences that they would then flag and return with questions for clarification or completion. An author who painstakingly submits correct copy should not assume that editors make only minor modifications.

B. Full-Image Documents

Full-image documents replicate the original as an electronic photograph (bitmapped image). In this case, the documents do not lose any of the information content, such as charts, photographs, or other graphics. Such an image consumes as much as 30 times more space than its ASCII equivalent (Barnes, 1992). Although these documents preserve the "look and feel" of the original along with the communication value and built-in intellectual content that editors and publishers provide with their publications, readers cannot perform a random search for specific words or phrases. Therefore, retrieval of information is only as good as the indexing that accompanies the document image.

The process of creating an electronic page image and the subsequent procedures to further manipulate it (e.g., index, sequence, store, display, or print it) involve elaborate technology and require much time and effort to implement. It also requires indexing to an agreed standard to provide access. Using a program such as Adobe Acrobat as an alternative preserves the "look and feel" of the printed page and permits random searches (Hudson, 1994). However, this option may not be suitable for older publications. It is a proprietary program that does not interface well with word processing programs. A different approach is to have both an ASCII and an image version available and link them, such as JSTOR does. Yet another approach is to create compound documents that provide searchable ASCII text with links to other file formats, such as graphics (for charts, tables, photos, illustrations, etc.), audio, or video. These last two solutions are costly in production.

C. Using Electronic Text

After receiving the text in electronic format, it must be converted into a usable format. Electronic files come in many different formats, which often complicate the conversion process. Many of the more powerful word processing programs can read and write files in a variety of formats or convert them through utility programs. Different typists may define paragraphs in different ways. These sorts of differences can increase the time and effort required to make the text consistent throughout an application. Sometimes, two or more conversion steps will be required. Publishers usually prefer to receive electronic documents in ASCII format, single spaced, with no special formatting, such as the indentation of paragraphs or headings or the use of print enhancements, such as bold or italic typeface. This makes it easier for them to convert it for use in their preferred layout program. However, those who undertake self-publication can choose whatever format they find most useful to achieve the desired results.

The publishers of *The American Revolution* and *Essential Documents of American History* both requested the submission of material in ASCII format. As the least common denominator, ASCII would provide the greatest flexibility to use the material in whatever authoring program the publishers selected. WordPerfect was used for submission of material, as all participants had compatible word processors.

1. Tagging

A markup language format such as SGML (Standard Generalized Markup Language) helps to achieve consistency of tagging between texts. Tags define the structure of a document and the purpose, rather than the appearance, of various elements. An accompanying file, called a DTD (Document Type Definition), specifies the layout of those elements. For example,

1. Character attributes or the codes that indicate bold or italic type, character fonts, color, and inverse video

2. Hierarchy or the basic structure of a document, usually expressed in book terms and including such elements as title and chapter heads

3. Links—cross references or hypermedia elements that the user clicks to initiate some action, such as jumping to another location, displaying a picture, or playing audio. These elements usually become the most difficult to add automatically to a file because the source file usually does not contain them (Lynch and Horton, 1997).

Such tagging simplifies the conversion process because only the DTD needs to be changed to modify the layout of a document. Frequently used DTDs can also be saved as style sheets, minimizing the conversion effort even further. HTML is a subset of SGML used to format documents for the World Wide Web (Boeri and Hensel, 1996). Publications designed for use with a Web browser would need to be tagged in HTML (Cole, 1997; Duncan, 1995; Goldie, 1997; Hensel and Boeri, 1997; Horton and Lynch, 1997; Lynch and Horton, 1997).

Authors who are accustomed to writing for linear publications may find it difficult and frustrating to write for hypertext (Bonime and Pohlman, 1997; Fisher, 1995). A reader can enter a product at virtually any point, and a writer cannot assume that a reader has read sections that occur elsewhere, either chronologically or logically. Consequently, common material may need frequent repetition. For example, in *The American Revolution*, publisher policy required the identification of characters with full names and dates at their first mention in each essay or caption.

2. Editorial Issues

The author was not quite ready to deal with one of the editorial issues—to produce a sanitized, politically correct approach to history—that emerged. Authors could not draw personal conclusions or inferences from their interpretations of the facts. Instead, they had to avoid politically incorrect topics and stick to interpretations to which most historians generally agreed. For example, an essay on the language of eighteenth-century America discussed why women were sometimes referred to as "baggage" (because they were required to travel with the baggage train). The managing editor eliminated this section because readers might take offense, seeing it as derogatory to women. Another section that discussed sanitation explained the meanings of the terms "head" and "throne." The passage was promptly deleted as potentially offensive but later included when the acquisitions editor resigned and her assistant took over the project. In contrast, some contributing authors used terms such as "Tories," "rebels," and "patriots," that convey a political stance to which the copy editors did not object.

III. Converting Audio

The digitization of audio, whether for music, sound effects, or speech, can take a variety of forms. It can consist of synthesized audio, CD audio, or MIDI (Musical Instrument Digital Interface). The selection of the type of audio depends on its intended use and on technical considerations related to that use (discussed toward the end of this section). The quality of the sound, however, depends on several factors, such as the frequency of sampling, amplitude, and the number of channels.

Sampling involves translating an analog waveform into a digital form by taking tiny (discrete) samples of the waveform at fixed intervals during sound capture (frequency). This is analogous to taking periodic "photographs" of the audio. The more frequent the "photographs," the better the quality or fidelity of the sound. Typical frequencies for digitized audio are: 44.1 kHz, 22.05 kHz, and 11.025 kHz (*Encyclopedia of Multimedia*, 1990; Miller, 1991).

Higher frequency also implies the recording of higher tones in the sound, otherwise known as amplitude. *Amplitude* refers to the distance between the top (or bottom) of an analog (continuous) waveform (sine wave), which represents the sound and its baseline. Frequency and amplitude determine the amount of information required to store each sample and consequently specify how precisely the sample gets measured. Digital sound files are large, regardless of the quality selected (Ratcliff, 1992). However, higher sampling rates produce much larger files than lower rates. The following formula can serve to estimate audio storage needs:

$$\text{(sampling rate} \times \text{bits per sample)} / 8 = \text{bytes/sec}$$

For example, a 1-minute monaural sound clip requires the following space:

Bits/sample	Sampling rate (kHz)	No. bytes required (MB/min)
8	11.025	0.66
8	22.05	1.32
16	44.1	5.292

The number of channels determines whether a recording produces one wave-form (called *monaural* or *mono*) or two waveforms (*stereo*). Stereo sound offers a richer listening experience than mono but requires twice the amount of storage space (Floyd, 1991).

A. Compact Disc Digital Audio

Compact disc audio (known as Red Book audio or CD-DA [Compact Disc Digital Audio]) represents the highest quality format but produces the largest files and uses the entire processing power of the CD-ROM drive.

In addition, CD-DA requires a lot of disc space. For example, 10 minutes of stereo digital audio can consume more than 100 MB of space. CD-ROM titles that use Red Book audio are often referred to as mixed-mode discs. They store the CD-DA sound separately from the other data on the disc and require a separate access when retrieving it. This means that a mixed-mode title must preload the program, image, and other data into memory (or into a cache area on the hard disk) and then dedicate the CD-ROM drive's circuitry to access the CD-DA sound as the application runs.

The choice of sound fidelity level for an application requires balancing sound quality against the storage space requirements for an application. From an audio perspective, it requires a reasonable fidelity level for the sound used; however, from a resource management perspective, the storage space for sound files is limited.

B. MIDI

MIDI expands a developer's options for including sound with a product (Rothstein, 1992). The MIDI specification defines a standard connection for computer control of musical instruments and devices. Any musical instrument with appropriate hardware interfaces and a microprocessor to convert MIDI messages can become a MIDI device. MIDI devices communicate with each other by sending messages through that interface. MIDI files can play through either an internal or an external synthesizer attached to the machine's MIDI port.

MIDI messages contain digital descriptions of a musical score—complete with the sequence of notes, timing, and instrument designations called *patches*. For each note, the MIDI file includes the key, channel number, duration, volume, and velocity (how quickly the key travels to its down position when struck). When a music synthesizer chipset plays MIDI messages, it interprets the symbols and produces music. MIDI sophistication is measured in terms such as number of simultaneous channels, simultaneous notes possible in each channel, instrument voices supported by each channel, and simultaneous voices and/or notes possible.

MIDI files have some strong benefits compared to waveform audio. Since MIDI files consist of a series of instructions, they require much less disk space. First, 1.8 seconds of waveform audio recorded at 8 bit, 22.05 kHz could require 41 KB, while 2 minutes of MIDI audio could use as little as 8 KB. Second, because MIDI files are so much smaller, the application developer can preload them much easier than a waveform file, giving greater flexibility in design and specifying when music occurs.

Although audio segments can be digitized with a sound card and accompanying software and a microphone or line input, the results may be rather poor if sound cards produced for the consumer market are relied upon. For best results, potential publishers should consider audio cards designed for professional musicians or for the audio industry. These are likely to be more expensive, but they offer more options and produce better results. MIDI audio will require a MIDI device, such as a keyboard with MIDI ports. However, the production of high-quality audio usually requires a good audio technician and a recording studio.

For *The American Revolution*, almost 3 hours of audio segments were collected. *Essential Documents of American History* did not use any audio or graphic elements. These audio segments ranged from military commands and sound effects, intended for random background sounds, to full-length pieces of period music that illustrated various themes and set different moods. Some of the audio mixed with narrated text was also intended to set the mood and to illustrate some of the culture of the period.

The publisher requested submission of audio on DAT (digital audio tape), a standard procedure for electronic publications. This required conversion from cassette tape, vinyl record, and CD onto DAT. Much of the material obtained from the Brigade of the American Revolution came with permission for use. Other material was submitted with copyright information.

The submitted selections were played on period instruments or reproductions and in a rendition or arrangement of the period. However, rather than use these audio tracks, the publisher elected to use familiar pieces, such as *Yankee Doodle*, played in a modern arrangement on modern instruments. Audio commentary on selected documents was also included, thus fitting in with the documentary approach of the series.

IV. Converting Graphics

A. Raster and Vector Graphics

The most frequently used digital images are known as bitmapped images or raster graphics. Bitmapped images consist of a set of bits in computer memory that define the color and intensity of each pixel in an image. They represent images as a matrix of dots, much like the photos in a newspaper. They typically reproduce images that contain lots of detail, shading, and color, such as photographs, film negatives, and other illustrations. Bitmapped images, which come in dozens of different formats (e.g., PCX, TIFF, PIC, BMP, GIF, JPEG), are transmitted continuously to the video screen, dot for dot, one line at a time, over and over again. The screen reflects instantly any changes made to the bitmaps, which generally display more quickly than complex vector graphic images.

Vector graphics, however, define the geometry of objects within the computer's memory. Rather than storing an image, the computer records a geometric description from which it can construct an image. In other words, the computer stores instructions that describe the dimension and shape of every line, circle, arc, or rectangle that makes up a drawing. It also saves the "object" as a list of points or as an equation that defines shapes on Cartesian coordinates. When it displays the image, software reads the instructions and converts them into shapes and colors for display on the screen.

Since vector graphics images consist of shapes, they cannot duplicate the same painted or photographic effects as bitmapped images. Some of the most common uses for vector graphics include line drawings, newspaper-style clip art, maps, CAD/CAM (Computer Assisted Design/Computer Assisted Modeling) illustrations, and architectural drawings.

Vector graphics are more manipulable than raster graphics, allowing the artist to work with each piece of the image separately. He or she can move the individual objects around on the screen, shrink, enlarge, rotate, or twist them—all without introducing distortion that usually occurs when attempting the same procedure with bitmaps. Vector graphic objects also maintain their unique identities when overlaying other objects. This means that vector graphics can overlay different backgrounds or change size or color independently of the other objects that share the same plane.

The main disadvantage of vector graphics, however, comes in the processing time it takes to recreate them. As the images get increasingly complicated, it takes the computer longer to interpret the instructions and construct the graphic. Developers often create complex images as vector graphics, then convert them to bitmaps for use in an application.

Raster graphics can load directly into memory for display, eliminating the time delay involved in building a vector graphic image. Bitmaps, however, require more disk space than vector graphics, since bitmaps have to specify information about each pixel displayed on the screen.

Developers can create bitmaps with "paint" programs, by taking pictures with a digital camera, by scanning photographs or flat art with a color scanner, or by digitizing video frames using a video camera and frame-grabbing equipment. Vector graphics, however, are generally created with "draw" programs, such as CAD/CAM programs.

Graphics can tax a computer system's performance capabilities severely. Adding video memory to a video adapter card or using a graphics accelerator can reduce the burden on the computer's microprocessor by shifting the tasks associated with processing images to the video card. Bitmapped images present particular challenges because they can cause an application to reach the limitations of the PC display system. To use them properly, the factors associated with resolution, image depth, and file size must be considered.

1. Resolution

The pixel matrix (TV screen or computer monitor) divides the image area into a uniform two-dimensional grid (screen resolution). *Screen resolution* determines the maximum image area of the computer screen, expressed in horizontal and vertical pixels, for a particular video mode. This corresponds to the number of samples and represents the spatial resolution to which the picture has been sampled. The more lines or columns, the more pixels, the bigger the sample, and the finer the spatial resolution (Kerlow, 1986).

Image resolution, expressed in horizontal and vertical pixels, determines the size of the digitized image. An image that has the same size as the screen resolution fills the screen, but the image resolution can differ substantially from the screen resolution. For example, if a 320-by-240 pixel image is displayed on a 640-by-480 pixel display, the digitized image only fills one half of the screen because the image size is one half the screen resolution. If the size of the image exceeds the screen resolution, the screen can display only a portion of the image. The display software then must support horizontal and vertical scrolling to see other portions of the image.

Pixel resolution, the ratio of a pixel's width to its height (also known as the pixel's aspect ratio), can become a factor when using images on different graphic display modes or computer hardware. Pixel resolution can cause unexpected distortions in an image when displayed on a machine with a different pixel resolution. For example, an image captured on a device that uses rectangular pixels with an aspect ratio of $1:2$ and later displayed on a device that uses square pixels with an aspect ratio of $1:1$ will manifest distortion. Fortunately, pixel resolution inconsistencies do not occur frequently, as most displays use square pixels with an aspect ratio of $1:1$. Also, most capture devices permit adjusting the pixel aspect ratio (Luther, 1991).

2. Color

A second factor involves the maximum number of colors used in an image (Bristow, 1994). In a digital system, image depth refers to the number of bits associated with each pixel in a bitmap. The more bits used to represent each pixel of an image, the greater the "depth" of the image and the more storage space it requires. Images that use 24 bits for each pixel (8 each for red, green, and blue [RGB] color components) can display more than 16 million color combinations ($2^{24} = 16,777,216$) for each pixel. This produces more color than the human eye can discern and contains more color than the phosphors in the monitor can display.

The process of sampling the tones in an image to create a bitmap also creates a *color palette*—a table of distinct color values. The digitizing software assigns each sample (each pixel in the bitmap) a numerical value corresponding to an entry in this palette (quantization). The number of colors in the palette depends on the image depth. Since numbers designate the colors, changing red to green simply involves searching for the red number and replacing it with the green number.

Developers can use a color enhancement called *dithering* to improve the appearance of bitmaps, whether monochrome, 16 color, or 256 color. Dithering allows representing an image using fewer colors than in the original. It uses a subset of the colors defined for a bitmap and varies the grouping of pixels to best recreate the effect of the lost colors. A good dithering method can create the illusion of having additional colors in a bitmap.

3. File Size

The third factor associated with bitmapped images involves their file size, which, in turn, affects the transfer time needed to find and copy an image file to computer memory (RAM) and display it on the screen. This often must happen simultaneously with other events (e.g., playing music, responding to keystrokes).

Developers have to take image size into account during the design of a product because it takes 2 seconds to transfer a full-screen, 256–color image from a CD-ROM to the monitor. A full-screen, 16-color bitmap requires at least 1 second of transfer time. Developers need to consider both the seek time and the transfer time for an image when they define the context in which the image will display. For example, to make the time less noticeable, they can preload images into memory while something else is happening (e.g., while the user reads text).

The size of the bitmap file relates directly to the number of bits in the image. The following formula shows how to calculate the amount of storage space that a bitmap requires:

$$\text{size in bytes} = (\text{height} \times \text{width} \times \text{color depth}) / 8$$

The height corresponds to the number of pixels displayed vertically. Width designates the number of pixels displayed horizontally. Color depth denotes the number of bits of color information stored per pixel. The division by 8 converts the number of bits to bytes (8 bits = 1 byte) (Luther, 1991).

The easiest way to make an image appear quickly is to reduce its size by reducing its width/height or by using images with a lower image depth. Data compression techniques, such as Run-Length Encoding (RLE), JPEG (Joint Photographic Experts Group), or other image compression technique can also reduce image size. However, not all compression techniques are mutually compatible. Also, some compression techniques do not lose any data (lossless compression), while other types discard redundant information to save space (lossy compression). Lossy compression techniques, although resulting in fairly good approximations of the original images, cannot restore the discarded data.

4. Image Quality

All pictures are not created equal; some are better suited for digitizing than others. For example, an image with a large section of clear blue sky may look like a good candidate in its original form. However, a picture with less sky showing may provide a better choice because the sky actually consists of dozens of shades of blue. The conversion software that converts this 16 million color image (24 bits) to 256 colors (8 bits) will probably reduce these dozens of blues to four or five shades, resulting in a striped or blotchy sky.

A good image enhancement program will allow blending the few barely noticeable blotches, but every extra step adds more time (cost) to the overall production process. Making a good choice will save touch-up time later in production, especially when the application's runtime palette size is limited to 16 or 256 colors.

An image's physical size presents another important characteristic. An image that is too small may have to be enlarged and distorted. However, if the original image is too large, it may have too much detail and require shrinking. Optimum size ranges between 3-by-5 and 8-by-10 inches. Other important factors to consider when choosing images include lighting, colors, contrast, and complexity (Ores, 1995).

B. Animation and Video

Animation and motion pictures basically involve displaying a series of still images in rapid succession to give the impression of motion. Animation generally implies drawn images while motion pictures usually involve photography. In each picture, the subject differs slightly from the previous picture (frame). Each picture flashes on the screen for a fraction of a second, but instead of seeing separate pictures, the eye sees smooth, continuous movement because of a condition called *persistence of vision*. When the eye sees an object under a bright light, the visual image of that object persists for one tenth of a second after the light has been turned off. Thus, each picture of the sequence appears before the preceding image has faded out.

Graphics are usually handled by a graphic artist at the publisher or sent to a service bureau. In the preparation of *The American Revolution*, the author visited most of the historic sites, national and state parks, museums, homes, and art galleries related to the topic to photograph the locations and objects or to identify paintings and portraits for which rights might need to be obtained. The author also attended many re-enactments, many on or near the locations where the events actually took place. This provided additional material to photograph and videotape. The publisher also employed an image researcher who worked primarily at the Library of Congress, obtaining images and illustrations from public domain materials. All of this material was submitted in black and white, even though colored versions existed.

1. Rights

The publisher claimed that some museums and art galleries refused to grant rights for use of the materials in multimedia CD-ROMs. It is possible that they did not want to pay a royalty for use of the material. For example, it was not possible to obtain images of the original Trumbull paintings, even though the images appear frequently in history and art books. Also, colorful mosaics of many of the paintings adorn the rotunda of the U.S. Capitol. Nonetheless, lithographs and other reproductions had to be relied on.

The Boston Museum of Fine Arts did not grant permission to use reproductions of John Singleton Copley's portraits unless they bore a watermark that would prevent copying for use in unauthorized applications.

Requests were submitted for multiple images to illustrate a point, anticipating possible problems in obtaining rights and hoping to get one or two. As a result, sometimes several were received and the author found himself in the position of having to use them all because the fees had been paid. This dilemma resulted in some topics having an overabundance of images, such as the battles at Lexington, Concord, and Bunker Hill.

As most of the historians and artists who covered the revolutionary period lived in the northern and middle colonies, there is an abundance of material covering the events from those viewpoints and concentrating on those areas. This situation can result in the under-representation of the events in the South and of the Southern campaign of the war, both in text and in media coverage. It was virtually impossible to obtain permissions for the few paintings identified for possible use on this topic.

2. Constraints

Budgetary constraints did not permit hiring a professional photographer; therefore, many of the images were taken on 35-mm slides by amateur photographers. Some of the photographs required touch-up work. For example, an image of a group of British grenadiers near their tent showed a bale of hay and part of a picnic cooler visible near the tent entrance. The author requested that these elements be overlaid with a caisson or a chest of clothes. However, shortly before production, the graphic artist was unable to do this and the slide was used as is. A request was made to add hot spots to the images to identify individuals and to caption objects but was denied on the grounds that it would take too much programming time to accomplish. Animated maps suffered a similar fate.

During the course of the project on *The American Revolution*, 17 hours of videotape taken at various re-enactments were compiled. The Brigade of the American Revolution, a national historical association dedicated to re-creating the life and times of the common soldiers of the war for independence, organized many of these events. They also provided several hours of video from their archives and granted permission for use in a noncommercial educational product. It was expected to take about 20 minutes of video clips to illustrate how battles were fought, how clothing was made, and how life was lived in eighteenth-century America.

V. Links

The final editorial step for *The American Revolution* involved linking the materials. The publisher had a group of in-house indexers work on all the various materials independently. This process caused difficulties in overall linking, much of which had to be done sight unseen. Because there are a number of errors that may creep into an electronic publication at various stages, it is important for someone to examine the finished product to uncover errors and to verify that the links do not lead to dead ends.

As copy editing proceeded at the same time as the linking, the copy editors could make changes that affected the linking. For example, an editor deleted some paragraphs discussing George Washington's farewell to his soldiers and the resignation of his commission that was intended to be linked to documents and images. A general link to his name was the only possible solution.

In other cases, the author had already created links that had to be deleted at the last minute because permissions had not arrived in time. This was particularly annoying for the memoirs of Joseph Plumb Martin, which contained unique material. The author worked from a copyrighted edition even though several public domain editions existed. The copyright holder refused permission shortly before the publication deadline, and it was too late to locate one of the public domain editions.

The author also wanted to include links to jump to related, contrasting, or unfamiliar elements. For example, Paul Revere is known for his midnight ride on the night of April 18, 1775, but few know of Sybil Ludington's midnight ride on April 26, 1777, or of Paul Revere's court martial for treason. Instead of a direct link between the two narratives of Revere's midnight ride and his court martial, an indirect one had to be created. The essay covering his midnight ride has a link to a picture, which, in turn, has a link to the essay discussing the fiasco in Penobscot Bay, which led to his court martial.

VI. Conclusion

This article has looked at the issues, decisions, and trade-offs related to the preparation of text, audio, and graphic content for electronic publication. There are many other issues related to electronic publishing that go beyond the scope of this article (Schuyler, 1996; Young, 1994). The selection of a publisher, the negotiation of a contract, and the selection of an authoring program can happen prior to or contemporaneous with the creative process. The storyboarding process and product design stage will determine how the elements relate to each other. The authoring process (as distinct from the creative process) will affect the product design, but certain programs may condition or preclude some design elements as will the delivery medium (Jarol, 1996; Joss, 1995; Kozel, 1997a,b). For example, delivery over the Internet will require different design considerations than a CD-ROM title.

Once a title has gone through the creative, editorial, and authoring stages, it is ready for the preproduction, prototyping, and production phases.

This article has covered the major issues related to preparation of an electronic manuscript. Authors must be aware of the technical aspects of text, audio, graphics, and links before they begin work on an electronic piece. Each aspect of production has its advantages and disadvantages and the choice of the technical specifications will depend on the requirements of the content and the author's preferences. Librarians need to understand these issues as they purchase and process electronic publications because libraries will be receiving more and more of these publications in the future.

References

Adam, J. A. (1992). Orchestrating graphics, text, sound, and movies. *IEEE Spectrum* **29**(3), S1–S2.

Anderson, C. J. (1990). *Creating Interactive Multimedia: A Practical Guide.* Scott, Foresman, Glenview, IL.

Barnes, J. (1992). Full text and full image . . . the full story. *Serials Perspective* **9**(1), 10–11.

Boeri, R. J., and Hensel, M. (1996). Corporate online/CD-ROM publishing: The design and tactical issues. *CD-ROM Professional* **9**(2), 77–79.

Bonime, A., and Pohlman, K. C. (1997). *Writing for New Media: The Essential Guide to Writing for Interactive Media, CD-ROMs, and the Web.* John Wiley, New York.

Bristow, C. (1994). Color trapping: Make sure you have the right stuff. *Folio: The Magazine for Magazine Management* **23**(3), 58.

Cole, J. O. (1997). Publishers' strategies for CD-ROM internet publishing. *EMedia Professional* **10**(1), 62–70.

Desmarais, N. (1996). Behind the scenes of multimedia publishing: Dream or nightmare? *Computers in Libraries* **16**(4), 61–65.

Duncan, R. (1995). Electronic publishing on the World-Wide Web. *PC Magazine* **14**(7), 257–261.

Fisher, S. (1995). *CD-ROM guide to multimedia authoring.* Academic Press, New York.

Floyd, S. (1991). *The IBM Multimedia Handbook.* Brady, New York.

Goldie, P. (1997). *Using SGML to create complex interactive documents for electronic publishing. IEEE Transactions on Professional Communication* **40**(2), 129ss.

Harrel, W. D. (1996). *The Multimedia Authoring Workshop.* Sybex, Alameda, CA.

Holsinger, E. (1991). How to build your own multimedia presentation. *PC World* **9**(11), 250ss.

Hudson, B. J. (1994). Soup to nuts CD-ROM creation: Hard lessons learned in cross-platform development. *CD-ROM Professional* **7**(2), 65–74.

Jarol, S. (1996). Beyond authoring systems: The making of explore the Grand Canyon. *CD-ROM Professional.* **9**(4), 80–85.

Joss, M. W. (1995). A trio of text-tagging, windows multimedia authoring tools for under $1000. *EMedia Professional* **8**(8), 72–80.

Kerlow, I. V. and Rosebush, J. (1986). *Computer graphics for designers and artists.* Van Nostrand Reinhold, New York.

Kozel, K. (1997a). Authoring a blind date: Are the tools up to it? *EMedia Professional* **10**(3), 64–65.

Kozel, K. (1997b). Authoring for uncertainty. *EMedia Professional.* **10**(11), 112–113.

Luther, A. (1991). *Digital Video in the PC Environment: Featuring DVI Technology.* Intertext Publications, McGraw-Hill, New York.

Lynch, P. J., and Horton, S. (1997). HTML vs. authoring tools for creating CD-ROMs. *Syllabus* **11**(3), 16–20, 43.

Maloney, J. (1992). Do-it-yourself multimedia. *Publish* **7**(7), 18.

Maughan, S. (1997). To CD or not CD: What publishers should consider when adapting books to CD-ROM. *Publishers Weekly* **243**(30), 154–155.

Miller, R. L. (1991). *Multimedia and Related Technologies: A Glossary of Terms.* Monitor Information Services, Falls Church, VA.

Ores, P. (1995). Optimizing graphics for use on the Web. *MacWEEK* **9**(44), 14–15.

Ratcliff, J. W. (1992). Audio compression: Digitized sound requires its own compression algorithms. *Dr. Dobbs Journal* **17**(7), 32–40.

Rothstein, J. (1992). MIDI: A comprehensive introduction. A-R Editions, Milwaukee, WI.

Schuyler, N. (1996). From concept to gold master disk. *Communication Arts* **38**(3), 190–194.

Stover, M. (1996). The librarian as publisher: A World Wide Web publishing project. *Computers in Libraries* **16**(9), 40–43.

Young, A. (1994). Cutting gold: A guide to in-house CD-ROM production. *CD-ROM Professional* **7**(1), 100–107.

Metropolitan Area Networks and the Future of Networking in the United Kingdom

D. G. Law
King's College London
London WC2R 2LS
United Kingdom

I. Introduction

Metropolitan area networks (MANs) are a sufficiently recent development that they may need some explanation (Kahn, 1996). Regrettably the definition of a MAN remains rather imprecise. In the United Kingdom they are regional/local networks set up by the Joint Information Systems Committee[1] (JISC) of the Higher Education Funding Councils,[2] with a management contract awarded to a local university. The MAN falls somewhere between a Local Area Network (LAN), which uses high-speed links to connect buildings that are close together (typically under 10 km) and usually form part of the same organization, and a Wide Area Network (WAN), which links different management domains independent of geography and at much slower speeds. A MAN aims to serve a geographic area beyond the scope of LAN technologies but is restricted by some well-defined community of interest, often a city and its surroundings. The MAN will provide interconnection between different sites of the same organization—and the typical British university is now a multicampus undertaking—as well as interconnecting different organi-

* This article is an expansion of a paper first presented at the Public Library Authorities Conference at Torquay in September 1997.

[1] The Higher Education Funding Councils (see below) recognize that some activities have to be carried out as a national level rather than in each of the countries forming the United Kingdom. These functions, such as networking and national information services, are then managed by Joint Committees of the Funding Councils. JISC is one such committee.

[2] State support for British universities is allocated by the Higher Education Funding Councils. The councils consist of government nominees from business, education, and public life and each has a permanent secretariat. There are four of these bodies, one for each of the constituent countries of the United Kingdom.

77

zation. Despite the name, MANs can link non-metropolitan areas and thus have the potential to cover the whole United Kingdom. An early and typical regional MAN is FaTMAN (Fife and Tayside Metropolitan Area Network), covering a mixture of rural and urban areas. The largest population center— Dundee—has a population of only 250,000 people. When set up in 1995, FaTMAN linked three universities—Abertay, Dundee, and St. Andrews— and was joined by the Northern College in 1996. The total length of the initial fiber optic network was nearly 48 km, with the link from Dundee to St. Andrews alone being 23 km. The data transfer rate is 155 Mb/sec, and it uses asynchronous transfer mode (ATM) technology. Although it does not yet link institutions from other sectors, it clearly has the capacity to offer high-speed data links outside urban areas.

II. MANs and Cross-Sectoral Networking

The exploration of the use of networks by libraries has hitherto been almost exclusively driven by higher education (HE) in the United Kingdom. This is partly due to accidents of funding and timing, but there is a clear and well-founded perception that HE has been reluctant to share either its experiences or its networks with other library sectors. In large measure this has been due to the Acceptable Use Policy, which guides the management and provision of the Joint Academic Network (JANET). JANET was set up in the mid-1980s to link all universities and it and its successor SuperJANET form the university and research network in the United Kingdom. The Acceptable Use Policy (http://www.ja.net/documents/use.html) has long been seen as either a defense for research or a barrier to cross-sectoral development, according to one's point of view. The policy states that "JANET is maintained to support teaching, learning and research. Only organisations whose predominant use of JANET falls into these categories, or whose use is approved by the JISC, will be permitted to make a connection." In particular this has been taken to exclude connection to public libraries, health service networks, and until very recently to schools. This may be compared with the Acceptable Use Policy for FaTMAN, which states that "FaTMAN is primarily maintained to support academic and related activities such as teaching, learning and research". (http://www.dundee.ac.uk/ITServices/fatman/aup.htm) This is clearly much more open in its approach and allows for almost any organization to join. At the least one might expect that links can be opened to further education colleges[3], schools, public libraries, and the National Health Service, all of which have proved contentious areas under the JANET policy. There is little evidence that any of the MANs are taking advantage of this new

[3] Further Education Colleges in the United Kingdom offer predominantly subdegree courses, often of a vocational nature. In some cases a few degree courses are offered.

freedom so far. An understandable caution has led to a concentration on connecting existing HE establishments and providing applications closely linked to HE needs. But in principle, any organization can "join" the MANs, subject to locally determined rules. This radical, if somewhat accidental shift of policy, offers MANs the opportunity to develop a central role in the growing range of national initiatives, which assume that what the Dearing Report[4] calls Communications and Information Technology (C&IT) will be central to the development of any enterprise.

Networks have, of course, existed in other sectors, but with a much narrower purpose or with much poorer funding. For example LANs were and are concerned with the administration and financial control of the parent body and by extension with the administration of the library service, rather than with the sharing of information. Similarly National Health Service networks are concerned principally with patient administration, which in part explains an obsession with secrecy on grounds of patient confidentiality. This leads to an inability to support interorganizational networking. Coupled with the introversion of HE, this led to many librarians misunderstanding the possibilities offered by networking. For too many libraries the goal became an Internet connection and a Compuserve or AOL account. The Internet became librarians equivalent of the cargo cults of Melanesia, which believe that the aping of Western society will bring material wealth or cargo. In the case of libraries the simple possession of Internet access is confused with the provision of an information service. A survey (Ormes and Dempsey, 1995) showed that only a handful of public libraries had Internet access. That has changed in recent months. The most publicized developments have come in public libraries, where Project Earl has offered a notable leadership role (Kilgour, 1996) since 1995. One good example of this is the development of "Ask a Librarian" (http://www.earl.org.uk/ask/index.html) a consortially based reference service somewhat akin to the U.S.-based Stumpers bulletin board for reference librarians. The advent of the Library and Information Commission, which is strongly committed to the advantages of cross-sectoral linkages has also begun to focus attention on such infrastructural prerequisites as digitization (Parry, 1997).

III. The National Scene

The potential for developing MANs has been evident since their inception (Law, 1996). But the perhaps theoretical ambitions of advocates of a UK national networking policy have been sharpened and overtaken by the election

[4]The Dearing Report is the result of an enquiry into the future of higher education by a commission chaired by Sir Ron Dearing and was published in late 1997.

of a new government that is aware of and supportive of the opportunities for the United Kingdom to be a leader in creating and shaping the information society. Networking in the United Kingdom is at a crossroads. A major network—JANET—exists for higher education. The government has announced three major new initiatives: the National Grid for Learning (Department for Employment and Education, 1997a), which will link all schools; the University for Industry, which will provide post-16 training linked to employment; and the People's Network for Public Libraries (Library and Information Commission, 1997). At the same time the Fryer Report (National Advisory Group for Continuing Education and Lifelong Learning, 1997) sees a continuum of lifelong learning that will require access to information from a variety of sources. A further report on the 25 school and college experiments constituting the Superhighway Initiative talks of the need "to organise the groupings of all schools into neighbourhood clusters" and to "encourage and support links between the schools and other local partners such as . . . libraries and colleges" (Department for Employment and Education, 1997b). These could operate as a series of separately planned and no doubt effective initiatives. However, the potential for bringing these activities together through the MANs is very real. The government is committed to regionally based politics and the MANs could provide a very elegant realization of a political ambition.

IV. MANs and the Internet: A Proposed Model

Anyone using the Internet in Europe knows that the United States ceases to exist in the afternoon. Although it may be technically possible to expand bandwidth to meet the desired capacity, there must be doubt as to whether this is either economic or effective. If it is far to early to predict the implosion of the Internet under its own weight, we can at least see different models beginning to emerge of how it can be made effective at the local level.

When considering the potential of the MAN it is instructive to consider the library as a paradigm for network content. What organizations do not do is to give every member a sum of money to be spent as they wish on data resources of more or less relevance to the mission of the parent body. What they have historically done is to employ information professionals to assemble a local collection that meets most of the day-to-day information needs of the organization and provides a back-up facility to provide that expensive, rarer or peripheral material that is needed from time to time (the interlibrary loan system). The prospect of the introduction of charges by JISC is beginning to concentrate thinking on the cost effectiveness of general Internet access in higher education. Quite apart from the telecommunications charges, use of the Internet is resource intensive in academic staff time spent finding data in an inadequately classified set of resources and in the inefficiencies that poor connectivity brings. The existing library model then elegantly transfers to the local networked environment. Although this might be considered to work for the fashionable intranet, it also applies to the closed grouping of a MAN.

Library tasks	Internet tasks
Acquisition	Resource discovery
Collection building	Local server farms
Classification	Knowledge management
Preservation	Long-term data sinks
User instruction	User instruction

This implies that MANs will have to begin developing views on such traditional areas as what in libraries would be called acquisitions policy. One of the best examples of this is the agreement of the University of Glasgow to host the Visible Human Data Set created by the National Library of Medicine. This is an image bank of growing importance to those involved in medical education. Initially the data was held only in the United States and it was ruinously expensive of bandwidth repeatedly to transfer—or often to attempt to transfer—the same image across the Atlantic Ocean. After a great deal of negotiation the National Library of Medicine agreed that a mirror site could be set up in the United Kingdom. One issue, which this acquisition opened, remains unresolved. usera will require some explicit or implicit assurance on data quality. yet there are no nationally or internationally agreed-upon guidelines or standards for running mirror sites. At the moment each dataset host has independently to negotiate the terms and conditions of mirroring to protect their product.

Since no MAN, as no library, would be able to meet the entirety of its community's data needs, provision will have to be made for the management of access to external data. Cacheing strategies are now relatively well understood and these too would form a significant plank of a MAN data strategy. In essence the cache works on the old library saw that the material most likely to be used tomorrow is the material used today. A computer cache then simply holds copies of the material taken by users from other networks for a specified period of time such as a week. All subsequent requests for data are pointed first at the cache before going outside the local network. Experiments in the United Kingdom at the University of Kent have shown that this makes dramatic savings in the need for international connections.

A. Acting Together to Meet Common Needs

Local information plans were created in an attempt to harness the cross-sectoral library resources of a region. MANs provide the opportunity to take a step beyond that and in addition to develop, increase, and make more available the resources of the region. An initial if scarcely original list demonstrates the sort of cross-sectoral activity, which is ideally suited to A MAN.

1. Some Library Needs

Shared catalogs
  Improved document delivery
Shared collections
  Shared digitization and purchase
  Shared archiving and storage
Shared services
  The 24-hour enquiry desk and teleworking
  Improved access to resources without compromising physical security

2. Institutional Common Needs

It takes little effort to work out that the range of potential benefits from the MAN stretch across the organization as a whole and not just the library. It has been shown that higher education can contribute as much as 10% of the local economy, and this is reflected in a whole range of relationships with the local community, all of which could be improved through a shared network.

- Student accommodation and some student supports is often linked to local authorities.
- Higher education has a large and active estate. Planning applications and related estates matters also link to local authorities.
- Electronic mail, diaries, and documents would facilitate the meetings that link schools, hospitals, local authorities, and industry.
- Most universities are now active in the health sector. Health care of students and staff as well as links to hospital trusts and the regional health authorities would be facilitated.
- Cross-domain links are becoming as important as cross-sectoral links. Work with museums, galleries, and archives, all with different curatorial traditions and a richness of media content, are to be encouraged and will be facilitated over MANs.
- Links to schools and further education colleges are inevitable as government policy increasingly regards education as a lifelong continuum of experience.

But the benefits are not exclusive to higher education:

- Information services for SMEs[5]
- Videoconferencing for any set of members

[5] Small and medium-sized enterprises (SMEs) is a term much favored by the European Union. In this context it refers to those businesses that are too small to have their own in-house information service.

- School and other student access to expensive university resources
- Presentation of cultural and heritage materials to the community at large

Such listings are neither exhaustive nor particularly original. Inevitably the growth of activity on MANs will develop from existing activities, but they will surely be strongest where local community-based services offer efficiency, effectiveness, and cost-benefit.

B. The London MAN and an Experiment in Developing Cross-Sectoral Activity

A specific proposal is being developed in the London area that aims to take forward cross-sectoral activity on the London MAN. Since the London MAN is potentially the largest in the country, covering 20% of HE institutions; for example, the initial project is concentrated in inner London, which contains a very rich mix of cultural, heritage, and educational organizations. The participants want to develop a platform where the general arguments in favor of MAN-based development can be given specificity.

The British Library Research and Innovation Centre (BLRIC) Digital Libraries Programme has awarded a consortium of London public library authorities (City of Westminster, Corporation of London, Royal Borough of Kensington and Chelsea) an award of £26,750 for a 4-month feasibility study into establishing a pilot project that will take a selection of London public libraries on to the London MAN. The hope is that by focusing on the common ground of heritage and cultural activities clear benefit can be shown to all parties. LASER[6] is the project coordinator and consultant to the project. The project steering committee has representatives from the Department of Culture, Media and Sport (DCMS), the University of London, the M25 Consortium of Higher Education Libraries,[7] the London 'MAN,' the participant public library authorities, a London Museum, and LASER. This broad-based grouping demonstrates that a wider perspective is beginning to develop.

The scoping study, which is of 4 months' duration, will

- Establish the detailed technical and networking configurations required by public libraries to become connected to the London MAN.

[6] LASER (London and South East Region) began life as one of the regional interlending cooperatives in the United Kingdom. It has grown and expanded its portfolio of activities into many other areas of information provision. While hardly an OCLC in embryo, it shares many of the same ambitions and attributes, albeit in a much smaller geographic area.

[7] The M25 is the motorway circling London, roughly equivalent to the Beltway in Washington, DC. The consortium links all the higher education libraries within the circle.

- Identify the capital and recurrent cost of the technical/networking and service components of a future pilot.
- Seek areas for collaboration/and or cross-domain developments with other departments within the local authority, the higher education sector in London, and other sectors such as museums, galleries, archives, business information, and the voluntary sector.
- Establish the feasibility, means, and time scale for developing and offering, sharing, and participating in all services on the London MAN.
- Show how public library participation in the London MAN and proposals for cross-sector developments might assist the recommendations for improving the services overall, assist the coordination/collaboration of London public library authorities, and the greater coordination of library and information services in London.
- Identify how the proposed pilot will be financed.
- Compare the situation and requirements of London public libraries in relation to the MAN with related developments in other parts of the United Kingdom.
- Evaluate how a pilot project in this area will provide input to policy and strategic discussion within London and at national level.

All of the partners are committed to cross-sectoral activity and perceive great potential in developing a London-based project that will show this.

V. Conclusion

The political climate in the United Kingdom is poised for a great strengthening of regional developments and initiatives. Separate Parliaments for England and Wales, the so-called Council of the Isles to link Northern Ireland and Eire with the mainland, and the growth of the Regional Development Agencies in England are all proposals actively promoted by the new government. At the same time the government seems prepared to contemplate a massive investment in networks as an essential element of infrastructure in creating an information society developing an information economy. Taken together the two factors suggest that regionally based cross-sectoral initiatives have the potential to deliver both great benefits to the participants and the new political orthodoxy.

References

Department for Education and Employment (1997a). *Connecting the Learning Society: National Grid for Learning.* (The Government's Consultation Paper.) London, DfEE. (http://www.open. gov.uk/dfee/grid/index.htm)

Department for Education and Employment (1997b). *Preparing for the Information Age: Synoptic Report of the Education Departments' Superhighways Initiative*. London, DfEE. (http://www.open. gov.uk/dfee/dfeehome.htm)

Kahn, M. (1996, October). *The Development of the London MAN*. Unpublished paper, University of London Computing Centre, London.

Kilgour, A. (1996). Interface: EARL. *Ariadne* 5. (http://www.ariadne.ac.uk/issue5/interface/ intro.html)

Law, D. (1996). A MAN for all reasons? *Ariadne* 2. (http://www.ariadne.ac.uk/issue2/derek/ intro.html)

Library and Information Commission. (1997). *New Library: The People's Network*. London, Library and Information Commission.

National Advisory Group for Continuing Education and Lifelong Learning. (1997). *Learning for the Twenty-First Century: First Report of the National Advisory Group for Continuing Education and Lifelong Learning (the Fryer Report)*. London, Department for Education and Employment.

Ormes, S., and Dempsey, L. (1995, December 20). *Library and Information Commission Public Library Internet Survey, Version 1.0*. UKOLN Report for the Library and Information Commission. (http://ukoln.bath.ac.uk/publib/lic.html)

Parry, D. (1997). *A Review of Digitisation Projects in Local Authority Libraries & Archives*. Final Report to the Library & Information Commission. NewCastle, Information North.

The Quest for Access to Images
History and Development

Christine L. Sundt
Visual Resources Collection
Architecture & Allied Arts Library
University of Oregon
Eugene, Oregon 97403

I. Introduction

Images occupy a special place in most libraries and, as dictated by their medium and content, usually require unique systems for organization and access. The growing interest in images as vehicles for communication among generations nurtured by television, videos, and instantaneous photography has reinforced the need to address the issue of access to images and to examine the proliferation of visual documentation within the "new media."

This article examines the complex history of access to image collections. It also focuses on the recent use of electronic resources, the World Wide Web, and in particular the Image Directory to overcome difficulties and challenges usually associated with image access.

II. Images Past

Finding an image to support study and research is anything but easy. As they are today, images were important in many academic disciplines. For some disciplines, such as art and architectural history, the image is essential—a necessary stand-in for an object or structure and a way to see and study a thing or place when physical access is impossible. By its very nature art is global. Being able to see, review, study, and compare art usually necessitates a mechanism to reproduce it. Since the early nineteenth century, the photograph or other photographic media, especially slides, have aided research, study, and teaching. Before then, hand- and mechanically produced images— woodcuts, engraving, lithographs, and offset prints, to name but a few—served the same function but at greater cost and often limited production.

ADVANCES IN LIBRARIANSHIP, VOL. 22

In the past, access to these diverse images and their descriptive data was a challenge. Gathering images together in one place and/or creating indices to these were among the most immediate solutions.

Collecting or amassing images is what led to the development of well-known and highly respected picture archives such as the Bettmann Archive (http://directory.compuserve.com/Forums/BETTMANN/Abstract.asp), Hulton Deutsch Collection (http://www.u-net.com/hulton/about.html), the Bridgeman Art Library (http://www.bridgeman.co.uk/), Harvard University Art Museums Visual Collections, and the Witt Library at the Courtauld Institute of Arts in London (http://ihr.sas.ac.uk/ihr/wp/court.html), along with the countless other picture collections in libraries, museums, archives, and organizations worldwide. The underpinnings of these collections were the guides to their contents. Also, highly skilled picture researchers navigated through the images in ways that the guides could not. The images, mostly photographs and illustrations, became the mainstay of commercial and educational publishing.

A. Image Resources: Historic Highlights

The development of access or informational guides to collections has a long and interesting history. Documentary paintings such as the well-known genre depicting a *Kunstkammer* (literally, art room; more accurately, a cabinet of curiosities) are among the earliest image reference tools (Lipp, 1994). Numerous early art collections are known today because of such paintings, meticulously reproducing the artworks or treasures and their collectors in the great houses of Europe. Johann Zoffany (1734/1735–1810), a German-born artist who studied in Italy and worked extensively in England, produced a number of such works. Best known among these works are "The Tribuna of the Uffizi" (illustrated at http://he.net/~mega/eng/egui/monu/uft.htm), (1772–1780; Royal Collection, Windsor Castle), "The Antique Room at the Royal Academy at New Somerset House" (Royal Academy of Art, London), and "Charles Townley's Library at 7 Park Street, Westminster" (1781–1783; Townley Hall Art Gallery). These works show the interiors of rooms filled with recognizable artworks being presented to visitors by their collectors.

Another medium for referencing artworks was through prints and their sale or publication. The public's desire to own copies of famous works by artists stimulated the practice of making or commissioning prints after the original works. In 1731/1732, William Hogarth (1697–1764) produced a series of moralizing oil paintings in London, called the "Harlot's Progress," with a companion set of engravings modeled after the originals. The success of the prints was sufficient to stimulate other morality-theme print series based on his original works, including the "Rake's Progress" (1735) and

"Marriage a la Mode" (1743–1745). The ease and efficiency of reproducing and, in some cases, pirating prints after original paintings led Hogarth to push for the passage of the Copyright Act in England in 1735 as a means of protecting artists from unauthorized copying of their works and the resulting loss of profits. The print as both an image document and a reasonable substitute for a costly oil painting by this time was well established.

With the invention of photography, the camera became the tool of choice for documenting and cataloging art and architecture. Artists such as Dante Gabriel Rossetti (1828–1882) engaged in photography as a means of promoting and publishing their works (Faxon, 1992). Photographers used their medium to capture the remains of past civilizations, such as ancient Rome (Wester, 1992). Even the great museums in London, namely the National Gallery, the British Museum, and the South Kensington Museum (now known as the Victoria and Albert Museum), used photography to create catalogs or documents of their holdings as well as to record important events at the museum. Hamber (1996), in writing about the British Museum, includes the following quotation of 1857:

> Photographic pictures of the ivory carvings would be valuable and interesting to the public, and would be the best inventory for the use of the Museum. . . . Mr. Hawkins would also wish that Photographic pictures should be made of all objects of antiquity acquired by the museum as the best mode for future identification. It would not be necessary that each object should form a separate picture but similar objects might be grouped together, which would save much expense. (p. 382)

Photography, introduced in 1839, was still a relatively new medium in 1857. The ease by which an image could be created is a factor in the profusion of photographic documents that remain from these early decades. Maintaining order and logic among these new documents was also necessary. Each collection of images had its own method for organization and retrieval, some abundantly detailed, others with only summary notes. The next apparent need was to assemble data about these images that would make them accessible to more than just the museum personnel. By the end of the nineteenth century, photographic study collections were being formed at museums and for teaching the arts at colleges and universities (Irvine, 1979).

1. The Carnegie Art Reference Set for Colleges

Teaching the "arts" opened new markets for photographic images. In 1923, recognizing that educators in that day were keen to "advocate a return to the Renaissance spirit which combines the study, enjoyment, and practice of the arts," the Carnegie Corporation produced the Carnegie Art Reference Set for Colleges (Carnegie Corp., 1939). The set consisted of 2,073 photographs and color prints, 45 large color facsimiles, several portfolios, and approximately 200 books. The images were selected to represent "standard material useful in teaching the evolution and appreciation of the arts, and were meant for students to study at their leisure." Each image, a photographic reproduction of art or architecture, had a fully descriptive label and a unique number. Based on the documentation in the handbook, the data were organized following the traditional chronology and methodology for the study of art history. The unique number on each image appears to have been arbitrarily assigned since it does not follow the logical ordering of names, places, or titles included in the handbook. Clearly the handbook was the key to the collection as well as the suggested classification for those 200 or more colleges and high schools in the United States and the "British Dominions" that were receiving this generous donation. For many of these institutions, the Carnegie set formed the nucleus of their image collections. Other institutions outside this select core were not so fortunate; their collections had to rely on other means to acquire images.

B. Image Acquisition

Even though the Carnegie set provided a foundation for images needed for an arts curriculum, the task of assembling other relevant materials had yet to be addressed. Two thousand photographs may appear to be a reasonable number of images that could be used for any given presentation, but what if the instructor wanted to talk about artists or places not provided in the set? What if several teachers needed to use the images simultaneously?

1. Resources for the Visual Arts

Educational "humanities" images—prints, slides, photographs, and film-strips—covering topics broadly from the arts to the sciences are a classroom staple (Roberts, 1994). Typically these images were used to describe and explain the meaning of art and the development of culture. They were displayed to enable study and discourse. They also served as a memory aid for the underlying works when access to those works was impossible because of the condition of the work (too fragile to handle, too large to perceive easily) or when the distance between the student and the object was too great.

For many years image sets such as the Carnegie set were skillfully developed by image producers or brokers who, in cooperation with textbook publishers, filled the needs of teachers and their students for inexpensive pictures or illustrations to supplement texts, especially when color reproductions were costly and thus prohibitive (Freeman, 1990b). Fine arts image producers worked directly with museums and at historical sites. They negotiated rights and permissions with the owners or holders of the artworks and brought in specialized photography equipment to render these objects "in the best possible light." Image brokers purchased their images from independent photographers and then sold copies. Their products were typically high-quality, well-documented color slides of artworks and architecture that were packaged and sold specifically for use in the classroom. Each company produced a catalog or distributed periodic notices regarding the availability of new materials. Some slides were sold only as sets, while others were available individually. The latter were identified by the object or place illustrated along with other defining information such as the medium of the original object, its size, the date it was made, and where the illustrated object or site is located.

Among the best known image producers and brokers for the fine arts were and continue to be Saskia Ltd. Cultural Documentation (http://www.-saskia.com/), Harthill Art Associates (St. Mary's, Ontario, Canada), Rosenthal Art Slides (a division of Davis Publications, Worcester, Massachusetts), Mini-Aids (Monterey, California), and Art on File (Seattle, Washington). Images could also be acquired directly from museums, archives, and libraries. These are marketed as slide sets or as individual images directly to schools, scholars, and publishers. Large and small institutions offer this service for reasonable prices. Producers and brokers of slides for the fine arts are listed and evaluated in the *Slide Buyers' Guide: An International Directory of Slide Sources for Art and Architecture* (Cashman, 1990).

Once acquired for the school, the task of preserving and providing access to the slides was the next major task. Over the years, collections at colleges and universities grew exponentially. Some of the largest are also today's most distinguished: Harvard University, Princeton University, Bryn Mawr College, Cornell University, and the University of Michigan, to name but a few (Irvine, 1979). Each institution over time established a unique system for arranging the images acquired from these diverse sources and later an equally idiosyncratic method for making their catalog accessible to users (Freeman, 1990a). Today classification systems are widely different, even though the fundamental goals are often the same.

2. Image-Finding Aids

Soon the need for resources that would enable librarians and scholars to locate new or additional images was recognized (Roberts, 1988). Three types of reference tools emerged: directories of sources, indexes to reproductions, and directories of collections and locations (Bunting, 1984). The list of possible titles that function as finding aids for images is too large to enumerate, and yet sources of images are anything but extensive; instead they are simultaneously summary, specific, elusive, and limited in scope. Each source usually has its own focus and purpose, but most lack the breadth and depth to be considered comprehensive and few actually include illustrations. Indexing illustrations, which indicates where to find pictures in previously published materials, is but one method to identify image sources. Since an image appearing in a publication is not suitable for reproduction or display, other avenues to the image were necessary. Furthermore, working through lists of titles of artworks reproduced elsewhere was extremely time consuming when no one tool encompassed the whole and the sources where the illustration could be found were not readily available to the searcher. Directories of collections or locations of image repositories were useful, but they represent yet another step in gathering data.

The explosion of interest in teaching the arts by the late 1960s and the need for slides for the classroom were recognized by the appearance of three new publications within a 2-year period. These are *Sources of Slides: The History of Art* (Metropolitan Museum of Art, 1970, 1973), *A Slide Buyer's Guide* (DeLaurier, 1972), and *A Handlist of Museum Sources for Slides and Photographs* (Petrini and Bromberger, 1972). These books offered the most direct link between the need for teaching resources and the sources that could provide them.

a. Sources of Slides: The History of Art (Metropolitan Museum of Art, 1970, 1973).
This 24-page booklet identified the major sources and vendors of slides relevant to the teaching of art at the time. Annotations identified each vendor's area of specialization or coverage. The major art museums of the world were also listed. The 1973 booklet was a revision by Donna C. Smidt and Doralynn Schlossman of the earlier publication.

b. A Slide Buyer's Guide (DeLaurier, 1972); Slide Buyers' Guide (Cashman, 1990).
First published in 1972, *A Slide Buyer's Guide* is now in its sixth edition, re-titled *Slide Buyers' Guide: An International Directory of Slide Sources for Art and Architecture* (Cashman, 1990). Nancy DeLaurier, the former slide curator at the University of Missouri, Kansas City, assembled data from questionnaires for the first through fourth editions. The survey method followed that of the Metropolitan Museum of Art's *Sources of Slides* (acknowledged), but more data was ultimately provided. *A Slide Buyer's Guide* was the first attempt to evaluate quality and compare prices based on actual experiences of colleges purchasing from these sources. Other editions followed in 1974, 1976, and 1978.

The fifth and sixth editions of the *Slide Buyers' Guide* (Cashman, 1985, 1990) were published by Libraries Unlimited for the Visual Resources Association. In the sixth edition's 308 entries, detailed information about the vendors and their practices are described. Included are scope, photography method, production, documentation, purchasing (prices and business practices), rental, other products, other sources, and evaluation. Name, subject indexing, and cross-referencing made this edition one of the most useful resources for image users. Information describing individual objects or works of art is not provided. At this time, the Visual Resources Association is sponsoring the development of the seventh-revised edition.

c. A Handlist of Museum Sources for Slides and Photographs (Petrini and Bromberger, 1972). This guide contains the results of an ambitious survey sent to museums around the world. The questionnaire covered both color slides and black-and-white photographs, their availability, cost, procedure for ordering, type of accompanying documentation, policy for further reproduction, and name of contact person. No index is provided.

Knowing where the work of art is maintained is required before any of these guides can be useful. If the collection where the work is held is not specified, then the search must continue elsewhere. If the place is known and the data about the object are complete, a letter could be sent to inquire about the availability of the reproduction of the work in question. A list of slides or reproductions was usually returned to the inquirer, along with instructions for ordering these materials.

Even though museums try to maintain reasonable documentation for every artifact in their charge, not every piece will have been reproduced as a slide; many are only documented as black-and-white prints, large-format transparencies, or negatives. None of these guides included detailed lists of individual works; instead searchers were told if and how such lists could be obtained.

Acquiring images has been a task that could take substantial time and resources because adequate research and reference tools have been lacking. The multidimensional tool that was obviously required to perform cross-checking and linking of data is one that obviously had to wait until new technologies could offer both the medium and a cost-effective method for delivery. Thus came the era of computer technology, digital imaging, and electronic information delivery.

III. Images Present

In the 1990s, the introduction of affordable, easily produced digital images has eased many of the technical restraints associated with image use and, as a result, the need for images has greatly increased. Images appear everywhere, in places where we expect to find them as well as in new venues. The World Wide Web is a good example. "What good is a website without images" could be the mantra for the latter decade of the twentieth century. Similarly, a textbook without images—high-quality color images—has little appeal to a generation that has only known color television and now digital imagery on the Web. With this profusion and accelerated interest, finding a number of images or even locating a specific image, often remains a daunting and time-consuming task. Access to images for scholarly, professional, and classroom use is anything but straightforward and the more images are used, the greater the task to provide access to them. The need for a reference tool for images is obvious, but the efforts to provide the same until now were generally less than satisfying. The reasons for developing the Image Directory as the image reference work for today's needs could be easily justified on these grounds alone.

A. The Image Directory

Introduced in October 1997, the Image Directory (http://www.imagedir. com) in its current iteration is an online catalog of information about art images—from paintings and sculpture to architecture, textiles, ethnographic objects, the decorative and applied arts, and even toys. Through the Image Directory, users are able to search the holdings of museums and image repositories worldwide with the aid of vocabularies, time lines, and eventually reference texts. It brings together data from diverse image sources into a single, easily searchable electronic format. Other formats, such as a print version, are also under consideration.

1. Inception

The concept of a directory of images was originally developed by this author for the "Initiative on Electronic Imaging and Information Standards," sponsored by the Getty Art History Information Program (now the Getty Information Institute), in Santa Monica, California, March 3–4, 1994, in the following statement:

> Access to images of art needed for both research and teaching is hampered because we do not have a comprehensive reference tool for images equivalent to *Books in Print*. It is impossible to conduct serious research or to develop meaningful courses without knowing where to locate all types of images—photographs, transparencies, slides, as well as digital image files.

This was presented as an example of a "barrier" to universal and comprehensive access to images and information on art, and submitted along with two other "barriers" prior to the meeting. Since each speaker was allowed to elaborate on only one "barrier," this author chose to focus not on the "access barrier" but on another important issue, namely the absence of a statement of understanding or guidelines regarding copyright and the use of images.

2. Goals

The Image Directory, envisioned as the ultimate image reference tool, amalgamates the functions of the analog image resources—the directories of sources, indexes to reproductions, and directories of collections and locations—and adds dynamic electronic features. The Image Directory strives to do what these and other guides and resources cannot do; that is, be authoritative, comprehensive, and specific, providing item-level data along with easy links to and from the owners or providers of the images. The online tool bridges different, wholly independent cataloging and description methodologies into a single search and retrieval system. Image owners, the best sources for authoritative data about their collections, are the primary contributors of information and at the same time the gatekeepers for their images.

Standardized data fields allow viewers to search across diverse collections, bringing together records and images that would otherwise be difficult to locate. Because the issues of rights for reproduction and use of images often require negotiation, this information had to be readily accessible along with any data about an image, its available formats, and its source. Different uses would engender different costs and conditions. This information needed to be clearly stated in the record. Although it would have been most desirable to include a thumbnail image in each record within the Image Directory, the image eventually was not a requirement for participation. The rich data submitted by the image owners could and would stand alone in some cases.

3. Data and Templates

The record core for each image record consists of 47 data fields. In determining how to interpret and field the data supplied by the image owners and providers, three standards were compared and evaluated: MARC (MAchine-Readable Cataloging), the Categories for the Description of Works of Art (CDWA) (Baca and Harpring, 1996), and the Visual Resources Association Core Record (McRae, 1997). These standards are recognized as important vehicles for resource sharing in the larger context of networked cultural heritage.

MARC has not been as widely used in museums and archives as it has been in libraries to store bibliographic data in an international data communications format. Nevertheless since libraries would be contributing data to the Image Directory database, this format, which provides a means for organizations to share cataloging information through its common structure for describing data, would have to be reconciled. Over the years archives and visual resources collections have experimented with MARC as well. Their pursuits and accomplishments are described by Gibbs and Stevens (1986) for the National Gallery of Art Photographic Archives, by Fink and Hennessey (1988) for the National Museum of American Art, by Abid, Lantz, Pearman, and Scheifele (1992) for the Slide and Photograph Collections at the Cleveland Museum of Art, and by Keefe (1990) for the Rensselaer Polytechnic Institute Architecture

Library's slide collection. Bower (1993) compared and analyzed documentation from 10 institutions, either using or considering MARC for use with descriptions of visual resources or original artworks to see how these efforts were proceeding and to share the findings with others in these communities.

CDWA (http://www.gii.getty.edu/cdwa/HOMEPAGE.HTM) is the culmination of the study of the Art Information Task Force (AITF), underwritten by the Getty Art History Information Program, now the Getty Information Institute, and a grant from the National Endowment for the Humanities to the College Art Association. The project, begun in 1990, sought to develop guidelines for describing works of art in the context of research and scholarship. The main purpose of the CDWA is to help formulate the content of art-related databases by defining the intellectual structure underlying the description of objects and images. As more institutions begin incorporating the CDWA guidelines into their collection management systems, the greater the need for strategies for sharing data systematically. The CDWA framework has been useful in developing the Image Directory fields and field tags.

The work of the Visual Resources Association in defining how the CDWA framework applies to photography documenting architecture and original art is embodied in the VRA Core Record (http://www.oberlin.edu/~art/vra/wc1.html). The aim of this project is to develop a core documentation standard that would lead to shared cataloging of image information in the future. The development of this and other standards such as the Dublin Core (http://purl.oclc.org/metadata/dublin_core/) will be closely monitored for their significance for the Image Directory.

Perhaps the single most important aspect of the Image Directory is that control over data remains with the image provider. When data is converted into the Image Directory template, the provider has an opportunity to review, correct, augment, or delete it. The reason governing this practice is because cultural objects usually lack firm documentation or identification. When compared to the holdings in most libraries, cultural heritage objects lack one important feature: an equivalent to a book's title page. Traditionally the responsibility for identifying or describing an object has been assumed by independent scholars who may or may not be affiliated with the repository where the object is maintained. As a result much of the information that relates to an object—attribution (authorship), title, date, meaning, and purpose—can be open to speculation and sometimes contradiction. However, the best, most authoritative and up-to-date information about the object should be found with the object, in the documentation maintained by the repository. The museum's, archive's, or library's—the image owners or providers—role in submitting data directly to the Image Directory is therefore significant in meeting the project's objectives and goals to be authoritative, comprehensive, and specific.

4. Participation

Any individual or institution having images of value or interest to others is eligible to participate in the Image Directory. Initial invitations were sent to museums and repositories having a record of selling or marketing images based on listings in the *Slide Buyer's Guide, 6th ed.* (Cashman, 1990). Others were contacted later on the basis of their size, location, and specialization in art. The benefits outlined in the initial contact letter included (1) educational: providing useful information about their institutions and resources in a single, easily accessible reference tool; (2) scholarly: being able to establish authority over the data describing their holdings without third-party intervention or interpretation; and (3) commercial: making their images available to both scholarly and commercial purchasers or users in a business-like manner through software designed to ensure secure communications and transactions.

To fulfill one of its most important missions, namely its educational mandate, may be the best reason for a museum or repository to contribute data to the Image Directory. The American Association of Museums (1992) identifies 10 principles, stating that for museums education is "at the center of their public service roles" (http://www.aam-us.org/eenv.htm). Participation in projects such as the Image Directory whose main audience is the image researcher can be seen as contributing to this important goal.

The third factor, the commercial aspect, or the need to find new revenue streams, is the one found most frequently mentioned as the driving force in many of today's museums (McLean, 1995). The Image Directory furnishes a vehicle by which the sale or licensing of images by the image owner can be facilitated.

Image owners and providers can submit data in whatever format they currently have available. Academic Press has accepted data in a variety of media—from printed books to index cards to text-based tables and electronic databases. When books are submitted, the data are scanned and then fielded into the Image Directory database. There is no charge for the data conversion service.

Images are an important part of the Image Directory but as mentioned earlier not a requirement. Some image owners have been reluctant to include images for fear that viewers will download copies. Others have submitted images that are watermarked or encrypted to discourage unauthorized use. For this reason only low-resolution (thumbnail) images are presented with the Image Directory data record.

No charges are levied for being included or participating in the Image Directory. Academic Press requires no initial fee from image owners or providers, no minimum number of records, and no annual quotas for records added or revised. The open policy regarding data submission is intended to provide the right incentives for image owners and providers to ensure that participation will be steady and long term. In addition, if participants should choose to withdraw from the Image Directory, there are no restrictions or penalties imposed.

5. Contracts and Licenses

The terms of the agreement between the Image Directory and an image owner are simple and straightforward. The use of image descriptions and low-resolution images (if provided) is nonexclusive and no copyright is claimed on the images. The agreement also covers record updates and modifications, use of materials provided by the image owner, and the conditions for terminating the agreement. Every effort is made to ensure that the terms of the contract are consistent with the goals and philosophy of the institution or individual providing data and images.

6. Querying the Database

Viewers at the Image Directory site are presented with two ways to find images: The first is a quick search and the second allows for a more complex, combined-field query. The quick query screen displays 6 criteria boxes, while the detailed query presents 20 boxes. For users who need assistance choosing search terms or spelling options for artists' or architects' names, two Getty Information Institute tools are included: the Art and Architecture Thesaurus (AAT) and the Union List of Artists Name.

The AAT (http://www.ahip.getty.edu/aat_browser/) is a comprehensive vocabulary of nearly 120,000 terms used for describing objects, textural materials, images, architecture, and material culture from antiquity to the present. It facilitates the use of terminology associated with the analysis and discussion of cultural history, encompassing the natural and built environments, furnishings, equipment, and artifacts. It is a system based on hierarchies and facets. Seven main categories or facets are further subdivided into 33 hierarchies or subfacets. Many of the terms include "scope notes" that provide definitions or comments that help the user to understand usage and application. This controlled vocabulary can be used either in the process of describing objects at the museum or repository by choosing terms for inclusion in a collections management database or by the end user of this data to build or refine query statements. Even with its predominantly Western bias, the AAT vocabulary extends well beyond the West to other cultures.

The Union List of Artists' Names (ULAN) database (http://www.ahip.-getty.edu/ulan_browser/) consists of more than 200,000 entries representing more than 100,000 artists (or "creators"), architects, craftspeople, and others. Coverage ranges from the ancient world to the modern period. Name variations, biographical information, and bibliographic sources are brought together in this dynamic reference tool.

Soon, a third and most recently released Getty tool, the Thesaurus of Geographic Names (TGN) (http://www.ahip.getty.edu/tgn_browser/) will be added to the Image Directory search screen. TGN contains nearly 1 million place names representing approximately 900,000 places. The thesaurus is composed of names and related information contributed by several Getty projects, including the Bibliography of the History of Art (BHA), the Foundation for Documents of Architecture (FDA), the Getty Center Photo Study Collection (GCPS), and the Getty Information Institute's Vocabulary Program (VP). Plans are in place to expand the list of TGN contributors to include more than just Getty data.

Eventually the AAT, TGN, and ULAN resources will be more seamlessly integrated into the Image Directory query structure similar to the way they are being used at the Getty Information Institute's a.ka. database project site (http://www.gii.getty.edu/index/aka.html).

Another tool to be found at the Image Directory site is the "Times and Places" feature, which incorporates maps and time lines from Gardner's *Art Through the Ages*. Plans to integrate "Times and Places" more dynamically and interactively into the data are being developed.

7. Audiences and Access

At this time, Academic Press has identified two primary audiences for the Image Directory. The first, the university and research library community around the world, is the traditional user of Academic Press projects. Through its IDEAL project, for example, almost 200 journals are distributed online, as full-text retrievable files. The Image Directory will be another database that could be made available to subscribers or site-license purchasers.

The second audience includes anyone who uses images, from publishers to television and film companies. Corporate art departments, producers, and agencies who typically purchase images from stock photography houses could have access to the Image Directory. The goal of the Image Directory is to help image "buyers" find the resources they need quickly and efficiently and to enable them to depend on this tool as they do on other electronic image sources.

After a free trial period that continues through early 1998, access will be available by site license, to individual users by subscription, or by a per-search or timed-usage fee.

B. The Image Directory in Context

The ease of putting up a website and making information available for all people to view has stimulated the countless resources that are now available on the Web. Individuals as well as institutions are now experimenting with this medium to see what gains can be realized and at what costs. Several other projects are noteworthy for their similarities to the Image Directory as well as their differences. Chief among these are Corbis, AMICO, and MDLC for their relationships both to museums and educational pursuits.

1. Corbis

Since 1989, Corbis (then known as Interactive Home Systems and later Continuum) has been working with museums to develop innovative uses for images. Corbis's mission is "to become the world's leading provider of visual content and services in the digital age" (http://www.corbis.com/com/about/). A leader in digital technology by virtue of its affiliation with Bill Gates and the Microsoft Corporation, Corbis is a broker of images, delivering high-quality images to its image-buying customers. The Corbis collection includes images from numerous world-class resources including the Bettmann Collection, LGI, and Starlight, in addition to great museums in Seattle, Philadelphia, Detroit, London, and Moscow, to name but a few. Participants sign a nonexclusive agreement that allows them to continue licensing their images to third parties, while Corbis has the right to use the images in their own products (Akiyama, 1997). Royalties resulting from image use are returned to the image owners, and advances are available to offset any costs incurred in preparing images for the Corbis archive.

2. AMICO

The Art Museum Image Consortium (AMICO) was founded by the Association of Art Museum Directors (AAMD) in 1997, with 23 museums representing AMICO's founding members. The brainchild of Maxwell Anderson, director of the Art Gallery of Ontario, Toronto, AMICO is a not-for-profit organization whose goal is to "build a shared library of digital documentation of their collections for licensing and distribution to the educational community" (http://www.amn.org/AMICO/AMICOinfo.html). The major North American art museums will be the target of this project.

At this time, museums are being invited to participate and examine the project's "framework documents" available for public comment at AAMD's Internet site, hosted by the Art Museum Network (AMN) (http://www.AMN.org). In the future, AMICO will also be marketing other products, which may include indexing and retrieval tools. Currently participants are engaged in a 1-year-long testbed project to learn how universities are using digital teaching and reference tools that will enable participating museums to meet the needs of their users. The consortium will be responsible for licensing the content of museums as a means of distributing museums' digital information to the educational community. The project will also enable museums to work together in defining license terms, to eliminate overhead costs of processing individual requests for single images, and to work toward standardizing digitizing and documentation procedures. Under this model, museums collaborating as vendors of digital images to the educational market mirror the efforts of libraries or library consortia with vendors of electronic information.

3. MDLC

The Museum Digital License Cooperative, Inc. (MDLC) is being developed by Geoffrey Samuels in cooperation with the American Association of Museums (AAM), Sun Microsystems, Cornell University, and the University of California at Berkeley (http://www.museumlicensing.org). Funding for this project is being sought from the private sector. This licensing project is open to all American museums, not just those specializing in art. Its first goal will be to develop an educational site license, but later it will expand its boundaries to include a commercial licensing arm. Because of the size of its constituency audience, its focus is being limited to the development of a digital library of images of nineteenth-century American culture. The notable benefit of this direction is the prospect of building on a critical mass of nineteenth-century American material already available in projects such as the Library of Congress "American Memory" (http://lcweb2.loc.gov/ammem/) and the Cornell–Michigan "Making of America" (http://www.umdl.umich.edu/moa/) initiatives. Another reason for choosing this timeframe is to minimize copyright problems, and the attendant rights and reproduction issues (Keshet, 1997).

Corbis, AMICO, and MDLC are not the only licensing initiatives to be recently developed, but they are by most accounts the most commonly discussed projects among museums and educational institutions at this time. Each embodies a noble purpose and goal and as such can be seen as being for the benefit of their communities. As libraries elect to offer more electronic resources to their patrons, licensing, instead of purchasing materials, will be a significant factor affecting their budgets and buying power. The fact remains that decisions still have to be made concerning sources and availability—in this case sources of images what would be available to patrons, whether for selecting teaching resources, for identifying research materials, or choosing illustrations for use in publications. The Image Directory's goal—to provide access to information about images—rather than to the image itself, means that data from any of the image collections or consortia can be included as data in the Image Directory.

IV. Obstacles and Resolution

The time that has elapsed between perceiving the need for an image equivalent to *Books in Print* and the realization of such services is explained by many factors. The first is technology or lack thereof, until now. Image data is dynamic and unwieldy. An object can be many things to different viewers and so too can the data describing it. The research and writing that has accompanied these objects over several centuries, before and after the introduction of standards, such as naming conventions, spelling, and access to diverse information through indices and guides is dauntingly abundant. Automation allows the researcher to traverse data and to find remedies for variances and the absence of standards. Pseudonyms and variant names are collected by tools such as ULAN, and specialized vocabularies made manageable by thesauri such as the AAT. Places in the world, along with their names and political associations throughout history, are documented in the just-released TGN. What had been a simple two-dimensional playing field in the analog world is now a three-dimensional matrix in which information can be accessed from many different directions using numerous strategies.

The second factor affecting these developments is the cooperation and collaboration of museums, archives, and repositories. Collecting organizations such as museums have lagged behind libraries in embracing technology in their collections management efforts. Each organization appears to proceed along a unique path even though their ultimate goal is to share data (Gross and Wilde, 1996; Jensen, 1997). In large organizations, each department or division might have its own unique system as well. Without a central system for managing information about the art or artifacts, institutions are sometimes reluctant to submit any data, claiming it to be incomplete or without proper verification. Funding issues are usually the primary reason driving technological delays along with the lack of adequate cataloging and documentation standards.

Today, many of these issues are being addressed in various initiatives, such as the Consortium for Computer Interchange of Museum Information (CIMI) (http://www.cimi.org/)—16 organizations working to solve problems relating to the electronic interchange of museum information; *Protecting Cultural Objects in the Global Information Society* (http://www.gii.getty.edu/pco/index.html)—a project seeking to implement worldwide common documentation standards to help prevent the illicit movement of cultural objects; *Census of Art and Architecture Known to the Renaissance* (http://www.gii.getty.-edu/giinew/index/census.html)—multimedia database documenting the knowledge and study of antique art and architecture by Renaissance artists, architects, and scholars; and *Distributed Database Initiative* (http://www.gii.getty.edu/giinew/index/distdata.html)—a project to foster broader information access and contribution to digital research collections by the international cultural heritage community. The Getty Information Institute, an agency of the J. Paul Getty Trust, has provided funding and support for many of these initiatives.

Finally, the question of what kinds of images should be distributed—format, quality, and medium—is fundamental. The delivery of digital images requires an understanding of this technology and its ramifications (Ester, 1991, 1994; Stam, 1997b). At the same time the needs of the user—the student, teacher, scholar, and all other image consumers—must be recognized (Stam, 1997a; Schmitt, 1988). Some museums question their ability to enter into commercial distribution of analog or digital images with limited resources and staff to handle requests; others find themselves concerned with ownership and rights issues that were never adequately explored when certain art and artifacts were acquired (Walsh, 1997).

The changing landscape occupied by today's classroom has brought about an understandable reexamination of the museum's role in supporting education and in dealing with the licensing of images rather than the sale of slides and photographs (Green, 1997). How much more could be expected to change before patterns can be understood and addressed with sufficient resources? To this end several testbed projects have been undertaken. One of the earliest, begun in 1995, to explore how museums can respond to the needs of images in higher education was the Museum Education Site Licensing (MESL) project (http://www.ahip.getty.edu/mesl/home.html). A joint collaboration between the Getty Information Institute and MUSE Educational Media, this initiative involved seven collecting institutions and seven universities working together to define terms and conditions for the educational use of digitized museum images and related information (Trant, 1996).

Among museum organizations, the Museum Computer Network (MCN) (http://www.mcn.edu/) has contributed significantly to the advancement of automation and technology in museums. Through its conferences, workshops, and publications, including *Spectra*, members learn about systems, resources, and methodologies that are working or being developed to meet new challenges. The evolvement of the Image Directory has been guided by knowledge gained from programs and information sponsored by organizations such as MCN.

The Image Directory is anything but static and, by the very nature of both technology and emerging developments in information access, will continue to evolve and expand its parameters. Presently, more than 100 museums, galleries, stock houses, and slide producers are contributing data. The participants include, for example, The Museum of Modern Art, the Rijksmuseum in Amsterdam, the Smithsonian Institution, the Brooklyn Museum of Art, the George Eastman House, and the San Francisco Museum of Modern Art, and the list grows weekly.

The Image Directory is a product of its time, depending as it does on the provision of data and the sustained interest among image owners and providers to create a perfect bridge between their images and the world at large. Time will also be the judge of its success. If the bridge is good, image seekers will find it and use it.

V. Conclusion

The vast wealth of images that comprise our artistic and cultural heritage certainly warrants the planning, expense, and energy associated with the image initiatives of the 1990s. With time, these new tools and services that now afford better access to images, their owners, and authorized distributors will be refined and even improved. In the end libraries and their patrons will find the quest for images much less of a challenge and much more an easy and logical route to important and unique resources in the library.

References

Abid, A., Lantz, E., Pearman, S. J., and Scheifele, E. (1992). Planning for automation of the slide and photograph collection at the Cleveland Museum of Art: A draft MARC/visual materials record. *VRA Bulletin* **19**(2), 17–21.

Akiyama, K. A. (1997). Rights and responsibilities in the digital age. *Visual Resources* **XII**, 261–267.

American Association of Museums. (1992). *Excellence and Equity: Education and the Public Dimension of Museums* (http://www.aam-us.org/eenv.htm)

Baca, M. and Harpring, P., eds. (1996). Art Information Task Force categories for the description of works of art. *Visual Resources* **XI**, 3–4.

Bower, J. (1993). The Visual Resources Association MARC mapping project. *Visual Resources* **IX**, 291–327.

Bunting, C. (1984). *Reference Tools for Fine Arts Visual Resources Collections* (Occasional Papers No. 4), Arts Library Society of North America.

Carnegie Corp. (1939). *The Carnegie Art Reference Set for Colleges.* Rudolf Lesch Fine Arts, New York.

Cashman, N. D., ed. (1985). *Slide Buyers' Guide: An International Directory of Slide Sources for Art and Architecture,* 5th ed. Libraries Unlimited, Englewood, CO.

Cashman, N. D., ed. (1990). *Slide Buyers' Guide: An International Directory of Slide Sources for Art and Architecture,* 6th ed. Libraries Unlimited, Englewood, CO.

DeLaurier, N., ed. (1972). *A Slide Buyer's Guide.* College Art Association, Commercial Slides Committee.

Ester, M. (1991). Image quality and viewer perception. *Visual Resources* **VII**, 327–352.

Ester, M. (1994). Digital images in the context of visual collections and scholarship. *Visual Resources* **X**, 11–24.

Faxon, A. C. (1992). Rossetti's reputation: a study of the dissemination of his art through photographs. *Visual Resources* **VIII**, 219–245.

Fink, E. E., and Hennessey, C. M. (1988). Testing the flexibility of the MARC format. *Visual Resources* **IV**, 373–388.

Freeman, C. C. (1990a). Visual collections as information centers. *Visual Resources* **VI**, 349–359.

Freeman, C. C. (1990b). Visual media in education: an informal history. *Visual Resources* **VI**, 327–340.

Gibbs, A., and Stevens, P. (1986). MARC and the computerization of the National Gallery of Art photographic archives. *Visual Resources* **III**, 185–208.

Gross, L., and Wilde, D. (1996). Creating a tool for sharing information and art objects. *Spectra* **24**(2), 36–37.

Hamber, A. J. (1996). *"A Higher Branch of the Art": Photographing the Fine Arts in England, 1839–1880.* Gordon and Breach Publishers.

Irvine, B. J. (1979). *Slide Libraries: A Guide for Academic Institutions, Museums, and Special Collections.* Libraries Unlimited, Littleton, CO.

Jensen, J. (1997). User centered design and usability testing interfaces for museum applications. *Spectra* **24**(3), 40–45.

Keefe, J. M. (1990). The use of the visual materials format for a slide library integrated into an OPAC, in *Beyond the Book: Extending MARC for Subject Access* (T. Petersen and P. Molholt, eds.). 25–41. G. K. Hall, Boston.

Keshet, A. (1997). Fair use, fair trade, and museum image licensing. *Visual Resources* **XII**, 281–289.

Lipp, A. (1994). Towards *The Electronic Kunst und Wunderkammer:* Spinning on the European Museums Network (EMN). *Visual Resources* **X**, 101–118.

McLean, F. (1995). A marketing revolution in museums? *Journal of Marketing Management* **11**, 601–616.

McRae, L. (1997). The core categories for visual resources: A progress report. *VRA Bulletin* **24**(3), 25–27.

Metropolitan Museum of Art (New York, NY). Photography and Slide Library. (1970). *Sources of Slides: The History of Art.* The Metropolitan Museum of Art, New York.

Metropolitan Museum of Art (New York, NY). Photography and Slide Library. (1973). *Sources of Slides: The History of Art.* The Metropolitan Museum of Art, New York.

Petrini, S., and Bromberger, J. (1972). *A Handlist of Museum Sources for Slides and Photographs.* University of California Press, Berkeley.

Roberts, H. E. (1988). "Do you have any pictures of . . . ?": Subject access to works of art in visual collections and book reproductions. *Art Documentation* **7**(3), 87–90.

Roberts, H. E. (1994). Second hand images: The role of surrogates in artistic and cultural exchange. *Visual Resources* **IX**, 335–346.

Roberts, H. E., ed. (1995). *Art History Through the Camera's Lens.* Gordon and Breach Publishers.

Schmitt, M., ed. (1988). *Object, Image, Inquiry: The Art Historian at Work.* The Getty Art History Information Program, Santa Monica, CA.

Stam, D. C. (1997a). How art historians look at information. *Art Documentation* **16**(2), 27–30. (reprint of the article originally published in the Winter 1984 issue).

Stam, D. C. (1997b). A Web-based model for providing access to museum information. *Spectra* **24**(3), 18–23.

Trant, J. (1996). The Museum Education Site Licensing (MESL) project: An update. *Spectra* **23**(3), 32–34.

Wallace, J. (1994). Project Chapman: The direct delivery of digital Smithsonian photographic images via the internet. *Visual Resources* **X**, 57–60.

Walsh, P. (1997). Art museums and copyright: A hidden dilemma. *Visual Resources* **XII**, 361–372.

Wester, S. (1992). Three nineteenth-century photographers of the ruins of ancient Rome. *Visual Resources* **VIII**, 343–354.

Web References

a.k.a. (http://www.gii.getty.edu/index/aka.html).

Art and Architecture Thesaurus (AAT) (http://www.ahip.getty.edu/aat_browser/)

Art Museum Image Conortium (AMICO) (http://www.amn.org/AMICO/AMICOinfo.html)

Art Museum Network (AMN) (http://www.AMN.org)

Bettmann Archive (http://directory.compuserve.com/Forums/BETTMANN/Abstract.asp)

Bridgeman Art Library (http://www.bridgeman.co.uk/)

Categories for the Description of Works of Art (CDWA) (http://www.gii.getty.edu/cdwa/HO-MEPAGE.HTM)

Consortium for Computer Interchange of Museum Information (CIMI) (http://www.cimi.org/)

Corbis (http://www.corbis.com/com/about/)

Cornell–Michigan Making of America (http://www.umdl.umich.edu/moa/)

Dublin Core (http://purl.oclc.org/metadata/dublin_core/)

Getty Information Institute. *Census of Art and Architecture Known to the Renaissance* (http://www.gii.getty.edu/giinew/index/census.html)

Getty Information Institute. *Distributed Database Initiative* (http://www.gii.getty.edu/giinew/index/distdata.html)

Getty Information Institute. *Protecting Cultural Objects in the Global Information Society* (http://www.gii.getty.edu/pco/index.html)

Green, D. L. (1997). *Museums Collaborate in New Marketing Ventures for Digital Images.* (http://www.arl.org/newsltr/193/intro.html)

Image Directory (http://www.imagedir.com)

Hulton Deutsch Collection (http://www.u-net.com/hulton/about.html)

Library of Congress American Memory (http://lcweb2.loc.gov/ammem/)

Museum Computer Network (MCN) (http://www.mcn.edu/)

Museum Education Site Licensing project (MESL) (http://www.ahip.getty.edu/mesl/home.html)

Saskia Ltd. Cultural Documentation (http://www.saskia.com/)

Thesaurus of Geographic Names (TGN) (http://www.ahip.getty.edu/tgn_browser/)

"The Tribuna of the Uffizi" (illustrated at http://he.net/~mega/eng/egui/monu/uft.htm)

Union List of Artists' Names (ULAN) (http://www.ahip.getty.edu/ulan_browser/)

Witt Library at the Courtauld Institute of Arts in London (http://ihr.sas.ac.uk/ihr/wp/court.html)

Visual Resources Association (VRA) Core Record (http://www.oberlin.edu/~art/vra/wc1.html)

Here Today, Gone Tomorrow

What Can Be Done to Assure Permanent Public Access to Electronic Government Information?

Daniel P. O'Mahony
Brown University Library
Providence, Rhode Island 02912

I. Introduction

On the night of January 10, 1921, a fire broke out at the U.S. Commerce Department in downtown Washington, DC. A night watchman traced the smell of smoke to the carpenter shop in the basement of the 11-story building. He immediately called for help, but the fire quickly swept through the basement and lower floors of the building. As an estimated crowd of 10,000 looked on, nearly all of the city's fire-fighting equipment and personnel fought for more than 3 hours to bring the blaze under control. When the final damage was assessed, fortuitously no human life was lost; the fire began less than an hour after the building's 1,200 workers had left for the day. But the fire had consumed virtually all of the documents of the 1890 U.S. census of population. These original records, stacked in the basement in an area outside the fireproof vaults, were completely destroyed by fire and water damage ("Census Papers Lost in Washington Fire," 11 January 1921).

This incident was one of the most catastrophic losses of government information this nation has ever suffered. In roughly 3 hours, the records of one of the most interesting and significant chapters in American experience were destroyed forever, leaving a gap in U.S. history that can never be replaced. Although the aggregate statistics from the 1890 census survive today, the loss of the information contained in the original census schedules continues to be mourned by historians, demographers, sociologists, genealogists, librarians, and other researchers.

Despite this vulnerability to accidental loss and physical deterioration, printed materials have been remarkably durable in sustaining the written historical record of government. Fortunately, fires, floods, earthquakes, wars, and other natural and human-made disasters have been relatively few and far between. Over the years, reliable systems have been developed to retain, preserve, and conserve the records and documents that tell the story of the United States's history. As a result, after more than two centuries, original copies of key documents such as the Declaration of Independence are available on display in Washington, DC, and are viewed by millions of visitors every year. Every day thousands of other people take advantage of copies of less famous but still important historical documents in libraries across the United States. Paper, along with its microfilmed surrogates, has withstood the test of time in meeting society's requirements for preservation and access.

The news of the tragic loss of the 1890 census was deeply felt at the time. The 1921 fire prompted renewed efforts to establish a safe and secure place for the permanent preservation of important government records, and eventually led to the creation of the National Archives in 1934.

Since that time, the nation has been relatively secure in the belief that the essential records of the federal government systematically are being identified and physically preserved for future researchers through the work of the National Archives in Washington, DC, and its regional offices. Equally important, the Government Printing Office's Superintendent of Documents, with its nationwide network of federal depository libraries, ensures that the public documents and publications created by the federal government are readily available to the general public for use today and in the future. The combined efforts of these and other partners have guaranteed continuous and permanent access to federal government information for all citizens. That is, until now.

Today the federal government increasingly relies on electronic means to create and disseminate information. Although there are distinct advantages and efficiencies gained by using electronic information technologies in the short run, the potential long-term costs and historical consequences may be staggering. Moreover, at present, there is no mechanism in place and no responsibility assigned within the federal government for systematically identifying, capturing, and permanently maintaining electronic information for future public use. More often than not, when an agency updates an Internet file or changes its website, the old or replaced information is lost forever. Thus, the public is now experiencing losses of government information, on a scale similar to that of the catastrophic fire of 1921, on what seems to be a weekly basis. Unless steps are taken soon to rectify the situation, one of the greatest ironies of the "information age" may be that there will be little or no information to survive from this period of time for the future.

II. The Challenge of Permanent Public Access in the Electronic Era

A. Preserving the Nation's History

Libraries and archives have worked together for centuries to preserve and provide access to the recorded knowledge of civilization. The traditional systems that have developed over time have done a venerable job in ensuring ongoing availability of information recorded on some type of tangible, physical media. In the realm of U.S. federal government information, three separate but complementary systems work in concert to ensure current and future access to government records, documents, and publications.

The first of these systems primarily serves the government itself. The National Archives and Records Administration (NARA), with its national facilities and system of 17 regional archives and records centers, works with federal agencies to identify the government's essential records of enduring historical value, and to preserve these materials for posterity (NARA, 1997). Items collected and preserved by NARA represent the raw materials of government—original papers, manuscripts, documents, photographs, and other documentary evidence.

The second is the informal "system" of national libraries, including the Library of Congress, the National Library of Medicine, the National Agricultural Library, and the recently established National Library of Education. These libraries work to develop comprehensive collections in their areas of expertise and include information from both government and nongovernment sources. The national libraries primarily serve government agencies and their respective specialized research communities, and serve as a "library of last resort" for others.

The third system differs from the first two in that its primary role is to serve the government information needs of the general public. The Federal Depository Library Program (FDLP) consists of nearly 1,400 depository libraries located in virtually every congressional district in the United States. Under the administration of the Superintendent of Documents within the Government Printing Office (GPO), these libraries collect federal publications based on the government information needs and interests of their local communities. Depository libraries make these collections available at no fee to users, and provide expert assistance and support services to help the public to find and use the government information they require or desire. At present, 53 of these libraries—the regional depository libraries—collect all of the public documents published by agencies of the U.S. government and retain them forever. These regional depositories (approximately one in each state) ensure that comprehensive collections of government publications continue to be readily available on an equitable basis for all citizens nationwide, regardless of their geographic location or economic condition.

Each of the three systems addresses unique and important aspects of ensuring that current and future users are able to identify, locate, and use information created by the federal government. Together, they work to guarantee the public's right to know—the right of all Americans to access information by and about their government to make informed decisions and to hold their government accountable for its actions. Further, they help fulfill a basic tenet of our democratic form of government, that information created at taxpayer expense should be made available for the free use of all citizens.

For more than a century, these systems have been successful in identifying, collecting, and caring for the published record of the federal government. In the print-on-paper era, preserving government information, for the most part, has meant preserving a physical artifact, either the book or document itself or, in some cases, a microfilmed reproduction of the book or document. Over time, libraries and archives have developed prudent and reliable means for ensuring that the materials in their custody will remain available for future users.

B. The FDLP and Permanent Public Access

Although each of the three previously discussed systems plays a key role in preserving the recorded history of the government, the responsibility for providing permanent *public* access to government information has been met primarily by the regional depository libraries of the Federal Depository Library Program. As cultural institutions dedicated to open public access, these libraries have been effective partners in providing broad public accessibility to physical collections of government publications.

The missions of NARA and the national libraries are, by necessity, narrowly focused. The roles they play are quite different from the FDLP. NARA, to be sure, is an invaluable national treasure that serves the government and the people by preserving the important collections of primary source records that reflect the official business of the federal government. In carrying out its charge, NARA makes the important distinction that "archival preservation of records is different than the preservation of publications, because of the differences in the basic nature of publications and records" (Thibodeau, 1997, p. 176). The national libraries, likewise, serve the United States through their vast collections for specialized research. Their role in the preservation of materials is more similar to an archive in that they concentrate on acquiring and retaining a single copy of the published literature within their scope for limited use by specialized researchers.

Neither NARA nor the national libraries is set up to handle the constant and diverse stream of questions and service demands for public information that flows through local depository libraries, or is it within their missions to do so. Meeting the everyday demands of continuous and permanent public access to government information for the general public has been the unique role of the FDLP. The statutory intent of the FDLP and its regional depository system is to ensure long-term availability of documents for the public, and the administrative policies and operational procedures of the FDLP work to fulfill that mandate.

In a nutshell, when a federal agency wants to print a publication it has created, it sends the order for the print job to the GPO. The Superintendent of Documents at the GPO reviews the print order and determines how many additional copies should be produced for the FDLP. All government publications, with very limited exceptions (i.e., national security documents, publications with no educational value or public interest), are to be included in the FDLP, and the FDLP copies of publications are paid for by GPO appropriations specifically designated for that purpose. Although selective depository libraries in the FDLP can choose among the titles and categories of publications they want to receive, and may discard certain publications in accordance with FDLP regulations, regional depositories receive one copy of every publication produced through the GPO and must keep these publications forever (Depository Library Act, 44 U.S.C. 1901–1916).

Thus, the GPO and FDLP work "behind the scenes" to centrally identify government publications and automatically produce and distribute those publications to depository libraries across the United States. The 53 geographically dispersed regional depositories in the FDLP are responsible for retaining these publications forever for continuous and permanent public access and use.

C. The Problems of Preserving Digital Government Information

Providing for future access to government information is as fundamental a need in the electronic environment as it is in the world of print publications. However, the traditional "tried and true" mechanisms in place for providing permanent public access to print materials do not work in the realm of electronic government information.

First, there currently is no comprehensive system or statutory responsibility within the federal government to identify, capture, retain, and provide continuous public access to electronic files of government information. Electronic information thrives in a decentralized environment; digital documents can be created, revised, uploaded, downloaded, and widely disseminated by anyone, in government or otherwise, with a PC and Internet access. Information on agency websites is in constant flux, and the whole concept of what constitutes a "publication" can be the subject of considerable discussion and debate. No one is responsible for keeping track of all of these files and all of these changes, and the rates of growth and change continue to increase at mind-boggling speeds. In essence, the technology has completely bypassed the traditional structures in place that have been charged with ensuring the preservation and permanent public access of government information.

This problem is exacerbated by the ubiquitous use of the World Wide Web to transmit government information. Federal agencies increasingly are using the Web to disseminate information to the public. Make no mistake— this essentially is a good thing. Users today have access to greater quantities of government information in more diverse formats and delivery mechanisms than ever before in history. It is estimated that the amount of electronic government information is doubling every year, and virtually every federal agency has a website to disseminate this information broadly (Sanders, 1997). It is highly suspect, however, whether much of this information still will be available for users in 5, 10, 20, or 100 years or more, especially the information that is available today in electronic format only. Currently, there are no governmentwide standards, policies, guidelines, or definitions that address the creation, dissemination, or preservation of electronic publications.

Aside from the sheer quantity and speed of electronic government information, preserving information in digital form presents other problems and concerns not encountered in the print world. "For hard copy records, preservation equals holding on to what you have. . . . For electronic records, holding on to what you have will eventually mean loss of records, because all of the technology on which the records originally depend eventually will become obsolete, making the records inaccessible" (Thibodeau, 1997, p. 176). Computer hardware generally is rendered obsolete within 3 years, and major software updates and revisions occur every 18 months on average (Sanders, 1997). Preserving access to digital information requires accounting for the disturbing fact that the machines and software necessary to use the information created today will not exist in the future.

NARA's Center for Electronic Records, in an attempt to deal with the problem of obsolescent technologies, requires federal agencies to submit files of electronic records in a format independent of the hardware and software used to create them, encoded in ASCII or EBCDIC. This means that any proprietary or special software encoding that originally may have been a part of the file must be stripped away before the file is accepted for preservation. NARA then creates two archival copies of the data on 3480-class tape cartridges for its holdings. Researchers who want to use these data files may order copies from the Center for Electronic Records, on either 9-track magnetic tape or on 3480-class tape cartridges, on a cost-recovery basis (Eaton and Hull, 1996).

NARA's procedures for digital information help address the critical need to preserve archival copies of these files, but they do little to meet the more general demands of permanent public access. ASCII files on magnetic tape may work well for high-level researchers, but most users of electronic government information do not have the hardware or technical sophistication to handle this format. Indeed, in many cases, it is the vendor-supplied software accompanying the data that makes the electronic product usable for the public in the first place.

In addition, the practice of translating data from one format to another presents serious questions regarding the integrity, authenticity, and usability of the information. Perhaps the greatest challenge in the transformation of electronic data "is to distinguish the essential attributes of electronic records, which must be preserved, from other attributes, which are merely artifacts of technology, and therefore can be discarded without loss of authenticity or alteration of meaning" (Thibodeau, 1997, p. 177). Developing a meaningful system of permanent public access will require establishing the means by which electronic government information will remain relevant and usable for all levels of users. It will mean developing ways to account for the rapid changes in the computer hardware and software used to create and access digital files without corrupting the integrity or authenticity of the underlying data.

Obsolescence and rapid change apply not only to the electronic data themselves, but also to the physical media used to store the data. Magnetic tapes, cartridges, computer diskettes, CD-ROMs, and other media that hold digital files are fragile and unstable. As these materials decompose, the data become irretrievable. To stave off the problem of physical deterioration of the digital files in its collection, NARA copies these files to new media every 10 years, or more frequently when necessary, "to prevent the physical loss of data or the technological obsolescence of the medium" (Eaton and Hull, 1996, p. 19). This is a painstaking and costly procedure, but it is essential to ensure that at least one viable copy of these files remains accessible in the future. However, this practice in no way can address the similar but more widespread problem faced by hundreds of depository libraries trying to manage growing and increasingly diverse digital collections. When the thousands of CD-ROMs that hold statistics from the 1990 census are no longer readable, how will the public's demands for this information be satisfied? To meet the immediate and future needs of users for electronic government information, the system of permanent public access must be able to ensure continued public access to government information, regardless of the storage or dissemination medium in use at any given time.

The problem of preserving and providing permanent public access to digital documents is complicated further because, for the most part, physical custody of these databases remains with government agencies, not libraries. The number of electronic publications produced by agencies on CD-ROM, and thus physically distributed to depository libraries, often represents only a small subset of the digital information that may be of use or of interest to the general public created by the agency. The issue of custody is especially troubling when one considers the tendency of most agencies to keep only the most recent information on their computer servers or websites. In the print world, depository libraries were able to fill this void by retaining in their collections copies of publications that agencies no longer kept in stock. (Indeed, one of the heaviest users of the FDLP is federal agencies looking for their own or other agencies' publications.) In an electronic environment, however, libraries often only have remote access to these databases and lack the opportunity to provide physical care or guardianship of the information. Generally, the only partner in a position to effectively preserve and provide ongoing access to electronic government information is the federal government itself.

Each day that the problems of electronic preservation and permanent public access go unresolved, alarming amounts of government information continue to be lost as databases come and go from agency websites, files are deleted from government computer servers, digital storage media deteriorate, and hardware and software become obsolete. The continuous and cumulative effects of this ongoing catastrophe are to deny taxpayers access to information they already paid for, to impair the public's ability to use government information already collected and compiled, to waste public and private resources in having to duplicate efforts to retrieve information previously available but now lost, and to allow the historical record of the nation to literally vanish before our eyes. Moreover, it severely undermines the potential promise and usefulness of new electronic technologies when the long-term consequence of their use is an ever-widening breach in our collected knowledge and information bank.

III. The Need for Statutory Authority

A. Legislation Reform Is a Top Priority

The unique advantages and capabilities of electronic information technologies are beyond question; in so many ways, electronic technologies have the potential for improving and enhancing public access to government information. Moreover, the ever-increasing proliferation of electronic government information underscores the wide acceptance of these technologies by both producers and users alike. It is clear that the electronic "genie" is out of the bottle, and no one is seriously suggesting that it would be to society's advantage to try to put the genie back.

At the same time, no one should believe that our societal and historical responsibilities can be abrogated simply because the means by which we choose to communicate at any point in time have changed. The obligation of a society to preserve its history is universal; and the duty of a democratic government to provide ongoing and permanent public access to its information is a constitutional priority.

The legal framework currently in place to provide for the preservation and permanent public access of government information has, in many ways, been rendered irrelevant by the advance of digital information technologies. The present law does not define the government's roles and responsibilities in this area, nor does it recognize the new and complex challenges inherent in dealing with these technologies. Revising federal law to ensure continuous and permanent access to all government information—both print and electronic—should be a top priority of Congress. This effort should be promoted and supported by all individuals and groups committed to education, research, maintaining the historical record, and preserving the public's right to know.

Legislative action is necessary to resolve this situation because the life cycle of electronic government information cuts across all branches and agencies of the federal government. Every government office is in the business of creating, acquiring, producing, and disseminating information to some degree; unless these offices are aware of their roles and responsibilities in preserving and providing access, this information can too easily be lost forever. Statutory authority must be clear in establishing the responsibility within the federal government to preserve and provide continuous and permanent public access to information created at public expense.

To be sure, it may be too early to attempt to describe exactly what a comprehensive system of permanent public access for electronic government information might look like. Few standards or guidelines are in place or are adhered to as yet, and there may be insufficient knowledge and experience at present to definitively satisfy all existing and future requirements. To wait any longer before formally addressing the problem, however, is imprudent. The complex and pervasive nature of this crisis requires coordinated, authoritative, and immediate action on the part of the government. This is a problem that will only get worse if it is ignored and left to continue. Instead, the law should be revised to establish the basic authority for developing the necessary structures, mechanisms, and procedures to successfully preserve and provide permanent public access to electronic government information.

B. The IAWG Proposal

The library community has been in the forefront of studying the issues and raising the concerns relating to electronic preservation and permanent public access of government information. As collectors, disseminators, navigators, and users of electronic government information, librarians have experienced first-hand the ramifications of this crisis and recognize the importance of working to resolve these issues.

In February 1997, seven national library associations joined forces to form the Inter-Association Working Group on Government Information Policy (IAWG). Begun at the urging of the leadership of the American Library Association (ALA), the IAWG brings together representatives from ALA and its divisions and roundtables, the American Association of Law Libraries, the Association of Research Libraries, the Chief Officers of State Library Agencies, the Medical Library Association, the Special Libraries Association, and the Urban Libraries Council. Together these associations represent more than 80,000 librarians, information specialists, library trustees, friends of libraries, and their institutions, all dedicated to public access to government information.

The purpose of the IAWG is to develop a legislative proposal for amending Title 44 of the United States Code to improve the Federal Depository Library Program and enhance public access to government information. A key goal of the IAWG in revising the law is to establish the affirmative responsibility of the federal government to preserve and provide permanent public access to electronic government information, and develop regulations and guidelines to ensure the authenticity of electronic government information (IAWG, 1997).

Under the IAWG proposal, the Superintendent of Documents would be responsible for coordinating the efforts of the federal government in establishing a system of permanent public access for electronic government information. This new responsibility builds on the current role of the Superintendent as the administrator of the FDLP, and extends into the electronic realm the program's responsibility to ensure public access to government information for future users. This is a natural and necessary extension of the public dissemination role of the Superintendent of Documents and the FDLP. This responsibility would be carried out in cooperation with agencies of all three branches of government, the National Archives and Records Administration and its Center for Electronic Records, the Library of Congress and the other national libraries, federal depository libraries, and other library partners. The resulting system would be a distributed arrangement including multiple partners based on official contractual agreements. This would provide for adequate redundancy to facilitate continuous and uninterrupted access to electronic resources, as well as provide the necessary assurance that electronic government information will be preserved in case of computer errors, human mistakes, or natural disasters.

Recognizing that such a system will take time to organize and develop, the IAWG proposal requires that, in the interim, federal agencies be responsible for maintaining the content and integrity of their own electronic government documents until the formal system of permanent public access has been established. Identifying and assigning this responsibility is important since every day more and more electronic government information is lost forever.

In addition, the IAWG proposal authorizes the Superintendent of Documents to obtain copies of or access to the electronic source files of government documents covered by the statute. This provides the superintendent with a mechanism for acquiring from agencies the underlying data of electronic publications. Thus, for example, if an agency decided to delete a document from its website, access to the source file would enable the superintendent to continue to provide public access to that data through the FDLP. Similarly, if an agency were to be reorganized or, as in the recent case of the Office of Technology Assessment, be abolished, the superintendent would be in a position to preserve and maintain ongoing access to this historical information.

Preserving and providing permanent public access to electronic government information will not happen by accident. It is a complex and costly endeavor, and it will require the best efforts of numerous partners in a concerted and coordinated fashion. Unlike printed materials that may be collected or saved after the fact, electronic information requires that a conscious, proactive decision be made from the outset—a commitment of organization and resources to keep this information viable for future users. Title 44 must be revised to fully recognize the responsibility of the federal government to provide the public with continuous and permanent access to electronic government information. To do otherwise is to ignore one of the fundamental obligations of government, and to deny future Americans their right to their history.

IV. The Role of Research Libraries in Providing Permanent Public Access to Electronic Government Information

The burden of providing permanent public access to electronic government information will not fall on the federal government alone. Just as in the print environment, libraries and other institutions must share in this responsibility if the overall system is to be successful. Today, the regional depository libraries of the FDLP devote considerable resources in preserving and maintaining their historical print collections. As research libraries committed to developing and servicing comprehensive collections of government documents, regional depositories have a special partnership with the federal government to ensure that future citizens have continuous access to the historical record of the government. New partnerships must develop in the electronic realm that parallel the shared commitments and obligations represented in the regional depository system of the FDLP.

New models for these relationships already are being formed. The GPO, building on its strategic plan to move the FDLP into an increasingly electronic environment, is developing the concept of a "collection plan" for electronic government information made available through the FDLP (GPO, 1996). Part of this plan envisions a collection manager at the GPO responsible for coordinating the various partnership agreements in place with libraries and other institutions that provide permanent public access to electronic government information (Aldrich, 1997).

GPO's first official permanent public access partnership was established in the spring of 1997 with the U.S. Department of State and the University of Illinois at Chicago Library (UIC, 1997). Under the conditions of a formal memorandum of understanding (MOU), the three parties work together to ensure that the electronic information available through the Department of State Foreign Affairs Network (DOSFAN) will be continuously accessible to current and future users. UIC and the State Department's Bureau of Public Affairs initiated the DOSFAN project in 1993 to provide broader access to the department's electronic news and information files.

Under the MOU, UIC manages the DOSFAN Electronic Research Collection, maintains custody of DOSFAN materials, provides online access to the Electronic Research Collection, and provides specific electronic reference services to U.S. foreign policy information. A key provision in the MOU is the recognition that the content of the information contained in the DOSFAN Electronic Research Collection is in the public domain. GPO is responsible for providing identifying pointers and bibliographic descriptions and access to DOSFAN materials through its locator and cataloging services.

The most important provision of the MOU regarding permanent public access is the requirement that UIC must provide GPO with an electronic copy of the DOSFAN Research Collection, and any UIC developed software necessary to access the collection, should UIC ever decide to discontinue support or services for the DOSFAN database (Aldrich, 1997). This agreement places the ultimate responsibility for providing permanent public access to these files with the federal government (in this case, the GPO). Further, it recognizes that circumstances and commitments at individual institutions may change over time, thus requiring a central coordinating role within the government for organizing and maintaining access to electronic files that the originating agency may no longer have an interest in or may not be able to support.

Another important case study worth examining that looks to take advantage of partnership relationships to provide for the preservation and permanent public access of electronic government information focuses on information from the U.S. Department of Agriculture (USDA). A number of agencies within the USDA have recently begun publishing exclusively in electronic format. In addition, the USDA has worked with the Albert R. Mann Library at Cornell University to develop the Economics and Statistics System, a digital core collection of research-level information in agricultural economics accessible over the Internet. These and other developments led the National Agricultural Library (NAL) and other key stakeholders to begin a process to develop a preservation plan for digital USDA publications (Frangakis, 1997).

In March 1997, NAL along with the Economic Research Service of the USDA, the GPO, Cornell University, and the Farm Foundation, sponsored a 2-day meeting in Washington, DC, of representatives from constituent organizations to identify the major elements and requirements that should be included in a preservation plan for USDA electronic information. The results of that meeting were an initial outline for a preservation plan and a preliminary action plan that will identify the steps necessary in the near term and over an extended period of time to move this initiative forward (Frangakis, 1997). This meeting represents an important model for other communities of interest to look to in developing cooperative approaches to dealing with the shared concerns of agencies, libraries, archives, users, and other interested parties in providing permanent public access to focused collections of electronic government information (Uhlir, 1997).

In the previous examples, research libraries play a critical role in providing essential services for preserving and providing permanent public access to electronic government information. This is a natural and logical extension of the basic mission and role of research libraries in the United States. One of the key differences in the electronic environment, however, is that these efforts, by definition, must be cooperative in concept and in practice. The overall task is too large, the resources required are too costly, and the decentralized nature of electronic dissemination and access is too dispersed for any one institution to act alone. The resulting model of a distributed system is made possible by the capabilities of electronic networked technologies. This underscores, however, the critical role of the federal government in centrally coordinating the responsibilities of preservation and access for the various arrangements that develop. Key concerns regarding public ownership, equitable access, and authenticity of government information can be addressed and administered adequately only by the government itself. Still, research libraries should fully explore the possibilities for creative partnerships that the new technologies afford them in enhancing their traditional services by providing permanent public access to selected collections of electronic government information.

V. Conclusion

In the PBS film by Terry Sanders, "Into the Future: On the Preservation of Knowledge in the Electronic Age," Donald Waters, Associate University Librarian at Yale University, describes preservation as an "obligatory one-way monologue with the future" (Sanders, 1997). In the traditional world of the printed word, the notion of preserving government documents conjures up images of carefully conserving old parchment manuscripts, brittle maps, or dusty leather-bound treaties or reports. Indeed, libraries and archives have worked throughout the history of the United States to ensure that the printed documentary record of the government has survived to date and will continue to be available for future generations.

Today, in the age of the computer, however, the volume and complexities of the digital information being created, and the seductive advantages in accessing electronic data, have distracted our attention from our obligations to the future. Already it is clear, however, that the consequences of our failings can be enormous. We no longer need to wait generations to discover problems or lapses in the preservation of the historical record, we stumble on them in just years or weeks, as electronic files disappear from the Web or digital media are rendered obsolete and unusable. Unless steps are taken soon to systematically rectify the situation, our "monologue with the future" may come to an abrupt and untimely end.

In 1822, James Madison wrote that "a popular government without popular information, or the means of acquiring it, is but a Prologue to a Farce or a Tragedy; or, perhaps, both" (Depository Library Council, 1996, p. vii). Over the years, Madison's words have served as the unofficial motto of the FDLP; they succinctly articulate the absolute necessity of providing the public with access to the information created by its government. But these very words survive with us today only because reliable mechanisms have been in place over the years to collect and preserve the printed records, documents, and publications created by and about the government. It is critical that Congress and the United States work to establish the legal authority and the necessary organizational systems and procedures to ensure continuous and permanent public access to electronic government information for Americans today and into the future.

References

Aldrich, D. (1997). Permanent access through partnerships: University of Illinois at Chicago, U.S. Government Printing Office, U.S. Department of State. In *Proceedings of the 6th Annual Federal Depository Library Conference*, pp. 179–181. U.S. Government Printing Office, Washington, DC.

"Census Papers Lost in Washington Fire," *New York Times*, 11 January 1921, p. 1; *Washington Post*, 11 January 1921, p. 1.

Depository Library Council (DLC). (1996). *Fulfilling Madison's Vision: The Federal Depository Library Program*. U.S. Government Printing Office, Washington, DC.

Eaton, F., and Hull, T. J. (1996). Preservation and archival issues for electronic records: The center for electronic records of the National Archives and Records Administration. In *Proceedings of the 5th Annual Federal Depository Library Conference*, pp. 18–21. U.S. Government Printing Office, Washington, DC.

Frangakis, E. (1997). Report on the meeting USDA digital publications: Creating a preservation action plan. In *Proceedings of the 6th Annual Federal Depository Library Conference*, pp. 41–44. U.S. Government Printing Office, Washington, DC.

Government Printing Office (GPO). (1996). *Study to Identify Measures Necessary for a Successful Transition to a More Electronic Federal Depository Library Program*. U.S. Government Printing Office, Washington, DC.

Inter-Association Working Group on Government Information Policy (IAWG). (1997). *Federal Information Access Act of 1997*. (http://www.library.berkeley.edu/GODORT/iawgpage.html)

National Archives and Records Administration (NARA). (1997). *Ready Access to Essential Evidence: The Strategic Plan of the National Archives and Records Administration, 1997–2007*. NARA, Washington, DC.

Sanders, T., prod. (1997).

"Into the Future: On the Preservation of Knowledge in the Electronic Age" (film). (Produced in cooperation with the Commission on Preservation and Access and the American Council of Learned Societies). American Film Foundation.

Thibodeau, K. (1997). Planning for preservation of digital information: An archival perspective. In *Proceedings of the 6th Annual Federal Depository Library Conference*, pp. 176–178. U.S. Government Printing Office, Washington, DC.

Uhlir, P. F. (1997). Key considerations in the long-term retention of digital information. In *Proceedings of the 6th Annual Federal Depository Library Conference*, pp. 45–50. U.S. Government Printing Office, Washington, DC.

University of Illinois at Chicago (UIC). (1997). *Department of State Foreign Affairs Network Electronic Research Collection*. (http://dosfan.lib.uic.edu)

Past, Present, and Future of Library Development (Fund-Raising)

Joan M. Hood
University Library
University of Illinois at Urbana–Champaign
Urbana, Illinois 61801

I. Introduction

A library is the heart of an educational institution, whether public or private, large or small. Support organizations, most often named "Library Friends" or "Associates," have existed for decades to assist libraries by providing additional sources of revenue, increasing visibility, and serving as advocates.

Personal and private support for academic libraries existed long before the formal establishment of library friends organizations. From their beginnings in the United States, academic libraries have enjoyed the support of innumerable friends. The oldest example is Harvard University, which was named for John Harvard in recognition of his bequest of 400 books and half of his estate in 1638.

Yale University's librarian, James T. Babb, often told the story of the founding of Yale College. According to tradition, 10 congregational ministers met in the home of Reverend Samuel Russel in 1701. Each clergyman brought choice volumes from his personal library. As the ministers gathered around a table in Mr. Russel's home, each placed his particular contribution on the table and intoned the words, "I give these books for the founding of a college in this colony" (Babb, 1966, p. 206).

Edward G. Holley, a distinguished library historian and Dean Emeritus of the School of Library Science at the University of North Carolina at Chapel Hill, suggests that it is no accident that Harvard and Yale currently have the two largest university libraries in the United States. "From the beginning there was a recognition of the principle that books and libraries are indispensable for the advancement of scholarship, culture, and learning" (Holley, 1980, p. 10). Holley (1980) adds that

no library has ever achieved significance without the support of those who understood that principle, whether they be librarians, faculty, donors, administrators, or legislators. Libraries exist because of those who understand their mission, who are sympathetic to that mission, and who give it their moral, political and economic support. (p. 10)

The first university library friends organization in the United States was founded at Harvard in 1925. It most likely was modeled on the first library support organization to call itself a friends group, La Société des Amis de la Bibliothèque Nationale et des Grandes Bibliothèques de France, which was founded in 1913 and with which Harvard's library director, Archibald Coolidge, had become familiar during a book-buying expedition to Europe (Wallace, 1962). By 1930, there were other library friends groups at private colleges in the East.

In analyzing the growth of friends groups from the 1930s to the present, it is obvious that there are fluctuations in the number of organizations. The number grows during periods of financial constraint and shrinks when there is ample funding.

The golden age for higher education in the United States was the 1950s and part of the 1960s. We began to see a downturn in funding in the 1970s that accelerated in the 1980s. True to form, we have seen an explosion of development activities in academic libraries since the early 1980s and in public universities during the 1990s. In the early 1990s, trend spotters predicted that the number one priority of higher educational institutions would be adequate funding. Indeed, libraries have been in the midst of the quest for additional revenue sources (Hood, 1991; Dewey, 1991).[1]

A. Friends of Libraries U.S.A.

For several years in the 1970s the American Library Association (ALA) included a Friends of Libraries Committee chaired by Sandy Dolnick. The first attempt at forming a link among existing groups was the publication in 1978 of the *Friends of Libraries National Notebook*, a quarterly newsletter. Its 70 subscribers included individuals, libraries, and organized friends groups in large and small libraries, both public and academic. An author luncheon was held during the annual ALA conference.

In 1979, from that core group Friends of Libraries U.S.A. (FOLUSA) was organized as a membership organization. The three incorporators of the new national group were Sandy Dolnick, Milwaukee, Wisconsin; Joan M. Hood, Coordinator, Library Friends, at the University of Illinois at Urbana–Champaign; and Robert Wedgeworth, Executive Director of the American Library Association. ALA served for many years as FOLUSA's mailing address and provided important office services. In 1994, all the office and financial functions were transferred to Philadelphia where Sandy Dolnick now serves

[1] Introduction reprinted with permission from Hood, J. M. (1991). *Library Friends*. Neal-Schuman Publishers, New York, pp 11–12.

as Executive Director. The two organizations continue to cooperate and to support each other's missions and goals.

In 1980, FOLUSA sponsored the *Friends of Libraries Sourcebook* (Dolnick, 1980), with the second edition printed in 1990 (Dolnick, 1990). ALA published the third edition (Dolnick, 1996), updating the previous two editions. The chapters range from getting organized, to fund-raising, advocacy, event planning, and library foundations. The information is presented by well-seasoned professionals who provide a practical approach to the topic of library friends groups.

Today as a network of more than 3,000 friends groups involving more than 1 million individuals, FOLUSA has become the national volunteer network of support for all types of libraries. It seeks to develop and support local and state groups, and it encourages grass roots advocacy.

Another important event in the history of library development also occurred in 1979. In November, the University of Illinois Graduate School of Library Science sponsored the 25th annual Allerton Park Institute at Robert Allerton Park in Monticello, Illinois. This silver jubilee conference was devoted to the works of auxiliary groups that support libraries through the donation of time, enthusiasm, advocacy efforts, money, and books.

Dr. Donald W. Krummel, Chair of the Conference, noted that the importance of the topic was evidenced by a capacity registration for the Institute. The 91 participants represented 32 states. The proceedings published in 1980 served as important resource material for developing both public and academic library support organizations (Krummel, 1980).

As the number of academic library development programs grew throughout the 1980s, a small group of library development officers decided to address a need for communication and instruction that they did not believe was being met at the time by existing organizations. Professional fund-raising groups such as the National Society of Fund Raising Executives (NSFRE) and the Council for the Advancement and Support of Education (CASE) existed but did not include specific sections for libraries. The ALA's Library Administration and Management Association (LAMA) had an active section on fundraising that focused on all types of libraries; however, it did not attract professionals in academic library development. ALA's Association of College and Research Libraries (ACRL) had not yet begun to address library development.

B. DORAL

An organization developed by a small group of professional library development officers is now known as Development Officers of Research Academic Libraries, North America (DORAL, N.A.). Its first meeting was held in the spring of 1987 at the University of Michigan. A fall meeting was held at the Johns Hopkins University. Founding members in 1987 included Sam Streit,

Brown University; Linda Safron, the Johns Hopkins University; Susan Jordan, Northwestern University; Joan Hood, University of Illinois at Urbana–Champaign; Barbara Dewey, University of Iowa; Mary Bailey Pierce, University of Miami; Betty Smith, University of Michigan; Linda Bowers, The Ohio State University; Deborah Riley, University of Wisconsin–Madison; and Chacona Johnson, Wayne State University.

The group has met every year since 1987 and consists of development officers whose primary responsibility is academic library development for institutions belonging to the Association of Research Libraries (ARL). The majority of DORAL members are development professionals rather than professional librarians.

DORAL is an informal organization with neither officers nor budget. It is comprised of 35 institutional representatives from public and private university libraries. Each year an institution takes a turn hosting the annual meeting, which provides a forum for discussing similar concerns and solutions.

Reflecting the growth of academic libraries' support activities, the organization quickly grew from 5 to 12 to 25 institutions. DORAL decided to cap the number of participating institutions at 35 to retain its informality for its roundtable discussion groups and for ease of organization. However, the membership wanted to offer assistance to newly formed library development operations and to those professionals entering the library development field. In 1992, the organization approached the ARL to see if it would be interested in assisting with the organization and implementation of fund-raising seminars. ARL's positive response resulted in DORAL joining with ARL's Office of Management Study (OMS) to organize professional seminars. To date there have been four seminars. The first was held in 1993 at the University of Chicago, followed by the 1994 Institute at Emory University, the 1995 Institute at the University of New Mexico, and the 1996 Institute at the University of Colorado.

DORAL encouraged the participants of the Institutes to form their own network for communication and support. In 1995, following the DORAL/OMS Institute at the University of New Mexico, previous participants joined together to form the Academic Library Advancement and Development Network (ALADN). Since that time ALADN has held three successful development conferences for academic libraries. Both ALADN and DORAL sponsor computer listservs.

C. Other Fund-Raising Efforts

In the 1970s, the Dallas (Texas) Public Library and the Tulsa (Oklahoma) Public Library began fundraising activities. In the mid-1980s, the Houston (Texas) Public Library made a major commitment to marketing, public relations, and fund-raising activities. For years the New York Public Library has rallied citizen support in addition to contributions from foundations and corporations and grants from the federal government.

LAMA in 1983 established the fund-raising and financial development section (FRFDS), which continues to hold meetings during ALA's midwinter and annual meetings. It provides an excellent opportunity for librarians and library development officers to exchange information and gain development expertise.

D. Fund-Raising Publications in the 1980s and Early 1990s

In 1984, Pierian Press published *Library Fundraising: Vital Margin for Excellence*, edited by Sul H. Lee. Susan G. Abernathy, in her chapter, describes gifts and grants at the Stanford University Libraries. She also talks about her preference for the term "development" rather than "fund-raising," because it suggests moving the entire library forward to a desired stage.

Also in this book Robin Downes discusses integrating fund-raising into the administration of university libraries, thereby having an impact on the goals, plans, and strategies. He uses the University of Houston (Texas) Library as a model. He concludes by summarizing that lasting fund-raising success must be built on a program with permanence, hence the importance of the integral nature of the development operation.

In 1987, Sandy Dolnick edited *Fundraising for Nonprofit Institutions, Foundations in Library and Information Science*, published by JAI Press. The intent of this book was to provide a different dimension to currently available material for libraries and other nonprofit institutions. The first section of the book deals with basic elements needed by any group searching for funds. The second half is comprised of case studies and portraits of nine distinctly different institutions and the way in which they raise money. The case studies include a public and an academic library, a health organization, a symphony orchestra, public television, a museum, and special fund-raising projects.

James Swan wrote *Fundraising for the Small Public Library, A How-To-Do-It Manual for Librarians* published by Neal-Schuman Publishers in 1990. It is a practical "how-to" book for small libraries. Mr. Swan walks the readers through the basics of fund-raising including a presentation of various techniques and events. He emphasizes the importance of a strategic vision and underscores the importance of making the "ask." Swan also underscores the benefits of friends groups that can help with volunteer service, public relations, and programming. Friends can assist with the passage of bond issues or tax referenda and can be effective advocates with city government officials and legislators. They can help the library become the focal point for community support.

In 1990, the *Journal of Library Administration* devoted volume 12, number 4, to library development. The introduction was written by Dwight F. Burlingame, Associate Director, Center on Philanthropy, Indiana University at Indianapolis. Burlingame states that the journal issue was intended for three groups: (1) leaders of libraries, librarians, board members, and friends; (2) those who wish to become involved in the support of libraries; and (3) academics and students of librarianship. The volume is a blend of theory and practice, including a history of philanthropy and the role of public relations in fund-raising. Burlingame states that academic libraries led the way in library fund-raising. Public relations played an important role in the 1950s, with the establishment of a public relations section in the LAMA Division of the ALA. He cites the 1976 fund-raising drive of the Dallas (Texas) Public Library and the establishment of the Tulsa City (Oklahoma) Library Trust in 1972 as significant development fund-raising activities for the public library sector. Other sections in the journal issue address special events, major donor prospects, annual funds, capital campaigns, endowment campaigns, and planned giving.

In the 1995 edition of *Library Fundraising: Models for Success*, edited by Dwight F. Burlingame, one of the models noted is the Tulsa City County Library (TCCL). The entry recounts the creation of the trust and its success with endowment fund growth from $13,970 in the founding year to more than $5 million by 1982. A National Endowment for the Humanities Challenge Grant was an integral part of the growth. In 1984, the Peggy V. Helmerich Distinguished Author Award was established, quickly becoming a focal point for the community. Distinguished authors such as Saul Bellow, John Updike, and Eudora Welty received the award. In 1991, the Anne V. Zarr Award for Young People's Literature was established by the trust.

In 1991, DORAL published *Raising Money for Academic and Research Libraries, A How-To-Do-It Manual for Librarians*, edited by Barbara I. Dewey. Vartan Gregorian, at that time President of Brown University and now President of the Carnegie Corporation, wrote in the book's foreword that

> Libraries are as old as civilization. From the clay tablets of Babylonia to the computers of modern research libraries, stretch more than 5,000 years of men's and women's insatiable desire to establish written immortality. It is, therefore, critical that colleges and universities across this nation and around the world recognize and promote libraries as worthy recipients of philanthropy. Our intellectual heritage depends on the success of this mission. It cannot be done by a single financial source. (Dewey, 1991, p. v)

In the following sections of DORAL's book, successful library development specialists provide readers with a grounding in topics related to fund-raising, with a specific focus on the academic and research library setting. Chapters address the fund-raising plan, library friends, donor relations, corporate and foundation support, planned giving, and public relations, along with the library campaign and development personnel.

E. Role of the Association of Research Libraries

Continuing its interest in the entire topic of library fund-raising, the ARL devoted its entire annual meeting in 1992 to the topic, the leadership role in library fund-raising. The proceedings were published in 1993 and offer a summation of some of the presenters' ideas.

ARL President-Elect, Susan Nutter, program convener and planner, opened the session with the following statement:

> While our libraries are dramatically changing, they're also facing serious funding inadequacies. As we are faced with the dual challenge of maintaining traditional resources while incorporating new information technologies into our collections, services, and operations, it has become increasingly difficult to find the support to maintain, let alone improve, collections, services, and staff. A significant and continuing decline in support for higher education, coupled with extraordinary increases in the cost of library materials and exacerbated by a weak economy, has prompted libraries to seek new funding networks. All of this is occurring at a time in library history when the real value and importance of the library to the university and to society is being understood and recognized. As a result, the use of libraries is skyrocketing. (Nutter, 1993, p. 3)

She then proceeded to cite the importance of external giving and mentioned that library directors must implement innovative and aggressive fund-raising approaches. Raising external funds will be imperative to the growth and maintenance of high-quality libraries. She stated that in the coming decades, fund-raising will make the difference between mediocrity and excellence for many of our libraries. Nutter (1993) went on to say that "few directors have been prepared either by training, experience, or temperament to undertake an ambitious development program (p. 4).

Stephen D. Elder, Senior Development Officer at the University of Redlands, California, discussed the art of designing a development strategy. He stated that a good development strategy starts with the development officer's clear understanding of his or her niche (i.e., the intersection of the organization's purposes and uniqueness). The second element is a strategic plan created by the leadership of the library. It forms the foundation for the development program. The third component is a strong development team that includes, for example, relationships with a central development office, university foundation, trust relations office, and development officers in other colleges. The next step is to identify prospects who will have the means and the inclination to support the library, create attractive giving opportunities, and begin developing individual strategies for each potential donor. Finally, the development strategist evaluates the fund-raising efforts in terms of meeting its goal. Mr. Elder and his co-author of *Becoming a Fund Raiser: The*

Principles and Practice of Library Development, Victoria Steele, suggest that the goal of a development program is to enhance the organization's independence (Steele and Elder, 1992). They maintain that this evaluation method is superior to the one that measures dollars raised, usually per annum and often in relation to previous years or other institutions. The dollar goal focuses too much on the bottom line and disregards several kinds of external factors that affect gift income.

Victoria Steele, Head of the Department of Special Collections at the University of Southern California, proposed an ethical framework for development in which she suggested that an individual may fashion a fundraising style compatible with his or her own personality and the institutional setting.

Joan M. Hood, Director of Library Development and Public Affairs for the University of Illinois at Urbana–Champaign, presented the essential components of a library development program. She mentioned that in the past, private funds for public institutions provided a margin of excellence that often took the form of funding for special projects or new technologies. Today, private contributions for many academic institutions are used to preserve and maintain universities, paying some of the essential costs formerly covered by state funding. Thus, many current library programs owe their existence to the availability of private funds.

She stated that for years we have heard about the difficulty of raising private funds for libraries. Unfortunately, many consultants assume this difficulty when discussing capital campaigns with university administrators and faculty members—that is, they do not include the library among potential "draws" for private donations.

Her experience at the University of Illinois, however, belied this attitude. From 1989–1992 fund-raising efforts at the University of Illinois at Urbana–Champaign raised more than $30 million for the Library System. This funding did not happen precipitously; it was the result of careful planning and implementation.

A successful library fund-raising effort is characterized by four elements: positioning, access, partnerships, and patience. The library must work hard to establish a central position for itself within the university structure, to ensure that it derives concrete benefits from its central role, and to be included in any capital campaign or special fund-raising project mounted on campus. The components of the library system (i.e., departmental libraries and divisions) directly support the teaching and research programs for all campus schools and colleges. It is vital to the success of the library's fund-raising program that the various deans and directors not only understand this relationship but give demonstrable support to maintaining the library's strength.

The university librarian is the key person for building relationships with the deans and directors of colleges and schools, as well as for developing positive relationships with the university's administrative leadership.

Clearly, the library has no graduates of its own; however, virtually all students and faculty derive benefit from the library's resources and services, and some will be willing to donate money earmarked for the library. The library should push for access to the university's central donor base and make sure this access is granted at the highest possible university level. Access will enable the library to identify, cultivate relations with, and solicit funds from alumni and other donors. The experience at Illinois indicates that the library expands the pool of donors to the university.

The function of the campus library cuts across all disciplines; it supports all academic and research programs throughout the university. The library should develop this mutuality into fund-raising partnerships with academic departments or colleges within the university.

The development of a fund-raising program is a long process carried out over years and even decades. The library should take a long view of the program, seeing it as a critical investment for the future rather than a quick fix for current library woes. Fund-raising activities require commitment and continuity of effort. A good plan will yield steady progress by developing strong library programs, linking efforts to larger campus fund-raising programs, and forming partnerships with the faculty and administrators to promote the value of the library on campus. Library fund-raisers will be better able to tap external resources for much-needed library funds.

F. Fund-Raising Publications in the 1990s

Although a number of articles and books had been written about library fund-raising, Steele and Elder (1992) took a different approach when writing *Becoming a Fund Raiser: The Principles and Practice of Library Development*, published by the ALA. The book is written for library directors who are the key element in a library fund-raising program. Successful fund-raising depends on the leadership and participation of the library director.

Various chapters examine librarians' attitudes about raising money, basic terms and concepts of fund-raising, the role of the library director in building a development organization, the library's strategic plan and the complementary development plan, and the evaluation of the fund-raising program.

Also, Hunt and Lee (1992) wrote *Fundraising for the 1990s, The Challenge Ahead, A Practical Guide for Library Fundraising: From Novice to Expert*, published by Genaway & Associates. These authors state that the book is a practical guide written for novices who need a "how-to" or "do-it-yourself" type of approach. Although the book draws heavily on previously published material written by development professionals and librarians, the real strength of the book is its organization. It draws together in a very readable and clear style the fundamentals of fund-raising and sources of support. Many of the original source references that Hunt and Lee cite in their publication are well worth reading.

In the 1990s, as capital and endowment campaigns have become a way of life for most universities, those libraries that had been successful in establishing annual funds programs and attracting major gifts were asked to document their experiences. In *Library Issues, Briefings for Faculty Administrators* published by the *Journal of Academic Librarianship* in July 1993, this author wrote an article, *Fundraising for Libraries: Four Important Elements* (Hood, 1993). She describes the importance of positioning the library vis-á-vis the campus, the critical point of having access to the alumni donor base, forming partnerships with other campus units, and having patience with the process.

II. Sources of Financial Support

A. Categories of Support

As the sources of financial support for libraries are examined, it can be seen that support comes from four different categories: individuals, corporations, foundations, and government agencies. In the 1997 publication of *Giving U.S.A.*, (1997, p. 16) it is noted that $150.7 billion was contributed to nonprofit organizations in the United States in 1996. Individuals, including bequests through estates, comprised 86.5% of the total; foundations contributed 7.8%, and corporations 5.6%. These percentages have remained relatively constant throughout the years. Compared with 1995 figures, we see that foundations increased slightly from 7.3%, and corporations increased from 5.1%.

As noted, individuals give nearly 90% of philanthropic dollars each year. Therefore, it behooves fund-raisers to spend the majority of their time identifying, cultivating and soliciting individuals who have a potential relationship to the library.

It is important to understand why individuals make gifts to any type of institution. Primarily, a donor gives to reinforce his or her self-image as a person helping society, to be a worthwhile member of a worthwhile group, to make a difference, and to provide continuity. They give to an institution because they believe in its mission. They trust and respect the leadership of the institution. In addition they have confidence in the stability of the organization. Donors also give because others are giving and because they are asked. Fund-raising is a business of relationships. Building relationships with individuals is one of the most critical parts of a strong library fund-raising program.

Corporations give to expand their markets and to provide high visibility for the company. Their support is intended to generate measurable accomplishments. Foundations are required to distribute a specified percentage of invested assets to retain U.S. Tax Code status. They award grants to eligible nonprofit organizations and support programs within their guidelines.

Education generally receives a higher percentage of corporate and foundation contributions than other sectors of nonprofit organizations. In 1995, 35% of corporate gifts were designated for education. The same year foundations gave 25% of their support to education, down from 29% in 1994. Eleven percent of all 1995 foundation grants went to higher education, down from 14% in 1994.

B. Corporate and Foundation Support

When exploring the corporate and foundation world, a helpful publication is *The "How To" Grants Manual: Successful Grantseeking Techniques for Obtaining Public and Private Grants*, third edition, written by David G. Bauer and published by Oryx Press. Bauer's thesis for moving an idea to a funded project is to develop a relationship with the grantor. In this edition of his well-written book, he provides insights and strategies for obtaining corporate, foundation, and federal grants by carefully reviewing the philosophy and the process for ultimate success. He emphasizes the importance of documenting a need showing that "there is a gap between what exists now and what ought to or could be" (Bauer, 1995, p. 6).

His sound fund-raising philosophy and its adaptation to corporate, foundation, and government grant-seeking provide a thorough framework for newcomers to the field, as well as a timely review for more experienced fund-raisers. The last section of the book lists current resources including electronic databases to aid in the required research necessary for the successful identification of sources.

A book targeted to proposal writing in library science and for libraries is *Getting Your Grant: A How-To-Do-It Manual for Librarians* (Crowe and Barber, 1993). This book discusses proposal writing in library science and library fund-raising in the United States.

There are more than 30,000 private foundations in the United States. In 1996, they distributed nearly $12 billion in grants to eligible nonprofit organizations. Foundations are nonprofit, nongovernment entities established under Section 501 (c) (3) of the U.S. Tax Act for the purpose of supporting educational, cultural, religious, health-related, and other nonprofit organizations. To maintain their status under the U.S. Tax Act, foundations are required to distribute a certain percentage of their invested assets each year. For several years, the amount to be distributed annually has been 5% of the foundation's invested assets. Because the return on foundations' investments has been extraordinarily high during the last 2 years, more funds have been distributed. Most foundations place their guidelines, regulations, and application procedures on the World Wide Web for easy access to the information. For example, the website for the Carnegie Corporation is (http://www.carnegie.org). If a foundations's Web address is not known, in most cases, it can be located at the Foundation Directory's site (http://www.fdncenter.org).

In the United States during the past 10 years we have seen the growth of library foundations, especially at public libraries or groups of public libraries. The public library foundation must become incorporated under U.S. federal tax guidelines. Incorporation means becoming a separate, not-for-profit organization seeking federal recognition. The status enables contributions made to the foundation to be legally tax deductible.

The library foundation exists primarily to solicit and accept gifts that will benefit the library. Such gifts are usually in the form of cash contributions, but they may be in the form of real property, such as farmland, houses, stocks, and other properties such as books or gifts-in-kind. As a not-for-profit entity, the foundation will need to form a governing board and to hold an annual meeting of all members of the foundation. Normally the board members are elected from the foundation members at the annual meeting.

The library foundation is different in many respects from a library friends group. The foundation's sole purpose is to raise money for the library. Fundraising is only one aspect of a friends group's activities. The friends group is a support organization for the library, but the support offered may range from volunteer service in the library, to helping the library in external affairs such as delivering materials or conducting a book sale, publicizing the local library through the community, advocacy, and fund-raising.

The William K. Kellogg Foundation in 1995 provided a 2-year grant of $100,000 to the ALA to provide fund-raising training for library directors and board members in small to mid-size libraries in four regions of the United States. ALA President Arthur Curley said, "In order to keep library doors open and maintain quality service and resources, libraries must look to the private sector as a means of support. This program will provide valuable training to library directors and board members seeking additional financial support (Curley, 1995, p. 190).

ALA is working with the Indiana University Center on Philanthropy to train teams of library directors and board members of 60 small to medium-size libraries to raise local funds. A clearinghouse including research information and sample library development programs will be developed for participating libraries. The goal of the program is to challenge public libraries to seek fund-raising as an integral part of their strategy and to help them develop the skills to undertake those activities.

In 1990, ALA established its own development office. It is the home of the aforementioned Kellogg Grant. A proposal was made to the ALA Executive Board in the fall of 1994 to establish a foundation known as the Fund for America's Libraries. The purpose of this 501 (c) (3) organization is "to seek and distribute resources to promote and improve libraries in America (Gaughan, 1995, p. 184).

In 1997, Bill and Melinda Gates formed the Gates Library Foundation to provide public libraries in low-income communities with computer hardware and software required for Internet access. The foundation also will provide computer training and support for public library personnel. More than $200 million in cash has been committed by the Gates Foundation with a software match by Microsoft.

Grant guidelines released in November 1997 indicate that over a 5-year period the foundation will work with approximately 1,000 individual libraries. Patty Stonesifer, President of the Gates Library Foundation, issued a statement that the program will be in three parts: statewide partnerships, an approach for urban library systems serving large low-income communities, and a program for individual library participation.

The Alabama Public Library Service (APLS) has been awarded the first statewide partnership that will bring computers and the Internet to more than 200 public libraries. As with many other foundations, the full text of guidelines, as well as application forms, are available at the Gates Library Foundation's website (http://www.glf.org/).

C. Federal, State, and Local Support

At the federal level, the National Endowment for the Humanities, the Department of Education, the Department of Defense through technological grants, and the Department of State have provided important grants and resources to academic and public libraries.

State libraries often have served as conduits for the administration of important federal construction and services grants, including Title II-C funds for research libraries. Many states provide substantial support to libraries individually and through consortia. At the local level, advocacy plays an important role to ensure that local authorities continue to understand the importance of public libraries in the accumulation of information and the citizen's right to access all types of material.

In reviewing the aforementioned categories of philanthropic giving by percentage, it is clear that individuals through current and deferred giving provide the bulk of private dollars for philanthropic purposes. Considerable time must be devoted to identifying and cultivating potential donors to the library.

Development officers need to understand the basic reasons why people give and what would motivate them to give to their library. They must understand the reasons corporations and foundations give to nonprofit organizations.

Library directors and development officers must be willing to spend the necessary time to identify, cultivate, and solicit gifts, as well as to put in place a meaningful stewardship program. As was mentioned earlier, the role of the library director is critical.

III. International Library Fund-Raising

In other sections of the world, fund-raising for libraries has developed at different levels. In Canada numerous libraries, both public and academic, have established support groups for fund-raising and advocacy. There is currently an effort to establish a national library friends group for Canada paralleling the efforts of Friends of Libraries U.S.A.

Recently the Friends of Libraries Australia was established. In New South Wales, Australia, the State Library has developed an extensive public relations and external funding program. Argyle Diamonds funded a major computer installation for the library at the University of Western Australia in Perth.

In 1986, C. Walter and Gerda B. Mortenson gave the Library at the University of Illinois at Urbana–Champaign a $2 million gift to establish a Professorship in International Library Programs. It was followed by a second gift of $2 million to establish the C. Walter and Gerda B. Mortenson Center for International Library Programs. Since that time, more than 250 librarians from more than 70 countries have spent amounts of time ranging from several weeks to 1 year or more at the University Library studying library management, automation, access techniques, fund-raising, and collection development.

In 1993, the author was invited to serve as a consultant to the Russian Ministry of Culture and the M. I. Rudomino All-Russia State Library for Foreign Literature in Moscow. She presented what were believed to be the first fund-raising seminars ever held in the former Soviet Union. They were certainly the first for library directors.

Returning on successive trips to Russia and Ukraine, she found fund-raising successes accomplished by library directors and librarians with vision and the willingness to take a risk. Lyudmila Pronina, Director of the Ryazin Regional Library, turned to the lace industry for private support. She then put in place a set of agreements with other local businesses and banks and cooperative arrangements with regional political authorities.

In 1996, Zoya Chalova, Director of the Mayakovsky Library in Saint Petersburg, estimated that 10% of her budget came from outside support. On Sakhalin Island in Russia's Far East, Tamara Danilenko, Director of the Regional Library for South Sakhalin, has created extensive links with the local business and immigrant communities to help secure needed books and equipment. The Sakhalin Energy Investment Company gave in 1996 the equivalent of $100,000 USD for automation, acquisitions, and language courses (Hood, 1996).

Information about private fund-raising for libraries was presented at the 1995 International Federation of Library Associations and Institutions (IFLA) Conference in Istanbul, Turkey, and in Beijing, China in 1996.

At the 1997, IFLA Conference in Copenhagen, Denmark, Virginia G. Young, author, consultant, and Past President of the American Library Trustee Association (ALTA), and the author co-chaired a start-up discussion group for Friends and Advocates of Libraries. More than 50 conference delegates representing numerous countries attended the meeting for a lively discussion of the importance of global cooperation in library fund-raising and advocacy efforts. An Advocates and Friends Discussion group will be held at the 1998 IFLA Conference in Amsterdam, the Netherlands.

Lessons can be learned from the fund-raising techniques now successfully employed in various parts of the world. Basic principles and successful experiences can be adapted to fit institutions and situations in other countries.

IV. Conclusion

Successful fund-raising depends on building relationships and developing partnerships, and by carefully cultivating a variety of sources including individuals, corporations, foundations, and government agencies. Libraries will need to reach out for new sources of financial support, while aggressively maintaining existing sources, to meet the continuing changes in the information age.

Throughout the United States there are positive signs that libraries of all types, public and academic, are increasing their external support. Because most gifts come from individuals, libraries are creating support groups such as library friends organizations and foundations to provide opportunities for building relationships and contributing funds and gifts-in-kind.

University libraries are part of major university campaigns to build endowments, secure technologies, create preservation funds, construct new facilities, remodel existing ones and support faculty/staff positions.

Because historically 80% of endowments are built with planned-giving vehicles and bequests, it is important that the library attract planned-giving funds over the years. Endowments are permanent funds and permit the library to plan with confidence for the future.

Development activities in libraries are becoming more professional each year. Large university libraries have specialized staff to direct and lead fund-raising efforts. Smaller academic and community college libraries are beginning to dedicate trained staff to this critical activity. Major public libraries have development officers. These people are essential for professional annual funds and major gift activities, as well as for planned-giving programs.

Because many people view libraries as basic to the fabric of our society, to freedom of information, to democracy, and to economic well-being, they believe that a donation to the library carries an impact for society at large, as well as for the academic or local community. A well-developed library fund-raising program should be able to attract external sources of funding based, at least in part, on an understanding of this basic motivation: Donors want to believe that their gifts will make a difference.

At the University of Illinois fund-raising has made a difference. In the last 7 years at the University of Illinois at Urbana–Champaign, $60 million in private funds has been raised for the University Library, $36 million for new construction and remodeling, the remainder for endowments and current use funds to support collections, preservation, collection access, new technologies, and personnel.

It did not happen overnight or without a plan. Over a period of 25 years the program grew from a friends group supporting solely rare books to an annual funds program assisting all 42 units within the library system. The Library's Office of Development and Public Affairs added a major gifts program and a planned-giving component. For the past 6 years the library has been part of the universitywide campaign. Its fund-raising and public affairs office is staffed by professionals who have the full support and cooperation of the university librarian.

Illinois' successful library fund-raising activities are emulated by countless U.S. public and private academic libraries across the country. The future for library development is bright.

References

Babb, J. T. (1966). The Yale University Library. *Library Trends* **15**, 206.

Bauer, D. G. (1995). *The "How To" Grants Manual: Successful Grant Seeking Techniques for Obtaining Public and Private Grants*, third edition, American Council on Education, Oryx Press, Phoenix.

Burlingame, D. F., ed. (1990). *Journal of Library Administration*, 12(4).

Burlingame, D. F., ed. (1995). *Library Fundraising: Models for Success.* American Library Association, Chicago.

Crowe, L. D. and Barber, P. (1993). *Getting Your Grant: A How-To-Do-It Manual for Librarians,* Neal-Schuman Publishers, New York.

Dewey, B. I., ed. (1991). *Raising Money for Academic and Research Libraries, A How-To-Do-It Manual for Librarians,* Neal-Schuman Publishers, New York.

Dolnick, S., ed. (1980). *Friends of Libraries Sourcebook.* American Library Association, Chicago.

Dolnick, S., ed. (1987). *Fundraising for Nonprofit Institutions, Foundations in Library and Information Science* (Volume 19). JAI Press, Greenwich, CT.

Dolnick, S., ed. (1990). *Friends of Libraries Sourcebook,* second edition. American Library Association, Chicago.

Dolnick, S., ed. (1996). *Friends of Libraries Sourcebook,* third edition, American Library Association, Chicago.

Gaughan, T. M. (1995). The fund for America's libraries. *American Libraries* **26,** 184.

Giving U.S.A., AAFRC Trust for Philanthropy, 1997 edition, New York.

Holley, E. G. (1980). *The Library and Its Friends, Organizing the Library's Support: Donors, Volunteers, Friends.* University of Illinois Graduate School of Library Science, University of Illinois, Urbana–Champaign.

Hood, J. M., (1993). Fundraising for libraries: Four important elements, library issues, briefings for faculty and administrators. *Journal of Academic Librarianship* (13)(6).

Hood, J. M. (1996). Library fund-raising update. *IFLA Journal,* vol. **22**(1), 46–47.

Hood, J. M. (1991). *Library Friends.* Neal-Schuman Publishers, New York, pp. 11–12.

Hunt, G. A., and Lee, H.-W. (1992). *Fundraising for the 1990s, The Challenge Ahead, A Practical Guide for Library Fundraising: From Novice to Expert.* Genaway & Associates, Canfield, OH.

Krummel, D. W., ed. (1980). *Organizing the Library's Support: Donors, Volunteers, Friends,* University of Illinois Graduate School of Library Science, Urbana–Champaign.

Lee, S. H., ed. (1984). *Library Fundraising: Vital Margin for Excellence.* Pierien Press, Ann Arbor, MI.

Nutter, S. K. (1993). *The Leadership Role in Library Fund Raising.* 120th membership meeting of the Association of Research Libraries, Charleston, SC, May 13–15, 1992.

Steele, V., and Elder, S. P. (1992). *Becoming a Fundraiser: The Principles and Practice of Library Development.* American Library Association, Chicago.

Swan, J. (1990). *Fundraising for the Small Public Library, A How-To-Do-It Manual for Librarians.* Neal-Schuman Publishers, New York.

Wallace, S. L., ed. (1962). *Friends of the Library: Organization and Activities.* ALA, Chicago.

Cooperation in the Field of Distance Education in Library and Information Science in Estonia

Sirje Virkus
Department of Information Studies
Tallinn University of Educational Sciences
EE0001 Tallinn
Estonia

I. Introduction

We are living in a period characterized by change. Economies and societies are changing at a speed never before experienced. The globalization of the economy, the information explosion, and advanced technology are factors that characterize the end of the twentieth century. Education must accommodate these changes since the ability to learn and lifelong learning are becoming increasingly important.

Higher education is in crisis in much of the world (Daniel, 1996). The challenge for higher education comes from the impact of technology, the ideas of the university as an instrument of social change, and the economics of education (St. Clair, 1997). Distance education (DE) is one of the many possible solutions that has been proposed to deal with these challenges.

II. Estonian Library Education

Change is also the most significant characteristic in Estonian librarianship and library and information science education. Estonian librarianship evolved in the first quarter of the twentieth century, influenced by German and Anglo-American librarianship. After the second World War it changed to conform with Soviet librarianship of the time (Lepik, 1997). After regaining independence in 1991, the Baltic states began a profound transformation of their societies, carrying out political, economic, and social reforms and integrating into European and world markets. The changes in the library network have taken place mainly in connection with the transformation of the economic structure, changes in the territorial and administrative situation, and the optimization of library services.

The history of professional library training in Estonia is 70 years old. Librarians' training became a regular issue for the Estonian Librarian Association (ELA) in the 1920s; in 1927, librarianship became an optional subject in the curriculum of Tartu University; 1944 saw the opening of the Department of Bibliography; and in 1954, the Faculty of Librarianship was established. Since 1965 it has been possible to get a degree in librarianship at Tallinn University of Educational Sciences (TUES), which was the Tallinn Teacher Training Institute until 1992 (Lepik, 1997).

Unified curricula, compulsory in the whole Soviet Union, did not allow librarians to prepare for the future information environment in which they had to work. The all-Union curricula could be adapted only to a small degree, and the content of education and its 4-year duration were rigidly prescribed for all the secondary and higher special-education institutions located in the territory of the Soviet Union. The transition to an Estonian curriculum for a 5-year undergraduate course took place in 1988.

Today TUES offers courses in information studies and graduates receive a bachelor's degree. Beginning with the autumn term of 1994, TUES began offering full-time university credit courses. Since 1991 it has become possible to take advanced degree courses at the Department of Information Studies of the TUES. These postgraduate studies lead to two degrees: Master of Information Sciences (MA) and Doctor of Philosophy in Humanities (PhD). It is the first time that either degree can be obtained in Estonia and in the Estonian language. Previously Estonian librarians had to seek advanced degrees outside Estonia and study in the Russian language (Lepik, 1997).

In the development of the new curricula in the Department of Information Studies, the practice and experience of several European and Scandinavian universities and library schools has been considered. The principles of new teaching and learning methods, namely distance learning, resource-based learning, and networked learning, are used in the context of continuing education and integrated into the curricula as well. Distance education provides the opportunity for people to respond dynamically to the demands of their environment and is boundless by nature, since physical distance does not have to be taken into account. It is therefore especially well suited for being developed through international cooperation.

III. Distance Education in Estonia

Distance higher education in Europe is at the beginning of the third phase in its evolution. In this third evolutionary phase, with complete multimedia openness, students will be able to individually choose the mix of media and teaching aids that best suits their learning style (Bang, 1995). Distance learning, flexible learning, resource-based learning, open learning, and computer-mediated learning are becoming commonplace in the progressive educator's vocabulary and are all used rather loosely to describe the alternatives to traditional educational provision. They reflect the shift from a teacher-centered to a learner-centered process, from a pedagogic approach to a facilitative one in which the focus is more on learning than on teaching and in which students are encouraged to pose questions and negotiate criteria for their own study and assessment. However, flexible learning is not an alternative term for the other terms (i.e., resource-based learning, open learning, computer-mediated learning). It is a generic title for all of these descriptions since it embraces all aspects of the other approaches. In any case, they are all subtly different from each other. The earliest origins of flexible learning were probably in distance learning. In resource-based learning, a newcomer to the field of flexible learning, there is a different emphasis. It makes learners aware of the wide range of resources available to assist them in acquiring knowledge and skills, and allows them to choose the appropriate resources to suit their own needs. The essential characteristics common to all definitions of open learning are that people are permitted to study at a time that suits them, at a place of their choice, and at their own pace. Open learning was originally conceived to meet the needs of people who found it difficult to attend courses in institutions but who wanted to take courses and obtain a degree and were unable to do so (Simmonds, 1995).

Distance education can not be separated from other modes of education. In Estonia there is no coherent model for the development of education. It can, however, be said that the major changes in the education field have been connected with university education. There is an obvious need in Estonia for providing education in the distance mode: Along with the rapid changes in Estonian society, a large number of people need training and retraining, and there is a need for new qualifications in both the private and the public sectors in Estonia. Universities have recently realized that distance education is very important in the strategy of the university to give adults lifelong learning opportunities. There has also been development in the DE policy at the institutional, national, and international level in Estonia (Virkus, 1997b).

Still the concept of modern distance education is not very well known in Estonia. Distance education is still associated, by most people, with the kind of correspondence education that was offered under the old regime and is often also associated with its most evident manifestation (i.e., technology). It is so even in the top-level education systems. In a society where education has long lacked any kind of information technology, all phenomena connected with modern educational technology easily have the charm of novelty. It is therefore important to convey an understanding of modern distance education to the Estonian education system ("Distance Education in Estonia, Latvia and Lithuania," 1993).

The ideas of modern distance education started to spread in Estonia in 1993. At their meeting on January 29, 1993, The Nordic Council of Ministers made a decision to support the Action Programme for the Baltic Countries and neighboring areas. In the Action Programme provision was made for educational projects in distance education. The Nordic Council of Ministers recognized explicitly that there exists a huge need for the training and retraining of considerable groups in both private and public sectors in the Baltic region. For this reason the council accepted an application from the President of the European Distance Education Network (EDEN) on behalf of the national associations of distance education in Finland, Norway, and Sweden to perform a feasibility study in the Baltic countries.

The aim of the feasibility study was to assess the state of art of distance education in the three Baltic states, as well as to identify the needs that exist for further development of distance education in the region ("Distance Education in Estonia, Latvia and Lithuania," 1993).

In March 1993, the Central and Eastern European countries proposed within the framework of the Working Group on regional initiatives in human resources, to establish a Regional Distance Education Network in cooperation with PHARE. (PHARE is the program of the European Union for the economic and social restructuring of the countries of Central and Eastern Europe. PHARE was the original designation for "Poland, Hungary Assistance for Restructuring Economies," which was later expanded to all countries of Eastern and Central Europe.) As a first step a feasibility study of the development of such a Regional Distance Education Network in Central and Eastern Europe was commissioned, and the European Association of Distance Teaching Universities (EADTU) was contracted to carry out this study with the Ministry of Culture and Education of Hungary as coordinator.

Feasibility studies on the development of modern distance education were carried out in 1993 by groups of experts engaged by The Nordic Council of Ministers and PHARE. In October 1993, at a seminar in Budapest for the official representatives of all 11 PHARE countries (Albania, Bulgaria, Czech Republic, Estonia, Hungary, Latvia, Lithuania, Poland, Romania, Slovak Republic, and Slovenia), it was agreed unanimously that a Regional Distance Education Network should be set up with a long-term perspective. Following up the feasibility study, a financing proposal for the pilot project PHARE Multi-Country Co-operation in Distance Education was approved in 1994. The pilot project aimed to

- Act as a catalyst for national policy formulation in the field of distance education through measures for increased awareness, staff development, the presentation of existing models, and mechanisms of distance education

- Establish a network of national contact points in the participating countries and develop the necessary infrastructure in all countries to allow them to cooperate on an equal basis
- Develop on an experimental basis two pilot courses (European Studies and Training of Distance Education Trainers), thereby testing the feasibility of joint development by the participating countries of core course modules, which can then be adapted to national requirements and contexts
- On the basis of the above items, define areas of common interests in which regional cooperation can produce an important added value, in terms of enhanced quality of outputs speed of development and/or economies of scale (Benders, 1996)

The establishment of the necessary infrastructure for distance education started in Estonia in 1994: The Estonian National Contact Point was established on November 7, 1994; regional centers were set up at TUES, the Tartu University, and the Tallinn Technical University; and training of the necessary staff for distance education began:

- Pilot projects, Train the Trainer in Distance Education and European Studies arranged in the framework of the PHARE Technical Assistance Program (TAP) for the Implementation of the Trans-Regional Component of the PHARE Pilot Project for Multi-Country Co-operation in Distance Education (June 1995–February 1996)
- FEUCODE (Finnish–Estonian University level Co-Operation in Distance Education) on methods and forms of distance education organized by Helsinki, Turu, Jyväskylä, and the Tartu University, TUES, and the Tallinn Technical University (1993–1995)
- Estonian–Swedish Project, Distance Education Methodology with Applications, organized by Linköping University and the Tallinn Technical University (April–November 1994)
- FEUCODE II (Finnish–Estonian University level Co-Operation in Distance Education) organized by Helsinki, Turu, Jyväskyklä, and the Tartu University, TUES, and the Tallinn Technical University for continuing professional education of the teachers on methods and forms of distance education (November 1995–June 1996)
- Project for tutor training arranged by Jyväskyklä University Center for Continuing Education (April–May 1996) (Virkus, 1997d)

After and during these pilot projects, training on distance education in different subject fields began. These fields included environmental sciences, projects for information professionals (the DE pilot project for school librarians [May 1996–June 1997], and the project on DE for Library and Information Professionals Information Technology in Libraries [1996–2000], etc.), training of trainers and, for example, teachers' e-mail skills. In addition to this, support was given by the Open Estonian Foundation to build up the network for the first stage of the distance education study centers by training 15 tutors and preparing the first DE course for teachers without pedagogical education.

Two study centers have been established in Estonia: one in Tartu and one in Tallinn as a consortium between TUES, the Tallinn Technical University, and the Estonian Business School. Some structures have been established in different universities of Estonia: Open Universities have been established in TUES, Tartu University, and Tallinn Technical University. Other organizations established during the project have included the Center of Educational Technology (1996), Telemedia Laboratory with ISDN facilities for teleconferencing (1996), and a computer lab of the Department of the Information Studies for offering DE courses for librarians and information professionals (1997) in TUES.

Estonian universities are as well prepared for distance education as conventional universities in other countries. The following conditions are fulfilled:

- A number of experts who are familiar with basic educational concepts
- Good contacts with high-quality DE and research centers in the world (Open Learning Foundation, New Brunswick University, Turku University, Gjovik College, etc.)
- Established cooperation among universities in Estonia
- People who are able to manage a system and subsystem of DE in Estonia (Henderikx, 1997)

In addition to this, an educational market has been developed. There exist private schools, universities, and training companies along with public schools and universities. Also a new round of educational legislation development was started in April 1996, new curricula are under development at all levels of education, structural changes in the universities have been started, and finally there is at least partial awareness of new concepts (Vilu, 1997). Most important, distance education in Estonia has developed from individual initiatives to the institutional level.

IV. Factors Inhibiting the Implementation of Distance Learning

There is a lack of national policy formulation in the DE field in Estonia. What is needed is more awareness, staff development, and the presentation and understanding of existing models and mechanisms of distance education. There is inadequate understanding of the educational needs of individuals and of society as a whole. There is also insufficient coordination of distance education at the institutional level, where major conditions (experts, cooperation, etc.) are fulfilled mainly at the level of individual or departmental initiatives; a lack of knowledge and skills of modern distance education; and a limited understanding of the possibilities of the new information and communication technology. Subject-oriented teaching and teacher-centered attitudes continue to be predominant. Some of the shortcomings are the lack of resources within institutions for operating DE courses effectively and the fact that there are only few active learners. The learners do not have an adequate understanding of the learning situation, their role and responsibility in it, and the need for self-guidance. They are also oriented to being furnished with knowledge instead of obtaining it themselves. Further, there is weakness in the learner support systems and a lack of teamwork skills. One of the major weaknesses is the stressful working conditions experienced by teachers in educational institutions. In compiling learning materials the teachers often find themselves in a closed circle because of the heavy teaching load. They do not have enough time for composing learning materials and the lack of learning materials does not allow for reduction of their teaching load. Finally there is a lack of the right balance between theory and practice in distance education.

V. Opportunities

The rapid development of the national telecommunication networks (Internet, ISDN, etc.) opens the possibility for making use of the most recent information technology in the DE field. Clarification of educational needs of distance education in cooperation with ministries, local governments, professonal unions, and other interested institutions is also needed. It is necessary to analyze the motivation and readiness of the potential target groups to participate in DE courses, to analyze the dynamics of the educational needs emerging from national development plans, and so on (Normak, 1997). Radical changes in attitudes are needed for training university teachers in DE methods, for integrating DE methods into academic research, and for creating an institutional DE environment. At the institutional level universities have to commit themselves to distance education and to adult education, and they must define their strategic management in the DE field and define an institutional framework to make structural progress. At the national level the financial support from the Ministry of Education is needed for integrating basic educational concepts into the DE practice in Estonia, for stimulating cooperation between universities and cooperation in developing courses. The Ministry of Education should encourage distance education, and DE structures should be promoted and supported by the government. Partnership in the region, with companies, with public agencies, and with institutions of higher learning will be important. At the European level there is a need to exchange good experiences between countries and to develop materials jointly, to exchange and adapt each others materials, and to exchange students and teaching staff (Henderikx, 1997).

VI. Obstacles

The number of obstacles is not as great as their possible influence. First, the biggest obstacle is the question of the quality of DE courses. There are new competitors in the market. Second, there is no overview in Estonia available, as to where and what is taught and who the teachers are. In Tallinn alone there are about 400 firms registered in the Enterprise Register offering education and training for adults. There is no information available on the qualification of teachers and quality of courses. The third big obstacle is that major changes in the process of teaching and learning are too slow. They are in danger of losing their grip on the rapidly developing technology. At the same time the financial, physical, and human resources are shrinking. Regulation and accreditation, or the lack of them, may affect DE in many ways. Finally there is the question of the effectiveness of teaching and the productivity of learning.

After all this there remain two simple questions: What is possible with the resources available in Estonia, and what kind of cooperation is needed from the partners outside? These are crucial questions for Estonian distance education and also for the development of education in general (Virkus, 1997c).

VII. Distance Education in Library and Information Science Education in Estonia

A. Pilot Project for School Librarians

To help the information professionals to meet new challenges, the Centre for Information Work was established within the Department of Information Studies at TUES in June 1995. For the transition from conventional learning to flexible learning, specially targeted pilot projects are used in the centre. The DE pilot project for school librarians was the first project in the centre attempting to adopt flexible learning methods. The project was meant for persons working in school libraries, media centers, or learning centers of K–12 schools. Steps in the design and development of courses, identification of areas of need, selection of appropriate learning media, and so on had already begun in 1995. The DE pilot project for school librarians started in May 1996, and finished in May 1997.

The aim of the project was to bring quality in service and continuing education to school librarians (K–12) in Estonia. This project also aimed to enable participants to become aware of the potential of network possibilities and to gain some basic skills about network information seeking and retrieval, publishing on the Internet via the World Wide Web, public relation and marketing, user education, and so on. Today from the computer at home or office the educator or learner can access hundreds of library catalogs, journal indexes, reference books, full text of journal articles and books, art exhibits, employment notices, and discussion groups. The learners in schools need help to convert information into knowledge, to avoid information overload, and to identify the best sources for the specific needs and abilities of each learner. It is hoped that the school library will play an active part in the educational process of every school in Estonia and will support the work of teachers and students showing how to make use of the modern information sources available to them.

1. Choice of Technology

Today there is a variety of technology available for transfer of knowledge from competence centers to specific target groups. This technology makes it possible to reach target groups, who, under normal circumstances, are disadvantaged regarding geography, finances, family, and job.

The Internet, commonly referred to as the information superhighway or cyberspace, is a relatively new medium for enhancing and delivering distance learning courses. Unlike traditional DE systems, which relied heavily on print-based materials supported by audiotape, telephone contact, videotape, color slides, and study pictures, the Internet gives increased access to graphics, sound, video files, and real-time communications. Teaching functions are directly related to the educational potential of the different technologies. Therefore, it is relevant to divide the previously mentioned technologies into technologies facilitating: presentation of the learning material, interaction between the learner and the learning material, and communication between the learner and the teacher/tutor or among the learners themselves (Bang, 1995).

The designer of distance learning programs has a lot of choices ranging from synchronous to asynchronous delivery systems. Choice of media will depend on the nature of the subject matter and skills to be covered, the knowledge level and prior skills of the learners, and the learners' access to replay equipment. The choice of instructional media depends greatly on the budget of course developers as well.

Given the relatively high degree of access that schools have to computing facilities and e-mail, electronic communication, especially the Internet, plays an important role in the promotion of DE to school librarians in Estonia. Many schools possess computers in Estonia, but computers are often used mainly to teach just mathematics and computing itself. Estonian schools are already much more better equipped with information technology than our public libraries and the online aspect of distance education will continue to grow in Estonia as the number of schools equipped with telecommunications equipment and computers increase (e.g., the project "Tiger Leap").

Teachers of informatics in schools will support and have already supported school librarians in their network learning activities. One reason for choosing the Internet was also that the Department of Information Studies has been involved with networking training since the beginning of 1994. The staff of the department is familiar with the possibilities of the Internet and has experience in using it. Using the Internet for DE is also relatively inexpensive compared with another media in Estonia.

Computer communication has been used to deliver course materials and in the area of communication between teacher and learner and between learners in different locations. Synchronous communication (e.g., talk software, CU-SeeMe technology) and asynchronous communication (e.g., e-mail, listserv and World Wide Web, telnet, ftp, gopher) have been used in the pilot project. Learning material have been distributed as ordinary mail (as ASCII files) or as attachments (for formatted documents) to learners. The learning materials also appear in the form of World Wide Web pages accessible over the Internet, and students are encouraged to explore and draw on the local and global networked information resources as well. A set of Web pages was created for the module with pointers to some useful information sources for school librarians.

To provide students with a common communication platform during courses and to enable all the group members to receive the same information, KR-LIST has been created for school librarians. It enables course discussions and sending questions or comments to teaching faculty or classmates as well. Students submit written assignments to teaching faculty through e-mail, and assignments are returned with comments and suggestions in the same fashion.

2. Content

The pilot project consisted of four modules, and topics covered included basic network concepts, Internet basic tools, services and search engines, network information seeking and retrieval, publishing on the Internet via the Web, public relations and marketing, user education, and so on. Each module consisted of 40 hours and included self-studying, face-to-face methods, and tutorial and group works. An introductory session of 16 hours was given during the first module using the traditional face-to-face method, and 12 hours were offered to prepare students for the telematics-based components of the course. Key aspects of DE were covered, and terms such as distance education, flexible learning, resource-based learning, and open learning were introduced to school librarians. An overview of challenges and school possibilities was given as well. In addition to face-to-face seminars, networking skills were spread through the electronic network.

Some of the advantages and difficulties experienced by now using the Internet for educational delivery are described as follows:

Advantages

1. Providing students with the ability to connect to educational resources when it is convenient for them.
2. Possibility for students to learn at their own pace.
3. Allowing students to explore the educational resources in an order that suits their needs.
4. Lower cost in electronic publication of course materials compared to printing the same materials.
5. Faster methods for electronically revising and redistributing course material compared to print materials.
6. Using the World Wide Web for delivering courses allows lecturers to develop a single platform, yet the content is accessible by students using a wide range of computing platforms and Web browsers able to provide links to previous electronic course modules or externally stored resources materials on the Internet.

Difficulties

1. School librarians' experiences in information and communication technology were relatively limited; only one librarian had previous practical network experience.
2. It seemed to the instructors that even when school librarians had access to computers and knowledge about them generally, they still needed considerable time to master the techniques involved in using e-mail for discussions and communication.
3. Not all students are suited for Internet-based education. It is often difficult for them to express themselves as well using the computer-based communication methods as they would in either direct conversation with their lecturers in classroom discussions. Thus, not all questions may be asked by the student when using computer-mediated communication.
4. Some students felt isolated, lacked confidence in their own abilities, and required careful support and encouragement. In general, students

have to be very highly motivated for personal competence development to study in isolation.

5. Cost of computer equipment and communications infrastructure lim-
   its the number of students that can afford an Internet-based course.
6. Poor technical support or tutorial help can lead to incorrect usage of
   software tools needed to do assignments.

B. Information Technology in Libraries

On September 20, 1996, the Department of Information Studies received
support from the Open Estonian Foundation to start the long-term project
DE for library and information professionals, called "Information Technology in Libraries." The aim of the project is to deliver continuing professional
education for library and information professionals using DE methods to
promote the realization of the development program of Estonian Library
Information System. According to the development program of the information system for Estonian libraries, "Estonian Library Information System,"
basic technology in Estonian libraries will be transferred to modern information technology during the period 1996–2005. As a result of that project,
1,500 workplaces with modern information technology will be established in
591 different Estonian libraries. This will increase significally the demand
for continuing professional education for library and information professionals with the knowledge and skills of modern information technology (Virkus, 1997a).

The analysis of the demand for training based on a questionnaire of the
ELA among the members of ELA in February 1996, demonstrated that
education and training is needed mostly in modern information technology
(e.g., computer handling, the generation and usage of computer-based databases, network training, integrated library systems, etc.).

A DE project is planned for the period 1997–2000, and includes three
stages: (1) distance education for the scientific libraries, (2) distance education
for central public libraries, and (3) distance education for other public libraries
and school libraries. The project includes different modules: basic computer
skills, integrated library systems, Internet basic tools, services and search
engines, information seeking and retrieval in Internet and commercial databases (Dialog, DataStar, etc.), generation of databases, electronic publishing,
methods of analyzing information, reference work, Estonian information
resources in network environment, user education and consulting, and so on.

In addition to technologies currently being used in pilot projects to
deliver DE to school librarians on the Internet, CU-SeeMe videoconferencing
software for the PC on the Internet will be used in this project. International
cooperation with Nordic countries has had an essential role in initiating and

developing distance education in Estonia: the Action Programme for the Baltic Countries and Neighboring Areas, a Feasibility Study, training of trainers, seminars and study visits, and personal contact with Nordic experts are just some of the resulting activities. On a regional level, since the autumn of 1993, Nordic–Baltic training of trainers seminars for library and information science academic staff have been organized. This long-term project (October 1993–April 1997) is an effective way to develop curricula and cooperate with Nordic and Baltic library and information science professionals.

Development of DE projects at the Department of Information Studies of TUES has received inspiration and support in the testing and use of modern information and communication technology as well as development of DE courses from colleagues in the following Nordic education institutions: Gjovik College in Norway and the Universities of Turku and Abo Akademi in Finland.

VIII. Conclusion

This article presents a brief overview of distance education as an important new field within the overall development of education in Estonia. The Department of Information Studies of TUES is currently exploring and developing new pedagogic models for learning to use electronic support and learner-centered approaches to provide education to remote students. This department has been very interested in the use of network possibilities for distance learning purposes. The DE pilot project for school librarians indicated obvious DE advantages in using the Internet, illustrated the difficulties in using this rapidly changing technology, and offered experiences to improve the quality of distance learning in the Department of Information Studies of TUES. In the future the long-term project, "Information Technology in Libraries, 1997–2000," will enable staff to apply the skills and knowledge of technology that they have obtained. Through this pilot project the technology will be tested and evaluated to develop methods for future use.

References

Bang, J. (1995). Curriculum, pedagogy and educational technologies. *EADTU-News* **18**, 35–42.

Benders, J. (1996). *A New Multi-Country Distance Education Network for Central Europe: Implementation of the Transregional Component of the PHARE Pilot Project for Multi-Country Co-operation in Distance Education Through Technical Assistance by European Association of Distance Teaching Universities (EADTU)*. PHARE Workshop, January 17.

Daniel, J. S. (1996). *Mega-Universities and Knowledge Media: Technology Strategies for Higher Education*. Kogan Page, London.

Distance Education in Estonia, Latvia and Lithuania. Report on a Feasibility Study to the Nordic Council of Ministers, Oslo, Norway (1993).

Henderikx, P. (1997). Interview for Infofoorum. *Infofoorum* **3**. (http://www.tpu.ee/~i-foorum/piet1.htm)

Lepik, A. (1997). Training of trainers and professional development: Estonian prospective. In *Human Development: Competencies for the Twenty-First Century: Papers of the IFLA CPERT Third International Conference on Continuing Professional Education for the Library and Information Professions* (P. Layzell and D. E. Weingand, eds.), pp. 105–113. (IFLA Publications 80/81). K. G. Saur, Muenchen.

Normak, P. (1997). Distance Education in the Tallinn University of Educational Sciences. *Infofoorum* **3**. (http://www.tpu.ee/~i-foorum/pee1.htm)

Simmonds, T. (1995). *Implementing and Managing Flexible Learning: Establishing Flexible Learning Programmes*. Pitman Publishing, London.

St. Clair, G. (1997). Coaching higher education for change. *The Journal of Academic Librarianship* **23**(4), 269–270.

Vilu, R. (1997). *Estonian Possibilities to Integrate into the European Distance Education Network*. Presentation at the international seminar at Tallinn University of Educational Sciences, Estonia, August 4–5.

Virkus, S. (1996). Distance education in library and information science education in Estonia. *Papers of the 5th Congress of Baltic Librarians "Independence and Libraries,"* Tallinn/Estonia, October 21–22.

Virkus, S. (1997a). Distance education as a new possiblity for librarians in Estonia. *Information Research: An Electronic Journal* **2**(4). (http://www.shef.ac.uk/uni/academic/I-M/is/lecturer/paper20.html)

Virkus, S. (1997b). Distance education as a new possibility for library and information science education in Estonia. In *Human Development: Competencies for the Twenty-First Century: Papers of the IFLA CPERT Third International Conference on Continuing Professional Education for the Library and Information Professions*, pp. 249–255. (IFLA Publications 80/81). K. G. Saur, München.

Virkus, S. (1997c). Distance education in Estonia. In *Distance Education in West Estonia: DECDEE-Project and Development Plan*, pp. 12–16. Eura Print, Turku.

Virkus, S. (1997d). Distance learning in a networked environment. *FID News Bulletin* **47**(1), 37–44.

Historiography and the Land-Grant University Library

Douglas J. Ernest
Morgan Library
Colorado State University
Fort Collins, Colorado 80523

I. Introduction

The significance of library history to practitioners has vexed library historians for the last several decades. This article investigates several aspects of this issue:

1. What has been the course of library historiographical thinking in the post–World War II era, as exemplified by its literature?
2. Has this thinking been reflected in studies devoted to the history of individual land-grant university libraries? These institutions appear to have been studied less than other academic libraries and, therefore, have been selected for examination in this article.
3. Can suggestions for changes in, or improvements to, the historiography of land-grant university libraries be made as a result of conclusions drawn from points (1) and (2)?

II. Literature Review

The literature of library historiography is, somewhat surprisingly, voluminous. For publications predating the mid-1980s, reference is made to Davis and Tucker (1989), a standard work identifying key sources in library historiography. For the period postdating Davis and Tucker, the author has selected items that appear to adhere most closely to themes identified in earlier literature.

A. The Early Years

Stewart (1943) began the debate by emphasizing that the history of college libraries in the nineteenth century was "unexplored" and then itemizing sources most productive for potential research. Of greater interest is Stewart's (1943) remark that "the library's relative position as a result of changes on the education scene" had been neglected (p. 231). This need to place the history of individual libraries in a larger context is one to which historiographers would return repeatedly.

Speaking at the inception of the Library History Round Table at the 1947 American Library Association (ALA) conference, Shores (1961) notes that relatively little library history had been produced in the first 70 years of the library profession in the United States. He attributed this inattention to the belief that librarians had been pragmatic pioneers who had to first carve out a place for their profession in American society. Now that the pioneer era had ended, he urges his colleagues to repair this deficiency. As the repository of the record of humanity, the library deserved a position second to none in the preservation of its own record.

McMullen (1952) characterizes librarians as "systematizers, blueprint-makers, counters, [and] planners" (p. 385), then emphasizes that these activities could be enhanced by library history. "If we are to operate our libraries wisely in the present, we need to know as much as possible about how libraries have been operated in the past" (McMullen, 1952, p. 385). He also notes that the history of library operations needs to be placed in larger contexts to be meaningful and concludes that library history could be valuable for problem solving, biographical interest, and the placement of libraries in a sociological perspective.

Writing at the same time, Shera (1952) takes a more philosophical and theoretical approach. He provides a threefold examination of library history: (1) the role of libraries in society, (2) the perceived decline in the use of history to understand libraries, and (3) the future course of library history. He then posits a case for the value of library history as a means to study and avoid the mistakes of the past, using examples such as the role public libraries attempted to play in the public education movement. Shera recognizes the difficulty of predicting the future by using the past as a guide but asserts that a greater danger lay in ignoring history altogether. A librarian who studied the past and current positions of the library within its community would serve that community better than a librarian oblivious to history.

Irwin (1958) asserts that an undue emphasis on the present in contemporary life and the need to acquire a mass of specialized information had led many library schools to drop their history courses. Admitting that history does not repeat itself and is an uncertain guide to the future, Irwin nevertheless asserts that a librarian with a knowledge of library history would lead a richer professional life. History lends perspective and understanding to a person's job duties, as well as sympathy for those gone before. He concludes by urging that librarians write their own history rather than leaving it to laypeople who might miss significant points.

Reichmann (1964) briefly examines the philosophy of history, indicating that the primary purpose of the discipline lay not in its utilitarian applications (if any) but, rather, in "the growth of understanding and in the intellectual satisfaction of recognizing . . . developments" (p. 35). He believes that librarians, as collectors of the printed word, have a natural affinity with historians but that American librarians were too interested in "pioneering" to devote much thought to history.

> We do like the word "pioneer"; . . . We are all continuously pioneering in readers' services, in technical services, in the application of machines, and so forth. The pioneer, of course, does not have the time, nor the interest to look backwards; for him the past is dead and of no consequence, and his main attention is focused on the future (Reichmann, 1964, p. 37)

The American belief in ongoing progress also hindered interest in the past. Reichmann ends on a realistic note by recognizing that history is only one tool among many disciplines and that many librarians would not devote themselves to it. He did hope that every library would have at least one staffer interested in history.

Echoing the complaints of his predecessors, Harris (1968) voices the opinion that American librarians show little concern for their past. He notes the difficulty of actually determining the influence of libraries, for there was no way to measure the effect of library books on the minds of their readers. Like other library historians, he asks that general studies, rather than histories of individual institutions, receive greater attention, while nevertheless noting that relatively few histories of academic libraries existed. The best work was being done by library school students producing theses and dissertations, as opposed to practitioners in individual libraries. Theses and dissertation topics, however, naturally focused on libraries physically situated near each library school. Harris also stresses two now familiar themes: (1) If library history were assigned any importance by the profession, it was for its supposedly utilitarian applications; and (2) the accepted methodology of library history meant an adherence to the idea of placing the library in its wider social context. Finally, it is well to note that Harris would become one of the more controversial and prolific contributors to library historiography in coming years.

Colson (1969) rises to the defense of history by likening it to individual human memory:

> The proper use of history is the thoughtful application of ideas in our memory to a problem which confronts us, whereby we may attempt a reasonable choice among the alternatives which may be available to us. History does not provide the alternatives, and it does not indicate the correct choice among them. (p. 68)

He adds that the library historian provides constructive criticism to a profession too given to "a concatenation of Babbitt-views of success" (Colson, 1969, p. 70). An understanding of history would allow librarians to change and progress; ignorance of it served only the status quo of complacent Babbitry.

B. The 1970s

In the 1970s, the scattered articles that had characterized library historiographical thought in earlier decades gave way to a more concerted effort that reflected an interest in the 1976 centennial of the ALA and, perhaps, the arrival of a greater number of professional library historians on the scene. Three relevant articles appeared in a single collection in 1971. McMullen (1971) provides library researchers with tips on the proper investigation and use of primary sources. Of greater interest from a historiographical viewpoint, he reports on the results of a sampling of 18 doctoral dissertations on American library history. McMullen's examination indicates that 73% of footnotes in these theses were to primary sources, presumably demonstrating that these doctoral researchers were well grounded in original source materials. However, McMullen's definition of "primary sources" is relatively broad, including government documents and, in certain instances, newspaper and journal articles.

The second article (Holley, 1971) also introduces the reader to a research problem, textual criticism, by citing practical examples. Holley notes that institutional annual reports tended to resemble propaganda but were too often among the few sources available. He also urges his readers to publish their work, rather than waiting until it was perfect, and indicates his pleasure at the recent establishment of the *Journal of Library History*, which provided a forum for the discipline.

Hagler (1971), the author of the third article, rejects the notion that library history needed to be utilitarian:

> history does not need the justification of such applicability to make it profitable—perhaps even essential—for the broadening and disciplining of the mind of both its writer and its reader, and for the improvement of the profession as a whole. (p. 130)

He goes on to indicate the need for more histories of individual organizations, as well as interpretive studies unifying the individual histories. He also expresses concern that too many histories appeared in theses or dissertations. Finally, Hagler laments that he was repeating admonitions expressed by Shera years earlier but expresses the hope that recent developments would free librarians from clerical tasks, enabling them to pursue historical research should they so choose.

Expanding on an article written initially in 1945, Shera (1973) first reviews the literature of American library history, then reiterates the need for an examination of librarianship, as opposed to individual institutional histories. Few histories had done so, despite the apparent maturation of the discipline and the rise of library doctoral programs. Insisting again that the sociological roots of libraries required scrutiny, Shera (1973) concludes:

> Though the past cannot provide all the answers to the problems of the present and the future, it is only the past we have, and as such it is our sole resource for an understanding of who and what we as librarians are. Only history can give us the key to our professional self-knowledge. (p. 151)

Harris (1975) moves the discussion to a more concept-oriented plane by noting differences in interpretation of library history between himself and other scholars. Harris characterizes his approach as "externalist," emphasizing that nineteenth-century librarians reflected, and acted on, beliefs held by a societal group he labels "authoritarian-elitists" (p. 108). Other historians were "internalist" in approach, assigning a more philosophical and societal role to librarians than Harris would concede. More noteworthy is the observation that library historiography had advanced to a point that a number of scholars were not only active but also capable of different conceptual approaches that could be controversial, as is seen.

Writing at the time of the ALA centennial, Colson (1976) examines the literature of American library history. Much had been achieved, but much remained to be done. He propounds two definitions of history: "one is of history as a past which is known, and needs only to be explained; the other is of history as a method of study" (Colson, 1976, p. 9). Too much of library historical work, particularly histories of individual libraries, fell into the first definition, whereas pursuit of history as a method was liberating, allowing one to discern both patterns and variations from patterns. Few library historical efforts had done so. Colson saw hope in the fact that more historical work was being executed by doctoral students. Such was the diversity of their efforts that Colson saw no trend toward a "new history." Indeed, he viewed an ongoing debate between Harris and critics of his ideas as one involving the need of the participants to identify with "revisionism" as much as an episode in revision of library history itself. He concludes with a warning that calls for library history to serve a utilitarian purpose were misplaced. Historical study might "assist in the development of . . . understanding, but only in the minds of librarians who are free from the past" (Colson, 1976, p. 18)—that is, those who realized that history served their own purposes rather than the reverse.

Concurrently, Harris (1976) defends the role of the revisionist in revisiting the historical record from generation to generation. He believes the task of the historian to be complex and time consuming, one that a pragmatic library profession tended not to attempt, but finds some comfort in the fact that a small group of scholars dedicated to the task seemed to be emerging. He urged library educators to stay abreast of the movement and to motivate their students to become aware of recent historical scholarship.

Shortly thereafter, Harris (1978) provides a defense of revisionist history from perceived attacks by opponents in the library world. Stating that the critics wanted to preserve a "liberal-progressive" view of American history that the revisionists had demolished, he castigates library historians for their amateurish and antiquarian concentration on details rather than interpretation. He saw the revisionists as concerned with values, while the more traditional library historians concerned themselves with the "consequences of library service" (Harris, 1978, p. 39). As a result, the profession was still largely interested in celebrating its past instead of engaging in its critical examination. Harris believed that revisionism would create a new consensus, not just destroy the old.

Dain (1978), who had been drawn into the debate over revisionism, agrees with Harris that library historians had been deficient in placing their institutions in a broader social context and that much could be achieved by emulating the methodology of the revisionists. However, she adds that history could never be an exact science; the historian must pursue truth, as it appears to him- or herself, and provide the documentation to support that vision of "truth." She provides a gentle admonition: "[I]f history can teach us anything, it is that there is no *one* [Dain's emphasis] road to such understanding" (Dain, 1978, p. 47).

McMullan (1978) provides an essay to which several other researchers responded. He examined 86 books and pamphlets published on library history since 1970 and found that 39% were devoted to individual institutions and 70% overall concerned with one or more libraries. About one fourth had been based on dissertations. Curiously, he warns against extensive interpretation of the historical record. McMullen then offers several tips designed to save authors from excessive dullness; echoing the methodology of the revisionists, he also recommended greater use of statistical data.

Reacting to McMullen's fear that modern interpreters would impose their own viewpoint on the past, Milum (1978) advocates, instead, that the library historian temper his or her interpretive decisions with "a more honest course which begins with careful reading, and resists unwarranted conjecture, open attack, and the venting of personal resentments" (p. 441). Milum also asserts that thoughtful reviewers served as a powerful deterrent to overzealous interpretation. Finally, she asks that McMullen's request for improved style not overshadow the need to avoid the "labor of love" so frequent among library histories.

Another, more laudatory comment on McMullen comes from Kraus (1978), who believed that the cause of library history had advanced in the preceding year: more was being written, publishing venues had improved, and critical editorial comment was increasingly evident. Still, Kraus concurs with McMullen that writing style needed improvement, blaming library schools for not inculcating stylistic skills among their students. He also asserted the importance of history for its ability to provide perspective "at a time when one problem seems to crowd another and another without end" (Kraus, 1978, p. 446). He concludes with a summary of library issues to be addressed by historians: (1) filling gaps among libraries not already having received attention, (2) analyzing collections, (3) developing biographies, and (4) documenting the influence of a library within its community.

The final comment on McMullen, that of Dickinson (1978), reiterates Milum's concern that McMullen's strictures on interpretation were misguided and, if followed literally, would create library history merely descriptive in nature. Agreeing in principle with McMullen's call for historians to make greater use of statistics, Dickinson also cautions that they not be overemphasized. Finally, he concurs that library history needed to be written with greater style and grace.

Surveying the literature of library historiography, Kaser (1978) concludes that the quantity of research had increased, with greater rigor also in evidence. Curiously, the number of studies of individual academic libraries had dropped over the preceding 15 years. Kaser agrees that such studies were needed before generalizations could be made:

> We cannot know what happens in libraries (*plural*) [Kaser's emphasis] until we know what happened in Library A, Library B, Library C, etc.; and this kind of descriptive, factual data is usually generated through unidimensional investigations. (Kaser, 1978, p. 186).

Kaser then addresses the utility of library history. He believed that the profession could benefit from historical research but only if that research were widely disseminated. A major benefit might be the lessening of the propensity of libraries to repeat past experiences and errors, forgetting the lessons to be learned. If nothing else, an understanding of history "might inhibit our inclination to label everything "new"" (Kaser, 1978, p. 195).

Fain's (1978) critique of the role of libraries within the public schools provides not only an example of revisionist history but also commentary on library historiography at large. She notes that, thanks to revisionism, no longer were libraries "automatically to be praised" (Fain, 1978, p. 348), nor could the complexities in library history be ignored. Finally, according to Fain, the significance of libraries is difficult to determine, "primarily because it is so much more difficult to assess the impact of books on individuals than it is to count the numbers of books on the shelves and to chronicle administrative growth" (Fain, 1978, p. 349).

C. The 1980s

By the early 1980s, the journal literature pertaining to library historiography began to reflect an increased emphasis on sophisticated and subtle theorizing,

subscribed to a "pluralist paradigm" in combination with a "positivist episte-mology"; together, they provided a specific view of the world in rather traditional terms. In effect, Harris' thesis was a restatement of the revisionist attack on the "progressive" view of American history. He summarizes:

> What emerges is a sense of the library as an institution embedded in a stratified ensemble of institutions functioning in the high cultural region, an ensemble of institutions dedicated to the creation, transmission, and reproduction of the hegemonic ideology. Such an interpre-tation challenges the "apolitical" conception of the library held by library professionals. (Harris, 1986, p. 241)

One need not agree with Harris' theory to recognize that his paper exemplified the use of social science methodologies outside the usual library history sphere.

Writing in a review essay, Herubel (1988) briefly examines trends in the historical world at large. He notes the importance for library historians to stay abreast of schools of thought, such as the collective point of view pro-pounded by Annales theorists, or deconstruction theory, exemplified by Der-rida. Like many other commentators, Herubel stresses that library topics should "integrate with the larger concerns of sociocultural, intellectual, and political history" (Herubel, 1988, p. 497), while maintaining a dialog with interested readers.

D. Recent Trends

Wiegand (1990) briefly traces the history of library historiography, asserting that historical research remained marginal to the profession at large. He lists several factors, including indifference among library schools, that contributed to this situation, grumbling that the attitudes of American librarians were "provincial and xenophobic" (Weigand, 1990, p. 108). Wiegand then enumer-ates several research areas requiring additional attention. One such area was the history of academic libraries. He concludes, "The report card on the state of American library history research is mixed" (Weigand, 1990, p. 110); much had been achieved by recent generations of scholars but much remained to do.

An article by Alston (1991) is more a protest against the alleged indiffer-ence to history at library schools than a prescription to achieve any change in the situation. Writing from the point of view of a Briton, he presents perhaps the most extravagant claim for library history by any commentator: "the very prosperity which we have enjoyed in the West . . . during the period since the Renaissance has only been possible because of libraries and their concern for the preservation and handing-on of knowledge, even when it seems to be of no particular relevance" (Alston, 1991, p. 46). Alston (1991) joins other historiographers in emphasizing that history must take note of the institutional framework of the individual library and that libraries are "a component in the social, economic and political developments of different civilisations" (p. 49).

In a survey of library historical articles and dissertations written during 1985–1987, Cox (1991) concludes that "such historical research has become more sophisticated in purpose and scope" and that "library history has moved beyond a preoccupation with commemorative institutional studies and biographies of professional leaders" (p. 576). Nevertheless, he considers that the use of primary sources could be expanded and chides the library profession for not paying enough attention to the collection and preservation of its own records. He suggests that the importance of documentation and the need to retain the historical record could be imparted to students by library schools.

Harris and Hannah (1992) express great alarm at the supposed decline in historical awareness among library professionals, contending that recent critics had labeled history as irrelevant; indeed, their indifference to tradition amounted to "ahistoricism." They attribute this attitude to adherence to ideas propounded by Daniel Bell and F. W. Lancaster, who predicated a postindustrial, paperless society in which libraries would be unnecessary. To this notion, Harris and Hannah retort that an acquaintance with history would indicate that libraries, as a cultural artifact with a 3000-year history, would not readily disappear. Led astray by their ahistoricism, critics of history were advancing theories without foundation.

Other observers also sought to justify the role history could play in the library profession. Genz (1993) states:

> All academic disciplines strive to make accurate predictions about probable outcomes. . . . In history, the process takes place backward in time rather than forward. History gives us collective memory, it provides us with ways of escaping narrow boundaries and provides us with perspective. History does not generate proofs, but possibilities. (p. 270)

She goes on to examine the question in light of emerging technologies and concludes that even if the book disappeared as a physical artifact, the study of texts and words in other formats would continue. Genz finishes by asking how the library profession could redefine itself in an era of change if it did not know from whence it came.

Addressing the issue of the utility of library history, Stieg (1993) avers that the profession could learn from its past experience, while admitting that it is not easy to draw the correct lessons from history. A library educator herself, Stieg (1993) then goes on to defend the role of history in the curricula, stating that it creates "professional identity":

> New librarians are the inheritors of [the] past and can better understand their own situations and therefore perform better if their outlook includes an appreciation of how our values came to be. (p. 277)

Harrison (1994) joins the chorus, claiming that library schools, including those in the United Kingdom, were neglecting history. Although the title of his article, "Why Library History?," implied a defense of the discipline, Harrison offers little rationale other than the need for leaders to be aware of the past whenever they began their tenure at an institutional post. Instead, he decries the tendency of librarians to neglect their own archival responsibilities, thus rendering the task of future historians more difficult.

Addressing himself to library educators, Carmichael (1995) repeats the complaint that history had fallen on hard times. Not only were educators and practicing librarians alike seemingly indifferent to the influence of history on the profession but also publishers were reluctant to accept book-length manuscripts in the discipline given low sales to libraries. To encourage potential authors, Carmichael then offers a "decalogue" of tips designed to assist publication. He reminds historians to reach beyond their immediate field to discover connections between librarianship and other fields, then sounds a utilitarian note:

> Library historians of every stripe need to be reminded that however intrinsically interesting their topics are, they also have a bearing on the current problems of libraries, publishers, and society. (Carmichael, 1995, p. 313)

At least one other statement had a familiar ring: "Librarians are quick to assimilate the new and are loathe to engage in basic redefinition and reinterpretation of the familiar" (Carmichael, 1995, p. 310).

E. Themes in the Literature

Certain themes emerge when historiographical thought in total is considered. First, most authorities consider that the library profession—driven by pragmatism, an emphasis on the present, and a fascination with the new—has neglected its own history. Some historians have gone so far as to label librarians "Babbitts," "provincial," and "xenophobic." Ignorance has led librarians to consider everything as "new." If they have assigned any importance to history, it is for its supposedly utilitarian aspect: Having learned the proper lessons from the past, one approaches the future with greater wisdom.

Second, driven to defend themselves, historians have advanced numerous justifications for the study of the past. Some take refuge in the argument that history does have a utilitarian value. They assert that knowledge of the past helps the librarian make wiser choices regarding future courses of action. True, history does not repeat itself, but at least it can provide some guidance to making the most appropriate choice among a group of alternatives. In addition, in time of rapid change, history can help librarians to either create or redefine their professional identity.

Others, however, scorn the idea that history has a utilitarian value and assert that it can be of little aid in predicting the future. Their attitude toward history is more aesthetic and, to some extent, more personal. To them, the study of history can itself be a goal, one that enriches professional life and the understanding of librarianship. It provides perspective, for history serves as our collective memory. In short, historical study is a path to intellectual satisfaction.

A focus on the problems inherent in library historiography represents a third theme. From the beginning, historiographers have stressed the need to place library history in a larger context, either institutional or societal, if not both. There have been frequent complaints that studies of individual libraries form too great a portion of the research undertaken and that such "little history" too frequently lacks context and is celebratory and uncritical in nature. Others fault library historians for failing to remain current with trends in the history profession and with making too little use of social science methods. Several have pointed out the difficulty, not yet satisfactorily resolved, of determining the effect of libraries and books on readers.

Not all historians agree with these assertions, and "little history," in particular, has had its defenders. Properly done, separate institutional histories provide data for those looking at the big picture. Historians attempting to reach conclusions in regard to particular aspects of the library scene need "little history" to provide a set of building blocks.

Yet another theme is that of change within historiographic thinking itself. In the years following the Second World War, library historians contented themselves with elaborating on the most pressing needs in the field. Articles on the subject were relatively few. The late 1960s then saw an increasing number of entries in the field, fueled in part by the approach of the ALA centennial in 1976. Research during the 1970s became more issue oriented, with historiographers disputing among themselves, particularly about revisionism. Nevertheless, the field seemed more stable than earlier, with the *Journal of Library History* (later *Libraries and Culture*), the Library History Round Table, and various conferences providing forums for discussion. By the 1980s, the results were apparent: Historiographic articles grew in length and sophistication and were more likely to incorporate social science methods.

Ironically, the 1990s saw a resurgence of concern over the future of history. This final theme, the supposed neglect of history by the library profession, had been sounded in earlier decades but lay dormant when historical research appeared to flourish in the 1970s and 1980s. The advent of electronic technology on a massive scale in the final decades of the twentieth century seemed to herald a renewed crisis, however. Some historians felt that library schools were no longer merely passively neglecting historical research but were actively questioning its relevance. "Ahistoricism," in league with the failure of libraries to organize and preserve their own archival records, threatened the future of historical research. Some believed that a wider dissemination of research to the profession would act as an antidote, while other historians claimed that a knowledge of the past would help librarians to define themselves in the metamorphosis from print to electronic publishing. Thus would history justify itself.

III. Histories of Land-Grant University Libraries

A. Parameters

The second investigation of this article is of the history of land-grant university libraries. I might note at the outset that several observers believe that histories of public libraries have, in general, received more attention than those of academic libraries. Stewart (1943) commented on this fact decades ago. Davis and Tucker (1989) indicate that the situation had been somewhat rectified but pointed out some limitations: "Many of these [histories of academic libraries], whose interpretive quality varies widely, discuss selected time periods, which are often determined by the tenure of chief administrators" (p. 129). They also note that many studies were the result of master's theses and doctoral dissertations.

Libraries in land-grant universities have received even less attention than other categories of academic libraries. The only historiographic survey, by Davis and Tucker (1994), is of recent vintage. After briefly reviewing general conditions at land-grant libraries, Davis and Tucker present short histories of 13 institutions: Auburn, Clemson, Colorado State, Iowa State, Kansas State, Michigan State, North Carolina State, Oklahoma State, Oregon State, Purdue, Texas A&M, Virginia Polytechnic, and Washington State. All were classified by Davis and Tucker (1994) as "land-grand universities with a major comprehensive public university in the same state" (p. 138), as opposed to comprehensive land grants such as the University of Minnesota and Ohio State. Six other institutions (Mississippi State, Montana State, New Mexico State, North Dakota State, South Dakota State, and Utah State) were similar to those studed by Davis and Tucker but were omitted because of their small size. The two authors also provide a statistical "snapshot" of the 13 primary institutions for 1900, 1930, and 1985. The comparative growth among the 13 could then be seen at a glance.

Davis and Tucker (1994) hypothesize that "The historiography of land-grant college libraries lags behind that of its more traditional counterparts" (p. 135). Their capsule histories, based on a variety of sources, reflected this reality. Articles from the *Encyclopedia of Library and Information Science*, unpublished items such as annual reports, and university histories were among the sources consulted. Only five discrete library histories appeared, of which three were monographs, one a dissertation, and one a master's thesis. This small number reinforces the notion that the number of histories for land-grant universities is relatively small.

To determine the historiographical significance of land-grant libraries, the author compares a number of historical works, applying two standards to select a group of publications for which valid comparisons could be made:

1. The institutions in question should be land-grant universities co-existing in the same state with a comprehensive public university. Nineteen such institutions exist, including the six excluded by Davis and Tucker.
2. Only monographs, dissertations, and theses were examined; as book-length studies, they were more likely to address historiographic concerns than briefer efforts, such as periodical articles, book chapters, unpublished reports, and encyclopedia articles, all of which were excluded.

With these standards in mind, the author identifies and examines 10 items in the chronological order in which they were written.

B. Examination of the Histories, 1929–1993

Brown (1929) was the first on the scene. His short (33-page) *History of the V.P.I. Library 1872–1928* appeared when he was librarian at that institution. Written in a straightforward manner, the volume includes statistical information—such as volume counts and expenditures—but says almost nothing about the land-grant status of V.P.I. (Virginia Polytechnic Institute). Brown does note the agricultural emphasis of the college and discusses the importance of government publications in the library but provides no references, no index, and no bibliography. Nearly half of the volume deals with Brown's tenure, which began in 1925; the author concludes with a plea for a new building.

Three decades later, Towne (1961) wrote the history of the Michigan State University library. He, too, was a director, having led Michigan State since 1932; indeed, he concentrates on the period from 1932 to 1959, covering the 80 years prior to 1932 only briefly. His emphasis is on the internal workings of the library, with considerable detail on cataloging, circulation, government documents, and other standard library units and tasks. Statistical information and the vicissitudes of physical buildings also receive attention. Towne takes little notice of library users but does devote some space to the land-grant, agricultural status of Michigan State. His volume lacks references and an index, but a two-page "Bibliographical Note" indicates sources. Interestingly, in his "Foreword," Towne defends his historical enterprise by asserting that any library history is worth writing, including that of Michigan State, even though that institution lacks the cachet of the University of Virginia library, which boasted Thomas Jefferson as a luminary and which recently had published its own history (Clemons, 1954). Towne did believe that Michigan State was more readily comparable with V.P.I. than with Virginia, although he appeared not to be aware of the history of the V.P.I. library.

Only a few years later, Carlson (1966) weighed in with a history of the library at Oregon State University. Like his two predecessors, he was writing from the perspective of a library director, his tenure having begun in 1945; approximately 40% of his account is devoted to the period from 1945 to 1966. The earlier years of this volume are enlivened by first-hand anecdotes from former student employees who had operated the library during the early years of the institution. These stories were gathered by Carlson's predecessor, Lucy Lewis, who thereby indicated an attentiveness to history perhaps unusual among her contemporaries. Carlson's admiration of Lewis and another early librarian, Ida Kidder, is evident. Otherwise, he follows the pattern set by Brown and Towne by examining staffing, buildings, collections, and budgets rather than focusing on users. Although Carlson pays little attention to the land-grant status of Oregon State, he does attend to the cooperative efforts of libraries in Oregon and the Northwest. The central role of Oregon State in a statewide library unification scheme makes an effort to examine the larger scene almost imperative for Carlson. Writing for the centennial of the library, Carlson ends his account abruptly with only a single paragraph to sum up events, rather than attempting an analysis of the first 100 years at Oregon State. He provides neither references nor a bibliography, stating that footnotes, "while perhaps giving the history an aura of scholarly accuracy, would also have cluttered it up substantially" (Carlson, 1966). Instead, he assures the reader of his adherence to accurate use of sources and objectivity.

An investigation of Washington State came from Gorchels (1971) a few years later. (Although his dissertation was copyrighted in 1973, its completion date was 2 years earlier.) Gorchels, an employee at the Washington State library for several years beginning in 1945, had access to a comparatively rich archival collection, including annual reports, correspondence, minutes, and book accession lists. Therefore, he examined the library in depth from 1892 to 1946, providing much detail on topics such as budgets, personnel, and accession of individual titles. Numerous tables accompany the text. Gorchels admitted that he was writing for an audience of academic librarians and Washington State devotees; and, indeed, portions of the text are of little interest to general readers, although the story of library director William Wirt

Foote's decades-long obsessive and indiscriminate collection development schemes includes many fascinating moments.

Gorchel's dissertation represents a quantum leap beyond its predecessors. The author not only examines the library but also discusses the university in depth. He provides a useful introduction to land-grant institutions and their founding legislation, and concludes with a lengthy comparison of the Washington State library with other land-grant libraries, both individually and collectively. Numerous tables display statistics about Washington State itself. His thorough bibliography points researchers to other relevant literature. Perhaps the only flaw in this dissertation is the lack of an index.

A master's thesis written by Bandy (1971) summarizes the history of the New Mexico State University library during its first 50 years, ending in 1939. Bandy begins well by discussing the land-grant legislation under which the university was founded but touches little on the subject later in the thesis. As expected, her thesis includes footnotes and a bibliography. Some of her material came from the university archives, while the remainder derived from college annual reports, catalogs, and the student newspaper. Bandy is rather uncritical in her approach; for example, she fails to comment on the possible deleterious effect on the library of rapid turnover in the head librarian position. The thesis concludes with a one-paragraph summation that says little beyond the fact that the library had become a recognized component of the university by 1939. Otherwise, her account adheres to the usual formula of buildings and collections.

Also traditional in its approach is a history of the Mississippi State University library by Peebles (1976). In fact, Peebles admitted that her account was as much a memoir as a history, for she had been on the library staff for decades. Her history is considerably more anecdotal than the others, although she retains the usual emphasis on staffing, buildings, and collections. In general, Peebles is uncritical, although stray comments hint that she might not have been fond of certain library directors. One wishes that she had gone into greater detail in regard to some episodes, such as political interference with higher education in Mississippi in the 1930s or the struggle for integration in the 1960s. Peebles' history leaves the reader feeling that Mississippi State has struggled more for support than have comparable land-grant institutions, but she makes no attempt at comparisons and scarcely mentions the land-grant status of the university. She does include a two-page bibliography and two pages of endnotes that indicate some use of archival sources.

Much more scholarly in approach is Schultz's *Making Something Happen* (1979), a history of the Texas A&M library. Schultz, a library employee, chose a format different from that of other institutional historians; rather than follow a chronological sequence, he devotes each of his nine chapters to a particular topic, including personnel, buildings, collections, funding, services, branch libraries, and special events. The initial chapter provides general background, while the concluding chapter analyzes the Texas A&M situation, with some comparison with other institutions and national standards. Endnotes accompany each chapter, and a 10-page bibliography directs the reader to both primary and secondary sources, including listings of books and articles pertaining to agricultural libraries, academic libraries, and library history.

The topical format chosen by Schultz fails to allow him to create a narrative flow and his study is, therefore, rather dry. One learns little of the personalities of library staffers, and student opinion of the library is subordinated to its operations. Given that Texas A&M remained an all-male institution until 1965 and that students doubled as military cadets, Schultz's lack of emphasis on library clientele is somewhat regrettable. He does, however, include some intriguing detail on branch libraries, including an engineering library that became a bone of contention in Texas politics. Despite some flaws, this history is among the more valuable examined, for it is scholarly in nature and does place Texas A&M in its land-grant context. Interestingly, Irene Hoadley, then library director at Texas A&M, states in the "Preface" that "Library histories are not as common as one might anticipate. . . . Many . . . libraries that have played an important role have not documented their development" (Schultz, 1979, p. v). Schultz's history was an attempt to fill that gap for Texas A&M.

Several years later, Brown (1987) produced a brief history of the library at South Dakota State University, basing his work on a more lengthy, but unpublished, paper created for the centennial of the university. Brown concentrates on such stock subjects as library directors, budgets, collections, and technological change but also briefly examines the standing of South Dakota State among its land-grant peers, thus showing some awareness of the larger scene. Readability of this history would have been improved had Brown elected to display some of the numerous statistics in tabular format, rather than in the text. No endnotes or sources are enumerated, although Brown states that he consulted annual and biennial library reports, as well as the unpublished work mentioned earlier. Perhaps the most glaring weakness of Brown's account lies in the fact that he pays almost no attention to the faculty and student clientele of the library.

Rouse (1992), another library director, produced a history of the Oklahoma State University as part of the centennial observances at that institution. Having had access to archival resources that appear to be comparatively rich, Rouse pursues his history in greater detail than usual for library histories, although he focuses on standard topics: buildings, collections, personnel, and budgets. Rouse adheres rather closely to a chronological sequence, at the cost of addressing larger themes or engaging in analysis. Like other library authors, he tends to be rather uncritical of his own institution. His account is heavily documented with endnotes and includes a bibliography of several pages, but it suffers for lack of any effort to compare the experience of Oklahoma State with that of other land grants. For example, he cites the histories of Peebles and Gorchels to trace the career of W. W. Foote—who was employed, in turn, by Mississippi State, Oklahoma State, and Washington State—but does not refer to Peebles or Gorchels for comparative purposes.

Littleton (1993) penned the final work to be considered in this article, a centenary history of the North Carolina State University library, of which Littleton had been director for a number of years. At the outset, he indicates his intention "to relate library history to relevant developments within the University and the larger society" (Littleton, 1993, p. iv); and, indeed, he often interjects summaries of events at both the university and the higher education community in North Carolina. However, he makes comparatively little note of societal happenings or of trends within the library community as a whole. For the most part, Littleton focuses on operations, buildings, committees, and staffing; this, in combination with a lack of narrative flow and a rather pedestrian writing style, makes his history read like an extended annual report. His work lacks endnotes, an index, and a bibliography, although he briefly lists the sources he consulted. The list comprises both secondary and primary materials. Perhaps the most interesting aspect of Litleton's history is the revelation that the library at North Carolina State has had an active friends group for many years. Such groups receive little mention in the histories of other land-grant university libraries.

C. Analysis

In general, these 10 histories share a number of characteristics. Most are relatively short; only those of Gorchels and Rouse number more than 200 pages each. One hundred pages is closer to the average, with two histories (those of V.P.I. and South Dakota State) well below that figure.

Those not written as a thesis or dissertation were all produced by local printers rather than commercial publishers, indicating that the perceived market for such histories is local in nature. Formats range from typescript, in several cases, to Rouse's book, which is casebound, printed, and sprinkled with well-reproduced photographs. Several histories were written as part of commemorative celebrations, such as centennial observances. In almost all cases, the authors were amateur historians employed at the library under discussion; several were library directors. With the exception of Schultz, all chose a chronological arrangement. The 10 histories represent a good cross-section in terms of geographic distribution, with institutions in the South, Midwest, and West all having received attention.

Those histories written in earlier decades lack such scholarly appurtances as endnotes, bibliographies, and indexes, a situation corrected to some extent in later works. Indexes still appear rather infrequently, but authors are more aware of the need to document their sources. Gorchels and Schultz, in particular, boast extensive and useful bibliographies. Reliance on primary resources also improved over time, although the availability of local archival resources is an important factor in their use by library historians. Some authors obviously benefited by having access to reasonably complete archival collections.

Historiographers have frequently chided library historians for writing "little history," with minimal effort to place their institutions in larger contexts. Regrettably, most land-grant library histories fall into this error. Their authors lean heavily toward standard topics, including personnel, buildings, budgets, and collections. Too frequently, these historians focus on the library and its operations almost to the exclusion of discussing the entire academic institution. In several instances, especially in the earlier works, little mention is made of the land-grant mission and its potential uniqueness. Only a couple of histories, those of Gorchels and Schultz, attempt much comparison with other libraries. Overwhelmingly, these histories tend to be rather uncritical in nature, with little emphasis on evaluation of either events or individuals. Controversies, when mentioned, generally are not examined for their possible significance, and fault is seldom attached to specific individuals.

A focus on library operations, so common in these histories, often comes at the expense of information about users. Aside from occasional anecdotes, students and faculty usually go unmentioned; and little regard is extended to the social role played by the library. The tendency to emphasize buildings, collections, and budgets is doubly unfortunate, for it often makes for rather dry reading. In some cases, even the library directors fail to come alive; the reader has no idea of their personalities. Anecdotes can obviously be overdone—and crowd out analysis—but recourse to an occasional human-interest story would brighten a number of these histories. As a further detriment, many authors lard their text with lengthy doses of statistical matter, rather than placing data in tables and thus improving readability.

Although individually the histories are often disappointing, collectively they present an illuminating view of land-grant libraries. Of course, certain problems are common to almost all of these histories: early struggles to establish a library of any size, unending budget woes, proliferation of departmental libraries across campus, and depressingly inadequate buildings. Surprisingly, most libraries also have rather distinctive aspects to their stories. Some saw long-term continuity among their library directors, while others experienced rapid turnover. Some individuals moved from library to library. W. W. Foote, for example, was employed successively at Mississippi State, Oklahoma State, and Washington State. Charlotte Baker left New Mexico

State for Colorado State. Some institutions, particularly those in Mississippi, Texas, and Oklahoma, had to deal with political interference from officials of the state. Foote, as noted earlier, set Washington State on a unique, almost bizarre, collection development pattern. Oregon State was the linchpin of a statewide library cooperative scheme for decades. In short, these institutions, properly observed, can boast of rich individual stories, while simultaneously providing much food for thought for the historian searching for common themes.

IV. The Author's Experience

The author of this article has, himself, written a history of the library in which he is employed (Ernest, 1996). Although direct comparison with other histories would be self-serving, thoughts on the process of writing such a history would seem to be in order:

1. The availability of archival resources bears directly on the themes of the history. The archives at Colorado State included annual reports of the librarian from the latter part of the nineteenth century to the present. For much of that time, however, little else emanating from the library had been retained. Reports from library staff, correspondence, and interoffice memos were notable by their scarcity. Thus for many years, the only point of view available was that of the head librarian. Conversely, by fortuitous circumstance, student views of the library were readily available. Some years earlier, Hansen (1977) had written a history of the university and, as part of the project, had compiled a handwritten chronological index to student newspapers. This index was made available to the present author and proved invaluable in retrieving student opinion over most of the life of the library. Otherwise, this component of the finished history would have been lacking.

2. As with many other library histories, this one was written to coincide with a commemorative occasion—the 125th anniversary of the university. Such a commemorative volume almost requires that the author bring the volume up to the present, a procedure that has a couple of obvious drawbacks. First, events within recent memory cannot be evaluated with any perspective; rather, they can only be documented with an an eye toward emphasizing those that appear to be of greater significance. Second, with all the actors still on the stage, candor becomes chancy. Ideally, the historian should be in the position to evaluate individuals and events as objectively as possible; but when

current events are in question, perhaps only a studied neutrality may be possible. Among the histories surveyed, only Gorchels' avoids this difficulty; his account ends more than 20 years before Gorchels began writing.

3. The time commitment for writing a library history can be substantial; in this author's case, the entire project consumed more than 3 years. In fact, publication occurred several months after 1995, the year of the 125th anniversary. Because the book was produced locally, delays were encountered that might have been avoided had the work been in the hands of a commercial publisher. For example, approximately 80 photographs were scattered throughout the text. The photos give the reader a visual break from time to time and make the volume more attractive. Still, selection of the photos and their placement in the text, with captions and credits, required lengthy and sometimes tedious work. In sum, no library historian should undertake a project of this sort without resigning him- or herself to a major time commitment. As an important corollary, institutional support, including funding, release time, and clerical assistance, should be secured from the start. Writing a library history can be rewarding, but it is inevitably laborious as well.

V. Conclusion

Revisiting some of the themes raised by historiographers over the years makes it evident that many of the histories of land-grant libraries exemplify these themes. Most authors have been professional librarians, but amateur historians, and have gravitated toward "little history." Too many accounts are uncritical in nature, offering little analysis of events or the actions and personalities of individuals. Few authors make much attempt to situate the library in a larger context; most are content to discuss only the library and the university of which it is a part, without reference to other libraries or universities, other land-grant institutions, or the national scene. In a few cases, little notice is taken of the land-grant milieu. Too frequently, such scholarly apparatus as a bibliography, endnotes/footnotes, or an index are lacking or rather sketchy.

Still, one can perhaps be too harsh concerning the intentions of these authors. Almost all were amateurs with a limited goal in mind; to expect them to meet the standards of historiographers is perhaps excessive. Furthermore, while most are uncritical in their approach, all attempt to be fair in assessing their material. None engage in cheerleading or glorification of the library or its parent institution. One also notices an improvement in research methods over the time these histories were compiled. Those published after 1970 show greater interest in adhering to accepted research methods and documentation. Finally, one cannot ignore their contribution to both "little history" and the library community at large. The more lengthy and detailed histories afford a glimpse into the unique circumstances that shaped individual libraries, while collectively many of the attributes that distinguish land-grant university libraries from other academic libraries can be discerned. Thus, these historians, despite some failings, as a group have made a real contribution to the history of academic libraries in the United States.

Reverting to the third question raised in the "Introduction" section of this article, how might the quality of land-grant library history be improved? Library history itself remains a discipline to which reasonable numbers of people are attracted, despite the supposed rise of ahistoricism, neglect by library schools, and the presumed indifference of the profession. Passet (1994) identifies 155 items, excluding dissertations and theses, that had been published in 1991–1992 related to library history, while Goedeken (1996) finds 208 for the period 1993–1994, again excluding dissertations and theses. Historians could also take encouragement from the fact that *Information Processing & Management* deemed history of enough importance to devote an entire issue to the subject. Its editor, Rayward (1996), defends history by stating, "a concern for context, precedents and antecedents, the attempt to achieve perspective, the notion of development—all are manifestations of the imperative of history" (p. 1).

Despite its flaws, library history thus appears to have achieved a degree of success and stability. Institutional history, however, has languished. Although Rouse's history of the Oklahoma State library received generally favorable notice, Hovde (1994) comments, "there is little attempt to place the library's development in the context of national trends" (p. 343), while Sowards (1993) states, "Because the history of the library makes up just one volume in a large series, issues of librarianship at times appear unconnected to campus trends at large" (p. 397). Nor do other academic libraries go unscathed. Passet (1994) observes that "few historians have attempted broad-based studies of academic library history" (p. 419). Goedeken (1996) is more severe. He takes to task the authors of histories of the libraries at the University of Colorado and Louisiana State University for failing to place their respective institutions in a larger context but reserved his sharpest fire for Littleton's account of the North Carolina State library, asserting that "the author's eyes seldom leave the interior of the library" (Goedeken, 1996, p. 613). Goedeken (1996) concludes: "If there is one consistent weakness in much of the material under review, it is the failure of authors to establish a larger context for their research and analysis" (p. 614).

It appears that authors of institutional histories have yet to heed the admonition that their work be related to broader contexts. A couple of reasons for this inattention can be advanced. First, institutional histories are almost always "labors of love." Their authors are usually students or employees of the library in question rather than professional historians. Their work normally receives only limited distribution, and they can expect to receive little remuneration for a project that can be both time consuming and laborious. Under such circumstances, it is perhaps not surprising that these amateur authors fail to place their histories in a larger framework or adhere to current historiographic trends.

Goedeken (1996) hints at the second problem when he states, "Scholarship going beyond investigating institutional library history is becoming increasingly prevalent" (p. 632). A glance at his compilation and that of Passet (1994) indicates that library historians are increasingly turning to a thematic approach rather than one based on individual institutions. It would be an exaggeration to assert that a stigma has been assigned to institutional histories, but it is apparent that the trend is definitely toward other themes. Furthermore, it seems likely that library historians with a more professional approach will be likely to pursue thematic and contextual issues, while institutional studies will fall by default to amateurs. Since the professionals in the field and their students will often be affiliated with library schools, any institutional studies they do undertake will probably be clustered in the vicinity of the school, a situation noted earlier by Harris (1968). Again, this clustering will mean that institutional histories written in other locales will of necessity be the work of amateurs.

The current lack of emphasis on institutional history and its relegation to authors untrained in historical methodology is unfortunate, for the importance of "little history" as a building block for broader studies has been acknowledged by virtually all observers for several decades. In the instance of land-grant university libraries as defined in this study, somewhat more than one half of the 19 possible institutions have been the object of a monographic-style history; but only those of Gorchels and Schultz and, perhaps, Rouse have met the criteria of a useful study as defined by most library historiographers. The other histories are not without value but are more noteworthy for their deficiencies. No immediate remedy for this situation appears at hand. Until institutional histories are considered worthwhile undertakings by professional library historians or their students, such histories will remain too few in number and will be the efforts of practitioners who too often lack the requisite training to maximize the value of the books they write.

References

Alston, R. C. (1991). Library history: A place in the education of librarians? *Library History: New Perspectives in Library History, The Leeds Conference Issue* **9**, 37–51.

Bandy, C. N. L. (1971). *The First Fifty Years of the New Mexico State University Library, 1889–1939.* Master's thesis, University of Oklahoma, Norman.

Brown, P. I. (1987). *South Dakota State University's Library: A History.* (Hilton M. Briggs Library Occasional Paper, Number 1.) H. M. Briggs Library, South Dakota State University, Brookings.

Brown, R. M. (1929). *History of the V.P.I. Library, 1872–1928.* V.P.I. Printing Department, Blacksburg, VA.

Carlson, W. H. (1966). *The Library of Oregon State University, Its Origins, Management, and Growth: A Centennial History.* Oregon State University Library, Corvallis.

Carmichael, J. V., Jr. (1995). Library history without walls. *Journal of Education for Library and Information Science* **36**, 309–318.

Clemons, H. (1954). *The University of Virginia Library, 1825–1950: Story of a Jeffersonian Foundation.* University of Virginia Library, Charlottesville, VA.

Colson, J. C. (1969). Speculations on the use of library history. *Journal of Library History* **4**, 65–71.

Colson, J. C. (1976). The writing of American library history, 1876–1976. *Library Trends* **25**, 7–21.

Cox, R. J. (1991). Library history and library archives in the United States. *Libraries and Culture* **26**, 569–593.

Dain, P. (1978). A response to issues raised by the ALHRT program "The nature and uses of library history." *Journal of Library History* **13**, 44–47.

Davies, D. W. (1981). Libraries and the two cultures. *Journal of Library History* **16**, 16–27.

Davis, D. G., and Tucker, J. M. (1989). *American Library History, A Comprehensive Guide to the Literature.* ABC Clio, Santa Barbara, CA.

Davis, D. G., and Tucker, J. M. (1994). Change and tradition in land-grant university libraries. In *For the Good of the Order: Essays in Honor of Edward G. Holley* (D. Williams, J. Budd, R. Martin, B. Moran, and F. Roper, eds.), pp. 135–160. JAI Press, Greenwich, CT.

Dickinson, D. C. (1978). Comment. *Journal of Library History* **13**, 448–450.

Ernest, D. J. (1996). *Agricultural Frontier to Electronic Frontier: A History of Colorado State University Libraries, 1870–1995.* Colorado State University, Fort Collins.

Fain, E. (1978). The library and American education: Education through secondary school. *Library Trends* **27**, 327–352.

Genz, M. D. (1993). Looking through a rearview mirror. *Journal of Education for Library and Information Science* **34**, 270–274.

Goedeken, E. A. (1996). The literature of American library history, 1993–1994. *Libraries and Culture* **31**, 603–644.

Gorchels, C. C. (1971). *A Land-Grant University Library: The History of the Library of Washington State University, 1892–1946.* PhD dissertation, Columbia University, New York.

Grotzinger, L. A. (1986). Ten years' work in library history: The monograph from 1975–1985. In *Library Science Annual, Volume 2* (B. S. Wynar, ed.), pp. 56–69. Libraries Unlimited, Littleton, CO.

Hagler, R. (1971). Needed research in library history. In *Research Methods in Librarianship: Historical and Bibliographical Methods in Library Research* (R. E. Stevens, ed.), pp. 128–137. Clive Bingley, London.

Hansen, J. E. (1977). *Democracy's College in the Centennial State, A History of Colorado State University.* Colorado State University, Fort Collins.

Harris, M. H. (1968). *A Guide to Research in American Library History.* Scarecrow Press, Metuchen, NJ.

Harris, M. H. (1975). Externalist or internalist frameworks for the interpretation of American library history—The continuing debate. *Journal of Library History* **10**, 106–110.

Harris, M. H. (1976). "The priest who slew the slayer and shall himself be slain": Revisionism in American library history. *Journal of Education for Librarianship* **16**, 229–231.

Harris, M. H. (1978). Antiquarianism, professional piety, and critical scholarship in recent American library historiography. *Journal of Library History* **13**, 37–43.

Harris, M. H. (1986). State, class, and cultural reproduction: Toward a theory of library service in the United States. In *Advances in Librarianship*, Volume 14 (W. Simonton, ed.), pp. 211–252. Academic Press, Orlando, FL.

Harris, M. H., and Hannah, S. (1992). Why do we study the history of libraries? A meditation on the perils of ahistoricism in the information era. *Library and Information Science Research* **14**, 123–130.

Harris, N. (1981). Cultural institutions and American modernization. *Journal of Library History* **16**, 28–47.

Harrison, K. C. (1994). Why library history? *Library Review* **43**, 9–13.

Herubel, J.-P. (1988). Clio's dark musings? A review essay. *Libraries and Culture* **23**, 493–498.

Holley, E. G. (1971). Textual criticism in library history. In *Research Methods in Librarianship: Historical and Bibliographical Methods in Library Research* (R. E. Stevens, ed.), pp. 95–105. Clive Bingley, London.

Hovde, D. M. (1994). [Review of] A history of the Oklahoma State University library. *Libraries and Culture* **29**, 343–344.

Irwin, R. (1958). Does library history matter? *Library Review* **128**, 510–513.

Kaser, D. (1978). Advances in American library history. In *Advances in Librarianship*, Volume 8 (M. R. Harris, ed.), pp. 181–199. Academic Press, ew York.

Kraus, J. W. (1978) Comment. *Journal of Library History* **13**, 445–447.

Littleton, I. T. (1993). *The D. H. Hill Library: An Informal History, 1887–1987*. North Carolina State University, Friends of the Library, Raleigh.

McMullen, H. (1952). Why read and write library history? *Wilson Library Bulletin* **26**, 385–386.

McMullen, H. (1971). Primary sources in library research. In *Research Methods in Librarianship: Historical and Bibliographical Methods in Library Research* (R. E. Stevens, ed.), pp. 23–41. Clive Bingley, London.

McMullen, H. (1978). The state of the art of writing library history. *Journal of Library History* **13**, 432–440.

Miksa, F. L. (1985). Machlup's categories of knowledge as a framework for viewing library and information science history. *Journal of Library History* **20**, 157–172.

Milum, B. (1978). Comment. *Journal of Library History* **13**, 441–444.

Passet, J. E. (1994). The literature of American library history, 1991–1992. *Libraries and Culture* **29**, 415–439.

Peebles, M. (1976). *Echoes, A History of the Mitchell Memorial Library, Mississippi State University*. Mississippi State University, Starkville.

Rayward, W. B. (1996). Introduction. *Information Processing & Management* **32**, 1–2.

Reichmann, F. (1964). Historical research and library science. *Library Trends* **13**, 31–41.

Rouse, R. (1992). *A History of the Oklahoma State University Library*. Oklahoma State University, Stillwater.

Schultz, C. R. (1979). *"Making Something Happen": Texas A&M University Libraries, 1876–1976*. Texas A&M University, College Station.

Shera, J. H. (1952). On the value of library history. *Library Quarterly* **22**, 240–251.

Shera, J. H. (1973). The literature of American library history. In *Knowing Books and Men: Knowing Computers, Too.* (J. H. Shera, ed.), pp. 124–161. Libraries Unlimited, Littleton, CO.

Shiflett, O. L. (1984). Clio's claim: The role of historical research in library and information science. *Library Trends* **32**, 385–406.

Shores, L. (1961). The importance of library history. In *An American Library History Reader: Contributions to Library Literature* (J. D. Marshall, ed.), pp. 3–7. The Shoe String Press, Hamden, CT.

Sowards, S. W. (1993). [Review of] A history of the Oklahoma State University Library. *Library Quarterly* **63**, 396–397.

Stewart, N. (1943). Sources for the study of American college library history, 1800–1876. *Library Quarterly* **13**, 227–231.

Stieg, M. F. (1993). The dangers of ahistoricism. *Journal of Education for Library and Information Science* **34**, 275–278.

Towne, J. E. (1961). *A History of the Michigan State University Library, 1855–1959*. University of Rochester Press for the Association of College and Research Libraries, Rochester, NY.

Wiegand, W. A. (1983). Psychohistory: A new frontier for library historians?—A review essay. *Journal of Library History* **18**, 464–472.

Wiegand, W. A. (1990). Library history research in the United States. *Libraries and Culture* **25**, 103–114.

Williams, R. V. (1984). Theoretical issues and constructs underlying the study of library development. *Libri* **34**, 1–16.

Index

ISBN 0-12-024622-8

90065